Cost–Benefit Analysis
5th Edition

Cost–benefit analysis (CBA) is the systematic and analytical process of comparing benefits and costs in evaluating the desirability of a project or programme – often of a social nature. CBA is fundamental to government decision making and is established as a formal technique for making informed decisions on the use of society's scarce resources. It attempts to answer such questions as whether a proposed project is worthwhile, the optimal scale of a proposed project and the relevant constraints. CBA can be applicable to transportation projects, environmental and agricultural projects, land-use planning, social welfare and educational programmes, urban renewal, health economics and others.

The timely 5th edition, examines new work in the discipline, with relevant examples and illustrations as well as new and expanded chapters, to include:

- non-market goods valuation
- the impact of uncertainty
- transportation economics
- investment appraisal
- environmental economics
- evaluation of programmes and services

The 5th edition continues to build on the successful approach of previous editions, with lucid explanation of key ideas, the simple but effective expository short chapters and an appendix on various useful statistical and mathematical concepts and derivatives.

Cost–Benefit Analysis (5th edition) will be a valuable source and guide to international funding agencies, governments and interested professional economists.

For this edition, **E.J. Mishan** has been joined by **Euston Quah** of Nanyang Technological University. New themes explored include the impact of game theory on CBA.

Cost–Benefit Analysis
5th edition

E.J. Mishan and Euston Quah

Routledge
Taylor & Francis Group

LONDON AND NEW YORK

First edition published 1976 by Allen & Unwin

Fifth published 2007
by Routledge
2 Park Square, Milton Park, Abingdon, Oxon OX14 4RN

Simultaneously published in the USA and Canada
by Routledge
270 Madison Ave, New York, NY 10016

Routledge is an imprint of the Taylor & Francis Group, an informa business

© 2007 E.J. Mishan and Euston Quah

Typeset in Times New Roman by
Newgen Imaging Systems (P) Ltd, Chennai, India
Printed and bound in Great Britain by
TJ International Ltd, Padstow, Cornwall

British Library Cataloguing in Publication Data
A catalogue record for this book is available from the British Library

Library of Congress Cataloging in Publication Data
A catalog record for this book has been requested

ISBN10: 0–415–35037–9   ISBN13: 978–0–415–35037–2 (hbk)
ISBN10: 0–415–34991–5   ISBN13: 978–0–415–34991–8 (pbk)
ISBN10: 0–203–69567–4   ISBN13: 978–0–203–69567–8 (ebk)

Contents

Preface to the fifth edition

Following precedent, this fifth edition of *Cost–Benefit Analysis* addresses itself primarily to the 'mature student', at least to the conscientious student, who is primarily concerned with understanding the rationale and the limitations of basic methods. The exposition, however, continues to remain informal, proceeding in the main through numerical illustrations and with only occasional recourse to simple notation.

Economists familiar with the fourth edition will at once notice that the several simplified examples of cost–benefit calculations, presented in its introductory Part I, have now been removed. At the time when the first edition was being prepared (1970), cost–benefit analysis was not so familiar a subject, and few economics departments included it in their list of courses. It seemed then advisable to prepare the students' minds for the need of the various techniques that were to follow. With the passage of time, we must recognize that initial presentations of simplified cost–benefit examples are no longer necessary.

In this new edition, therefore, we have reverted to the more traditional practice of beginning a textbook with an introductory Part I on Scope and method; in our case, a decision that has required, *inter alia*, the removal of some chapters of the fourth edition, and parts of some other chapters, to this introductory Part I, where they are now more comfortably lodged, for it is incumbent in this Part I that the authors make clear just how the economist's conceptions of costs and benefits differ from those employed in the business world. To the layman and the politician, the notion of gains and losses may seem evident enough for transactions between a limited number of people. It is far from evident, however, when calculations of gains and losses have to be made for whole communities, whether or not the individuals are directly engaged in some project or programme.

As for the remaining parts in this fifth edition, apart from correcting some minor errors in the fourth edition, some rearrangement of the chapters has taken place and, occasionally, what appeared there as two consecutive chapters has been combined here to form a single chapter: all this, and more, in the endeavour to make the exposition in this new edition more lucid and concise.

It may be noted, in particular, that Part IV (on 'External effects') now ends with an extended chapter in which the possibly quite different outcomes from using a calculation based on the CV^{21} measure, instead of the CV^{12} measure, are elaborated and illustrated. Again, in our Part V (on 'Investment criteria'), a searching comparison of the implications and the limitations of the various criteria in common use cannot be undertaken without taking up far more space than any of the other parts. In this connection, the two chapters devoted to explaining the proposed normalization procedure (in compounding net benefits forward to a terminal date), regarded as a technique superior to any of the popular discounted-present-value criteria for evaluating a stream of net benefits, have been entirely re-written to make it more comprehensible.

After much reflection, it seemed to us that some of the chapters in the fourth edition, in particular that on the Scitovsky Paradox and that on Second-Best, would be better relegated to expanded Appendices. There they are included with a number of other Appendices that, although not central to a proper exposition of cost–benefit analysis, touch on sources of misunderstanding or of common error in some popular treatments of the subject.

It may be unnecessary to remark that no significant theoretical novelty is to be found in this edition, or indeed in earlier editions. Inasmuch as cost–benefit analysis is, in fact, no more than an assembly of concepts and techniques culled from mainstream economic theory, in particular from that branch known as Welfare Economics, it is not surprising that the subject itself cannot boast of theoretical innovation.

Apart from proposals for the gathering and refinement of data, the development of cost–benefit analysis over the years has centred, in the main, on controversies over the propriety of concepts, over proxies for their measurement and over the appropriateness of the techniques employed to determine the ranking of alternative public projects. With regard to all such issues, our overriding concern remains that of examining the validity of the key concepts in use, of making explicit the limitations of the usual proxies adopted for their measurement and of checking for consistency the various techniques employed in any cost–benefit calculation.

We are aware, of course, that although purporting to be both a guide to, and a critique of, cost–benefit methods, this resulting volume is somewhat slimmer than other popular cost–benefit manuals. There are several reasons for this. One is that we are studiously economical in our choice of tables, diagrams and other such schema that seem to exert a fascination on some writers. Another is that we do not undertake to test the reader's understanding of the material in each chapter by including pages of questions (and answers). Although we do not deny that repeated elaboration of such features can be helpful in impressing on the more plastic minds of beginners who are eager to be inducted into 'the mysteries of the craft', there is always the danger that the sheer mass of material and formulae in these bulkier manuals may also act to intimidate or to bewilder hapless students so that, in the end, they 'cannot see the woods for the trees'.

We also note that, in some of the more ambitious textbooks, there are extended reports of cost–benefit studies already undertaken for existing programmes or projects. Their value, however, is limited unless the methods used in such studies are also subjected to fastidious examination. Since this, in fact, is not the case, the reader might like to know that a companion volume to this fifth edition is currently being prepared, one that, indeed, subjects the selected case studies to critical assessment.

The co-author of this fifth edition, Professor Euston Quah, needs no introduction to economists who keep abreast of the growing literature in Environmental Economics. He is currently editor of *The Singapore Economic Review* and, in the past few years, has been active in arranging cost–benefit courses for the cohorts of economics students at the National University of Singapore: courses that have been based on the material now contained in the present edition, which has, incidentally, benefited from students' 'feedback'. We should like to acknowledge Dr Lim Boon Tiong from the National University of Singapore for his invaluable advice, as well as Mr Lim Sze How for all the fieldwork and multitude of tasks that he has undertaken in the course of writing and organizing the material used in this book, and it is indeed to his credit that things got organized. We should also like to thank Ms Khatini binte Anuar for much of the secretarial work that accompanied this project and, last but not least, we must thank Robert Langham and colleagues at Routledge for their suggestions and support throughout.

E.J.M. and E.Q.

Part I

Scope and method

1 Introductory remarks[1]

1 No textbook can provide detailed guidance on every aspect of gathering and processing data on the variety of programmes and projects in which cost–benefit analysis (CBA) may be employed. Indeed, attempts by authors to put together increasingly comprehensive textbooks on the subject result in so overloading the students' minds that they 'cannot see the wood for the trees'.

In this introductory text, however, we continue the policy of earlier editions in focusing the student's attention on the crucial concepts and, unavoidably, also on the controversies they engender. The purpose of this stratagem is to enable the conscientious student initially to understand what ideally he should be seeking to measure before resorting to a considered choice among the proxies available or contrived. Our aim, that is, is primarily to sharpen the student's insight into the rationale of the basic fundamental concepts, in the endeavour to develop his judgement in appraising the validity and the usefulness of the diverse techniques employed or proposed in the economic valuation of projects.

2 Let us be clear from the start that the sort of question a CBA sets out to answer is whether one or a number of projects or programmes should be undertaken and, if investable funds are limited, which one, two or more among these specific projects that would otherwise qualify for admission should be selected. Another question that CBA sometimes addresses is that of determining the level at which a plant should operate or the combination of outputs it should produce. In this introductory volume, however, we follow custom in confining our attention chiefly to the former question, about the choice of investment projects.

But why bother with CBA at all? What is wrong with deciding whether or not to undertake any specific investment or to choose among a number of specific investment opportunities, guided simply by proper accounting practices and, therefore, guided ultimately by reference to profitability. The answer is provided by the familiar thesis that what counts as benefits (or profits) and costs to personnel engaged in the activity of a particular segment of the economy – be it a firm, an industry or any private or public organization – does not necessarily coincide

1 A brief history background of CBA is provided in Appendix 1.

with, indeed, is unlikely to coincide with, all the benefits and costs experienced by the individuals residing within an area subject to a CBA. The area to which the analysis is addressed is often the economy of a whole country or nation state. But it can also be a region that encompasses a number of contiguous countries or, alternatively, one or more provinces of a country or even a single town or city. This problem is called the accounting stance. In order to avoid unnecessary verbiage, however, we shall assume henceforth that the area in question is that of the whole country and therefore speak of 'the economy as a whole' or 'society as a whole'.

A private enterprise, or even a public enterprise, comprises only a segment of the economy, often a very small segment. More importantly, whatever the means it employs in pursuing its objectives – whether rules of thumb or more formalized techniques such as mathematical programming or operations research – the private enterprise, at least, is guided by ordinary commercial criteria that require revenues to exceed costs. The fact that its activities are guided by the profit motive, however, is not to deny that it confers benefits on a large number of people other than its shareholders. It also confers benefits on its employees, on consumers, and – through the taxes it pays – on the general public. Yet the benefits enjoyed by these four groups continue to exist only for as long as they coincide with the yielding of profits to the enterprise. If it makes losses, the enterprise cannot survive unless it receives a public subsidy. If it is to survive unaided as a private concern and, moreover, to expand the scale of its operations, it must, over a period of time, produce profits large enough either to attract investors or to finance its own expansion.

There is, of course, the metaphor of the 'invisible hand', the *deus ex machina* discovered by Adam Smith that so directs the self-seeking proclivities of the business world that it confers benefits on society as a whole. And one can, indeed, lay down simple and sufficient conditions under which the uncompromising pursuit of profits acts always to serve the public interest. These conditions can be boiled down to two: that all effects relevant to the welfare of all individuals be properly priced on the market, and that perfect competition prevail in all economic activities.

3   Once we depart from this ideal economic setting, however, the set of outputs and prices to which the economy tends may not serve the public so well as some other set of outputs and prices. In addition to this possible misallocation of resources among the goods being produced, it is also possible that certain goods that can be economically justified are not produced at all, while others that cannot be economically justified continue to be produced. If, for example, technical conditions and the size of the market are such that a number of goods can be produced only under conditions of increasing returns to scale (falling average cost), it is possible that, although some of these goods will be produced by monopolies charging prices above marginal cost, other such goods will not be produced, as there is no single price at which the monopolist can make any profit. But the production of these latter goods is not necessarily uneconomic. It may simply be the case that the monopolist who sells each good at a single price cannot transfer enough of the benefits from his potential customers to make the venture worthwhile.

Again, certain goods with beneficial, though unpriced, spillover effects also qualify for production on economic grounds; but they cannot be produced at a profit as long as the beneficial spillovers remain unpriced. The reverse is also true and more significant: profitable commercial activities sometimes produce noxious spillover effects to such an extent that, on a more comprehensive pricing criterion, they would be regarded as uneconomic.

The economist engaged in the cost–benefit appraisal of a project is not, in essence then, asking a different sort of question from that being asked by the accountant of a private firm. Rather, the same sort of question is being asked about a wider group of people – who comprise society – and is being asked more searchingly. Instead of asking whether the owners of the enterprise will become better off by the firm's engaging in one activity rather than another, the economist asks whether, by undertaking this project rather than not undertaking it, or by undertaking instead any of a number of alternative projects, net benefits will accrue to a society consisting of all the individuals who reside or work within the area in question.

Broadly speaking, for the more precise concept of revenue to the private firm, the economist substitutes the less precise yet meaningful concept of *social benefit*. For the costs of the private firm, the economist substitutes the concept of *opportunity cost* – the social value foregone when the resources in question are moved away from alternative economic activities into the specific project. For the profit of the firm, the economist substitutes the concept of *excess social benefit over cost* or, in short, net social benefit.

It may be mentioned in passing that it is just possible that within the accounting stance in question the economist is instructed to include benefits that accrue only to a specific group, say to those who are disabled, indigent or single parent families. Irrespective, however, of the political desirability of such an objective, collecting such specific data alone may prove so costly as to raise questions about its feasibility.

Again, it may be held that there are difficulties in calculating the value of benefits that accrue to individuals, or to those members of a family who do not themselves make economic decisions. Yet the economist may reasonably accept as the value of such benefits those that may be calculated from the decisions on their behalf taken by others.

4 Returning to the notion of net social benefit, or excess social benefit over cost which is to be estimated by a CBA, it may be recognized as one referred to in the literature on welfare economics as a *potential* Pareto improvement or, earlier still, as a 'test of hypothetical compensation'. The project in question, that is, may be regarded as an economic improvement if its implementation produces an excess of benefits over losses for the community: one, that is, for which a costless redistribution of the benefits could make every one affected by the project better off.[2]

More formally, however, the cost–benefit criterion to be adopted can be expressed in simple notation form as $\Sigma V_i > 0$, where $V_1, V_2, \ldots, V_n$ are the net valuations of each of the n persons affected by the project, where a positive V valuation indicates a net benefit, and a negative V valuation a net loss to the person. Clearly, if the aggregate valuations sum to a positive figure, the aggregate of benefits exceeds the losses, and a potential Pareto improvement is realized. (More precise measures of such valuations in the form of compensating variations will be introduced later.)

The above criterion is better regarded as necessary though perhaps not sufficient, inasmuch as it may have to meet some additional political requirement, say, that ΣV exceed a certain figure or else exceed a given benefit–cost ratio.

Another reason why our $\Sigma V > 0$ above may be deemed insufficient is that, as it stands, it makes no provision for the distributional impact of the project. Since a number of ways have been proposed for attaching distributional or other weights to the valuations, none of which, however, we find acceptable, we defer these proposals, and our objections to them, to Chapter 3.

In the meantime, although the criterion we have adopted (simply that the sum of all valuations be positive) is straightforward enough,[3] our difficulties begin once we start to trace all the repercussions and bring them into the calculations. These difficulties, which require extended treatment, are to be found chiefly in the concepts and measurement of consumer surplus and rent, in the distinctions between shadow prices and transfer payments, in evaluating a range of spillover effects, in the choice of investment criteria, and in proposals for dealing with future uncertainty. They are dealt with in that order in the parts that follow.

5   Finally, the reader will appreciate that the techniques employed in CBA can be put to related uses. Public funds used for the financing of education or medical

---

2 Although this potential Pareto improvement involves no more than an exercise in positive economics, some economists would regard it as having normative implications independent of any political decision. Both the reasons that may be advanced for this view and those for rejecting it will be discussed in Appendix 2.

3 It has frequently been alleged that the Arrow Theorem invalidates the validity of welfare economics and, by extension, that also of CBA. This is a misunderstanding of the scope of that theorem.

The intransitivity that may occur when majority decisions are used to rank alternative policies – an intransitivity easily demonstrated by an example, say, of three alternative policies, A, B, C, to be ranked by three persons (or groups) – can have political implications for countries where decisions are reached by majority rule. But in economics, where persons are assumed not merely to be able to rank alternatives, but also to assign money valuations to units of goods and bads, this sort of intransitivity does not arise.

The possible contradiction in the so-called Kaldor–Hicks test, first pointed out by Scitovsky (1941), however, has no affinity with the above theorem. It arises rather from the relationship between the set of market prices and the distribution of the community's income, as explained in Appendix 3.

services, recreational facilities, the building of dams or irrigation works, the provision of tools, technical equipment and advice, and the establishing of industries or information centres are different ways in which the state can help others to help themselves. Of course, none of these ways might meet a strict cost–benefit criterion. Yet, some or all of them might be regarded by society as superior to direct cash transfers. The economist can then contribute to such decisions to the extent of selecting – within the limits of a number of seemingly equally appropriate ways of helping these less privileged groups – those opportunities that yield the maximum social benefit per dollar transferred in such ways to these groups. Clearly, the discounted present value (DPV) of the maximum benefit per dollar invested in these socially approved ways may turn out to be less than a dollar. But such projects do have the merit of encouraging people to help themselves – an intangible benefit, no less important just because it cannot easily be quantified.

Similar calculations arise when transfers in kind are not the immediate goal, the beneficiaries being a mixed income group or the greater part of the community. The economist in such cases is required to restrict his estimates to the 'cost-effectiveness' of a number of alternative projects, any one of which is thought to be politically desirable. Should the government wish to discover the resource costs involved (though *not* the benefits) of maintaining alternative standards of water purity along different stretches of the Delaware Estuary, the economist would be able to provide cost estimates, leaving it to the community to decide, through the political process, just which standards to adopt. Another example of cost-effectiveness would be the comparison of the social costs of alternative airport sites, on the assumption – possibly unwarranted – that the airport site confers benefits that more than cover all the social costs.

2   Cost-effective analysis

1   The analysis of cost-effectiveness is effectively comprehended within the techniques of CBA. Yet, although a knowledge of cost–benefit techniques more than suffices for a calculation of cost-effectiveness, it is important to make explicit the difference in political constraints involved in the latter and therefore in its prescriptive significance.

First, let us highlight the basic distinction between the two by a simple illustration. Let V^a be the net value person (or group) A places on the project in question; say it is $+100$. And let V^b be the net value placed on it by B, say -80. For this project that affects only A and B, the cost–benefit calculation is simply $V^a + V^b$, or $100 - 80$ which equals $+20$. In contrast a cost-effectiveness analysis would contain only V^b, a cost of 80, provided, however, that B enjoys no benefit but suffers only a loss of 80 and that A enjoys only a benefit of 100.

If, instead, A suffers a cost of 40 to be set against a gain of 140 (net gain of 100), and B suffers a loss of 110 to be set against a gain of 30 (net loss of 80), the aggregate cost of the project to A and B would be $40 + 110$, a total cost of 150. It should be manifest that we could equally have calculated only the benefits conferred on A and B by the project without any reference to the cost. Thus, in the preceding example the aggregate benefits alone would be 140 plus 30, a total of 170.

Although a benefit-effectiveness calculation may occasionally be required, a cost-effectiveness calculation is the more common. In the latter case, the problem facing the economist is that of discovering the lowest cost of achieving a particular objective regarded as desirable by the community. An example could be that of reducing the effluent poured into a river or lake to some pre-determined level. Another example would be that of estimating the lowest cost of saving a life in undertaking a specific project. A ready presumption of cost-effectiveness is that aggregate benefits must be so high as to make a project proposal desirable in itself and/or the fact that political considerations dominate the decision.

Whether or not the project in question will be undertaken may no longer depend upon a CBA which also calculates the benefit of the project. The decision whether to proceed may now depend only on the political process which takes account only of the information on costs.

2 It should be obvious that, in order for the problem to have an economic dimension, there must be more than one way of achieving the required change. In the first example, that of reducing effluent by a given volume, say E, we may suppose that there are two factories, A and B, pouring effluent into a lake, each having a distinct rising marginal cost curve of effluent-reduction. We assume that factory A is the more efficient in effluent-reduction in that its marginal cost for any given volume of effluent-removal is below that of factory B. Nonetheless, unless very little effluent is to be removed, it would generally be uneconomic to let factory A alone curb the entire amount of the effluent decided upon. The marginal cost of reducing effluent can be made lower by eventually bringing in factory B at the point where its initial marginal cost of effluent-reduction is just below that reached by factory A. As the student suspects – and as is illustrated in Chapter 19 – the optimal contributions of the two factories in reducing the required amount of effluent must be such that their marginal costs are equal. This condition ensures that the effluent is removed at least cost.

The same least-cost condition has to be met if, instead of a problem of removing effluent where two methods for doing so are available, the problem is that of preventing a given number of deaths from a particular disease. In such a case, however, the least-cost calculation will depend not only on the degree of risk reduction specified, but also on coverage of diseases, for whatever the least cost happens to be, the economist is at liberty to point out that, for this same cost, a yet greater number of lives may be saved if some of this money, at least, were spent on other potentially fatal diseases.

Thus, suppose a test for lung cancer costs $1,000 per patient, and it is known from long experience that, on a first test, of every 10,000 patients tested, 100 will be shown to have the disease. Therefore, a first test costing $10 million reveals 100 of these 10,000 persons to be afflicted with lung cancer. Assuming there are no false positives and yet a slight chance of a false negative, a repetition of the test (or of a somewhat different test costing the same as the original) on the remaining 9,900 patients at a total cost of almost $10 million discovers yet another 10 patients to be suffering from lung cancer. A third test on the remaining 9,890 patients, again at almost the same cost, reveals only one more patient with the disease. The decision makers may wonder if the second and third tests are worthwhile, assuming always that there is a good chance of saving a person's life if lung cancer is detected by the test.

The economist can help in this respect by calculating the marginal cost of detecting lung cancer in a patient. A first test, which costs $10 million discovers 100 lung-cancer victims. The 'marginal cost' of a detected cancer (in such a case, marginal cost being the average cost of detecting cancer in the 100 patients suffering from lung cancer) is, therefore, equal to $100,000. A second test, which costs almost as much as the first, discovers an additional 10 lung cancers with the 'marginal cost' of a detected cancer now being close to $1 million. A third test, which detects only one cancer, shows a marginal cost of nearly $10 million, as shown in Table 2.1.

Table 2.1 Cost of detection for lung cancer

Number of tests conducted on group of 10,000 patients	Total cost of test	Number of cancer victims discovered	Cost per detected cancer victims
1st test	$10 million	100	$100,000
2nd test	$10 million	10	$1 million
3rd test	$10 million	1	$10 million

Incurring a sum close to $10 million in order to save the life of one additional patient may gratify our humanitarian impulses, yet it would be economically inefficient if this sum could be used in some other way that would save more than a single life. Whatever the sum appropriated specifically for carrying out tests that would enable lives to be saved, the largest number of lives would be saved if that sum were allocated among the different disease tests on the equi-marginal principle.

3   It should be emphasized, however that useful as a cost-effective analysis can be, a cost-*benefit* analysis is effectively superior. In our first example of effluent reduction, the economic calculation of the many benefits of reducing the level of effluent may reveal that it far exceeds the implicit value held by decision makers. In the second example, a calculation of the value of human life, or of reducing the risk of death, may warrant a far larger sum than is currently set aside for testing patients for fatal diseases. In sum, economic valuation of the benefits of a programme in addition to the calculation of its cost will provide all the relevant economic information necessary to enable policy makers to make more judicious decisions.

3 Proposals for weighting money valuations

1   In this chapter, we shall examine those proposals which, if adopted in a cost–benefit calculation, would entail a departure from a potential Pareto criterion as represented $\Sigma V > 0$ (aggregate money valuation). These proposals arise in connection with equity and distribution and also in the treatment of so-called merit goods, of intangibles and of the social rate of discount.

2   The impact of large investment projects on the *distribution* of welfare has recently attracted some attention.

One form of response to this concern has been an attempt to incorporate distributional effects into a cost–benefit calculation by effectively expressing gains and losses in terms of utility rather than in terms of money. For each dollar of gain or loss to a specified income group, there corresponds a particular marginal utility: the higher the income group, the lower the marginal utility of a dollar gain or loss.

Having transformed all the Vs into utility terms into Us, the resulting cost–benefit criterion is met when the aggregate gains in terms of utility exceed aggregate losses, i.e. when $\Sigma U > 0$. Clearly, a cost–benefit criterion in money valuation terms, $\Sigma V > 0$, may be met which, however, fails the valuation in utility terms, $\Sigma U > 0$, and vice versa. The particular weighting systems that have been proposed are of necessity somewhat arbitrary, and all assume diminishing marginal utility of income.

One method is that of positing a particular form of the utility–income relation. If, for example, one adopts a function that results in a constant elasticity of *minus* 2 with respect to income, a 1 per cent increase in income is to be associated with a fall of 2 per cent in the level of the utility indicator.

Another method of weighting, that of calculating a set of weights from the marginal rates of income tax, derives from the premise that the object of a progressive income tax is to share the 'real' burden of any increment of tax equally among all income groups. Thus, if on the marginal dollar of income, the 'rich' (say those in the $100,000 to $500,000 bracket) pay 80 cents, and the 'not so rich' (say those in the $10,000 to $25,000 bracket) pay 10 cents, it may be inferred that 80 cents for the rich has a utility that is equal to 10 cents for the not-so-rich or that an additional dollar to the rich is worth only $1/8$ as much as an additional dollar is worth to the not-so-rich.

A third method of weighting would be to calculate the set of weights as a result of the ratio between the income of the different income groups and that of the average national income. Thus, assuming the average national income is $50,000, the weight for the rich (income of $200,000) would be $50,000/$200,000 which equals $1/4$ and that of the poor (income of $10,000) would be $50,000/$10,000 which equals 5. It can be seen that there is an inverse relationship between the weight and income, and this is so reflected

Alternatively, the weighting system can be made dependent upon political decisions taken in the recent past. One way of doing this, proposed by Weisbrod (1968), rests on the assumption that all public projects that were adopted, notwithstanding their failure to meet cost–benefit criteria, were adopted as a result of an implicit set of utility weights attaching to the earnings of different groups. By comparing a number of such projects, these utility weights can be made explicit and, perhaps, become incorporated into the economist's cost–benefit criterion.

Again, although they differ from the actual techniques used by Weisbrod, the proposals advanced by Dasgupta *et al.* (1972) also defer to prevailing political agenda in giving expression to distributional, regional or merit priorities and in deriving particular prices such as the social rate of discount. Such proposals amount to the employment of what we may call politico-weights, their purpose being to reflect – and therefore unavoidably to promote – the government's planning objectives or political priorities.

Finally, we can use sensitivity testing to work out a range of alternatives weights. If a change in the weights results in an insignificant change in the CBA, we can deduce that the model used is robust. What this implies is that the CBA is relatively reliable and that the imposition of weights to account for income distribution is not a serious issue. Conversely, if a small change in the set of weights greatly alters the result of the CBA, this becomes a serious issue, as the final result is very sensitive to the change of weight, especially when the reliability of the set of weights is unknown.

It cannot be emphasized too often however, that CBA as generally practised is to be regarded as no more than economically informative calculations in the service of those having to make social or political decisions. It is then clearly understood that the outcome of a cost–benefit calculation is, of itself, not socially decisive. It does not meet even conventional welfare economics criteria for an improvement in social welfare, in as much as these criteria also have regard to distributional considerations. It is certainly not to be thought of as an alternative to the government's economic policy or as overriding it – although it may properly be seen as a corrective to economic policy or, at least, as an aid in reaching political decisions. A CBA as understood here, and quite generally, is conducted solely in terms of economic valuation and therefore, by definition, excludes distributional effects or existing social predilections in favour of certain groups or regions or types of goods. It may have to ignore intangible spillovers simply because, for some, they defy measurement – although in such instances the economist must make this omission explicit and, in addition, provide whatever information is available.

Of the occasional influence of a project on broad social goals, CBA can only draw public attention to the fact. In sum, a well-conducted cost–benefit study can be only a part, though an important part, of the data necessary for informed collective decisions.

Attempts to work more into the technique of CBA, to endow it with greater self-sufficiency for policy purposes, by recourse to distributional weights or national parameters formulated by reference to political decisions or, at any rate, by reference to non-economic considerations, are to be resisted by economists in that they entail the following disadvantages.

First, there is the obvious difficulty of securing widespread acceptance of a given set of distributional weights or of any other weights.

If the weights are chosen through the political process or from political priorities, they may vary from one year to the next and from one country to another, according to the composition of legislators, political fashions or the exigencies of bureaucrats.

Whether and to what extent such politico-weights do, in fact, vary over time, it has to be acknowledged that they are selected or deduced so as effectively to vindicate the policies or projects favoured by the government in question.[1] Such a 'politically massaged' CBA may help ensure political consistency in the government's selection of projects, yet it does so only by jettisoning the economic rationale of the basic cost–benefit criterion, $\Sigma V > 0$.

If, however, the weights are to be chosen by the economist, they are perforce arbitrary. They will vary with the social climate and are also likely to encounter squabbles among economists, or between social groups and economists. And since some projects will be sanctioned on one set of weights and rejected using another set, one can anticipate some political in-fighting over the weights to be adopted. In this way, a continuing search by economists for an ideal set of weights may result in the public's discrediting the employment of cost–benefit techniques or, indeed, of economic measurement generally.

Second, the proposed utility-weighted criteria are at variance with the allocative principles by which the perfectly competitive economy is vindicated. It is sometimes argued that conventional CBA carries an implicit weighting system,

---

1 Once political valuations are believed pertinent for some items, there is no clear case for limiting the extent of political intervention for that purpose. If decision makers can attach weights to merit goods, why not to ordinary goods also on the argument that, as among ordinary goods, some have smaller social merit than others? If they can attach a valuation to accidents or loss of life, why not also to a wide range of spillover effects? And if so much can be justified, there seems to be no logical reason against going further and having political decisions override all market prices and subjective valuations. Indeed, there is no reason why each and every investment project should not be approved or rejected directly by the political process, democratic or otherwise. With such a dispensation, the economist could entertain the public by cleverly explicating the implicit prices or weights that could justify any particular investment decision so that it could compare them with those corresponding to some other investment decisions.

namely, that one dollar is equal to one 'util', irrespective of who gains or loses the dollar, or that a dollar gained or lost has the same value for both poor and rich. But the rationale of the conventional CBA is not to be interpreted as having any affinity with a social goal of maximizing or increasing aggregate utility. No interpersonal comparisons of utility are to be invoked. As frequently indicated, cost–benefit methods derive their rationale from the concept of a potential Pareto improvement – the social value of output being so increased that (by costless redistributions of net gains) everyone *can* be made better off by the change in question.

This much being granted, a traditional CBA can be properly regarded as an extension of an efficient price system; certainly it enables the economist to select projects and programmes that are estimated to produce an excess of social benefit over resource cost and, indeed, of opportunity cost. If, however, the economist elects to use a contrived cost–benefit criterion, using a system of weights and possibly also politically directed valuations, so departing from the traditional $\Sigma V > 0$ criterion, then clearly projects and programmes may be sanctioned even though the value of the benefits they confer fall short of the costs incurred – so that their introduction implies that everyone, via costless redistribution, can be made worse off. Such contrived cost–benefit criteria therefore entail a departure from the norms of allocative efficiency.

Third, no matter how accurate or acceptable are the set of utility-weights proposed, their incorporation into a CBA does not, in general, serve the purpose for which they are presumably designed – to promote equity, or at least to guard against projects that are distributionally regressive. For whatever the set of weights employed, the resulting utility-weighted cost–benefit criterion could still admit projects that make the rich richer and the poor poorer, especially if the rich persons affected by the project are numerous or are made very much richer.

Although the device of incorporating utility weights into a CBA as a means of enforcing the claims of equity or distribution is evidently unsatisfactory, distributional and other social goals must be respected by the economist who offers advice to society. The least he should do is to point up the distributional implications wherever they appear significant. And since he need not affect to be so unworldly as to be in ignorance of society's commitment to greater equality, or to its declared aversion to measures that harden the lot of the poor, the economist can afford, on occasion, to be more emphatic. In particular, wherever an investment project that appears to be advantageous by ordinary cost–benefit criteria causes particular hardship to some groups, the economist should consider the practical possibilities of adequate compensation.

3   It is frequently alleged that a CBA or, for that matter, a competitive economy, ignores considerations of the social merit of certain goods, services or activities, an allegation that no perceptive economist would deny.

To some extent, their omission in a particular cost–benefit calculation may be ascribed to seemingly insuperable difficulties in their evaluation (although, as indicated earlier, all available information about them should be made explicit). Wherever the range of benefits of such good things as better health, improved education or expanded recreational facilities can be satisfactorily measured, wholly or in part, they will, of course, be included in the calculation, and what cannot be included will be described.

On the other hand, merit goods or merit benefits, such as national pride, more civic participation, better community relations or the alleviation of poverty, though they might notionally be brought 'into relation with the measuring rod of money' are likely to elude all economists' attempts to translate them into unequivocal money valuations.

Socially desirable goods of this latter sort are some times measured by what have come to be known as social indicators, the units proposed varying from one good to another. Health, for instance, might include longevity, infant mortality, reduction in diseases, improved weight control and so on. The measurement of poverty might include the proportion of families living below some index of 'real' income, existing on a sub-standard diet or occupying sub-standard low-cost housing.

Wherever programmes are expected to have significant welfare effects that cannot realistically be evaluated, the measurements of the appropriate social indicators should be drawn to the attention of the decision makers in addition, therefore, to the calculated benefits.

There can be yet other intangible welfare effects on the community for which no social indicators are feasible: they may serve to augment civic pride or to promote self-confidence, objectives deemed desirable by society and therefore, if necessary, to be drawn to the attention of the public body that commissions the CBA.

4   There is, finally, the proposal that the economic valuation of some goods or of the benefits to particular groups or regions be raised or lowered in order to reflect the declared or the inferred national objectives. Thus, if for broad policy objectives, the government looks more favourably on benefits accruing to area A residents than on benefits accruing to area B residents, a dollar of benefits to the residents of area A will carry a greater weight than a dollar of benefits to the residents of area B. In addition to some doubts about the implications of this practice aired in footnote 1, it is unsatisfactory on other grounds.

Wherever a public body commissions a CBA, it presumably expects an independent economic assessment which it treats as an important input in arriving at a political decision that also takes into account other desiderata. And in this regard only a wholly independent economic assessment will serve, one that is raised on a single criterion, a potential Pareto improvement, formalised here as $\Sigma V > 0$.

Were an estimation of the relevant ΣV to reveal a net loss, it would be properly regarded as telling against the introduction of the project. Yet, such an economic assessment is, of itself, not decisive. There may be countervailing considerations turning on equity or other social merits to set against it.

If, however, instead of a wholly economic assessment based on ΣV, the proposed evaluation of the project or programme is one in which the valuations of benefits and losses are transformed by a weighting scheme putatively designed to express the government's national objectives and priorities then, in so far as it is successful in expressing them, all government-proposed programmes will be approved. Were it otherwise, were government proposed programmes to be rejected by this contrived criterion, the only conclusion that could reasonably be drawn would be that the weights initially assigned were faulty, or that the government's priorities are inconsistent.

Therefore, any government or any decision maker prepared to sanction the use of a cost–benefit assessment built on politico-weights should be made aware that such an assessment acts as little more than a mirror which reflects its own political priorities and biases. Consequently, such an assessment can no longer act as a check to political ambition. On the contrary, it acts only to reinforce, indeed, to vindicate it.

5   As we shall discover in later chapters, there are substantial difficulties in discovering an acceptable rate at which society as a whole can be deemed to discount the future. The difficulties arise not because society is too large a group, or because of large differences between them of income and wealth. Such differences do not prevent the economist from calculating the valuation of other goods and bads.

The difficulties arise for a number of related reasons: capital markets tend to be imperfect; in advanced economies, rates of return vary widely according to risk and length of investment; and then there is the existence of progressive income tax. Concerning the latter, even supposing that everyone in the community had the same rate of time preference, say 6 per cent per annum, the introduction of a progressive income tax system would alter the requirements of different income groups. Imposing a 40 per cent income tax on the marginal incomes of the wealthy would result in their requiring a 10 per cent premium in order to induce them to postpone x consumption until next year. Those paying 20 per cent income tax on their marginal incomes, in contrast, would require only a 7.5 per cent premium to induce them to postpone x for a year, and so on. Again, for any given rate of return on investment, a portion may be paid out, part of which may be consumed and part invested, the remainder of the investment return being reinvested either in the same project or in some others.

Notwithstanding such difficulties, the economist must endeavour to calculate appropriate rates of discount, based ultimately on individual valuations only, if he is to offer an independent economic assessment to the political decision maker – an injunction that is consistent with our arguments for disallowing into our economic criterion all social or political weights or valuation. It follows that any arbitrary or politically inspired rate of discount proposed as being appropriate for public projects or programmes has to be rejected, for its employment could well sanction projects that would fail the economist's $\Sigma V > 0$ criterion, and vice versa.

Moreover, where the *de facto* decision maker is virtually a dictator or a powerful bureaucrat though perhaps a humane bureaucrat, the idea of empowering him to set crucial prices or, specifically, the social rate of discount has even less social warrant. In poor countries, for instance, the bureaucrat is likely to be one among the group imbued with 'Western ideas' of the desirability of rapid economic growth. He is likely to think of himself as the custodian of future generations, charged with the sacred task of transforming a 'backward' economy into a 'modern' economy in the face of the resentment, inertia and 'superstition' of the masses. In the endeavour to achieve a faster rate of economic growth than that which would accord with existing behaviour patterns in the mass of people, the 'policy maker' will be prone to adopt a social rate of discount for the guidance of economic decisions that is appreciably lower than that which is in realistic relation to people's actual time preference, or to the rates of return that would emerge under ideal economic institutions. Too low a discount rate may also arguably affect efficiency in the use of scarce money resources in terms of forgone opportunities. It may also encourage too much public investment over private investment.

6 While eschewing politically determined weights or parameters in any criterion of economic efficiency (based, as it is, wholly on individuals' valuations) we can hardly avoid the incidence of political constraints in any cost–benefit calculation. As such constraints do not entail arbitrary or non-economic valuations, they act only to circumscribe the range of calculations and are to be construed as information on how the government, as decision maker, proposes to act or is expected to act. To be sure, the government may not act wisely in as much as it violates mainstream economic norms. In undertaking a CBA, however, the economist is in no way endorsing government policies or the particular constraints proposed in the designated project. Indeed, he may go on record as opposing them, notwithstanding which he is obliged to accept them. For he is seeking to discover whether, within the proposed constraints, the introduction of the project or programme in question will yet realize a potential Pareto improvement.

Political constraints may include the location of the project, the level of operation of one or more plants over a given period, restrictions on exports of the product or even the sort of workers to be employed. In addition, they may include restrictions on the distribution of the goods produced by the project and, in respect of any money portion of the returns over time to the investment, the proportions to be either reinvested in the project or invested in other enterprises.

Thus the economist, in evaluating a project, does not claim to be achieving optimal results. He is not claiming that nothing better can be done. On the contrary, he will readily agree that better can be done (for the economy at large as well as for the outcome of the project he is concerned with) if certain political or administrative constraints were to be modified or removed. But by making provision in his cost–benefit calculations for the constraints that are expected to prevail over the project's lifetime, the economist is addressing himself specifically to the question: what difference does it make to the economy if, under the constraints likely to be operative over the relevant time period, this specific investment project is introduced? In particular, does the project, under these conditions, bring about a potential Pareto improvement?

7   A question that often arises is that of how to treat the various ways in which the project or programme can be financed. After all, the \$500 million, say, that is required for the project can be provided by raising that sum on the open market or by borrowing it from the Treasury or by a reduction in government expenditures on health, education, pensions, etc., or else from additional taxes, whether excise or income taxes – or, of course, any combination of these.

The ways in which the necessary funds are to be raised also come under the category of political constraints which the economist perforce has to accept. And inasmuch as any designated way of raising the required funds entails the foregoing of some existing stream of benefits (one that would have been generated if, instead, the sum in question had not been withdrawn to finance the project), these foregone streams of benefits are to be thought of as opportunity costs.

A calculation of these opportunity costs is not, however, included in the economist's brief – not unless he is directed otherwise by the decision maker. He need confine himself only to estimating the ΣV of the project under consideration, in order to determine whether the aggregate is positive.

Although the above remarks may seem self-evident to some students, they can bear emphasis in as much as the notion, and proposed measurement, of what is sometimes referred to as the 'excess burden' or 'deadweight burden' on society incurred when the necessary funds are raised by an (increase in) income tax or by an excise tax continues to appear in some currently used cost–benefit textbooks. This rather old-fashioned but persistent concept is something of 'a green mare's nest' notwithstanding that the analytic errors involved have been treated at length in the more fastidious literature on welfare economics.[2]

Finally, although the treatment of all aspects of the subject in this volume is related to a cost–benefit criterion based on the concept of a potential Pareto improvement, we cannot stress too often that such a criterion might well conflict with the law or with popular opinion. The law might well forbid the undertaking of certain enterprises that can realize a potential or even an actual Pareto improvement. For example, gladiatorial contests, public exhibitions of obscenity, the sale of hallucinatory drugs might be forbidden by laws expressive of public opinion, even though every person directly affected might freely choose to participate.

The reverse is no less likely: the law may enact measures that do not realize a potential Pareto improvement. Issues over which feelings run high – for example, the choice within a country between several regions which are to receive government subsidies in order to encourage industrial or environmental development – can sometimes be more satisfactorily resolved through the political process. In addition, it has to be borne in mind that political decisions can modify the legal framework within which economic behaviour is circumscribed and,

---

2 See in particular Chapters 31–34 in Mishan (1981), also Appendix 4 on the theory of Second Best.

consequently, economic valuations also. In particular, they can determine which of the two groups representing opposing interests – as occurs in any development that creates adverse spillover effects – has the legal obligation to compensate the other. As we shall see, such a decision can make a significant difference to the valuation of such spillovers.

Part II

Basic concepts of benefits and costs

4 Measurements of consumer surplus

1 A favourite sport among the earlier generation of economists was that of taking pot shots at the still-floating concept or measurement of consumer surplus in the endeavour to sink it beneath the waves.[1] It is as well that such endeavours have failed to do so. Notwithstanding some ill-considered judgements about the uses of consumer surplus by some highly regarded economists some two score years ago,[2] it is a concept so crucial to allocative economics generally, and CBA in particular, that there is everything to be said for clarifying the concept itself and the ways it can be measured.

What makes the concept effectively unsinkable is the fact that even the most ardent critic cannot deny that 'there is something in it'. After all, if he agrees that in mainstream economics one values the worth of a thing to a person by what he is willing to pay for it, he has only to take a small step before stumbling on the consumer surplus concept (Carson *et al.*, 1993).

Thus, if a man is willing to pay as much as $25 for a litre of cider, the economist has to concede that it is worth no less to him than $25. If, however, he buys that litre at $15, he is obviously better off than if he had indeed to pay the $25 that he is willing to pay. And it makes sense to say that, when he buys the litre of cider at $15, which is $10 less than the $25 he is willing to pay, he makes a saving of $10 which may properly be regarded as a measure of his gain – that is, of his consumer surplus.

Again, if we now suppose that, at the price of $15, the man buys ten litres of cider each month, and the price is then lowered to $10 a litre, there is a cost-saving of $5 on each of the ten litres he habitually bought. Thus, in the limiting case in which he continues to buy only ten litres at the lower price, he will find himself

---

1 There have been critiques based on inconsistency, intransitivity, and multiplicity. An appraisal of the main critiques can be found in Mishan (1977a).

2 For instance, Little (1957) stated that it was no more than 'a theoretical toy' (p. 180) and, according to Samuelson (1963), 'The subject is of historical and doctrinal interest with a limited amount of appeal as a purely mathematical puzzle' (p. 195). This latter remark could be said with some truth about quite a number of topics in contemporary economics, but it certainly cannot be accepted as sound judgement of the consumer surplus concept. Without it, how can the economist rationalize the free use of parks, bridges or roads, or the use of two-part tariffs?

with an additional sum of $50 (10 × $5) each month, which he can spend on other goods. Such an example alone is enough to vindicate the concept of consumer surplus. There can, however, be arguments about how exactly to measure it.

2 Let us put these arguments aside for the present and adopt in this and the following two chapters a simple common-sense definition of consumer surplus traceable to the French engineer Dupuit (1844): the consumer surplus of a person is measured by the most he would pay for a thing less the amount he actually pays for it.

Let us now consider a single person's demand curve for a good x. In the ordinary way, we interpret this curve as a locus of the maximum amount of x that the person will want to buy at any given price. This demand curve, however, may just as well be interpreted differently – as the most the person will pay for each successive unit of x. If the good x is a litre of milk, we can ask what is the most the person will pay for one litre of milk per week: then, what is the most he will pay for a second litre and so on, as depicted in Figure 4.1 for the first ten litres.

These successive amounts of money, which we can speak of as margin valuations, are plotted in the figure as the heights of successive columns. If the price of a litre of milk is equal to P, say 20 cents, then the person makes a gain or surplus on each successive litre of milk bought per week up to and including the seventh litre. He does not buy an eighth litre, since its worth to him is less than the price he would have to pay for it. Thus, the figure illustrates the case in which the man makes the largest consumer surplus by buying seven litres of milk a 20 cents, so spending $1.40 per week on milk. The area contained in the shaded parts of the columns above the price line is a sum of money equal to the person's consumer surplus.

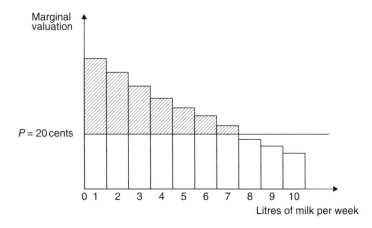

Figure 4.1

3   Once perfect divisibility is assumed, the stepped outline of the columns gives way to a smooth demand curve. From a point on the vertical or price axis the horizontal distance to the curve measures the maximum amount of the good the person will buy at that price. The market demand curve, being a horizontal summation of all the individual demand curves, can be regarded as the marginal valuation curve for society. For example, the height *QR* in Figure 4.2, corresponding to output *OQ*, gives the maximum value some person in society is willing to pay for the *Q*th unit of the good – which, for that person, may be the first, second or *n*th unit of the good bought. But to each of the total number of units purchased, which total is measured as a distance along the quantity axis, there corresponds some individual's maximum valuation. The whole area under the demand curve, therefore, corresponds to society's maximum valuation for the quantity in question. If, say, *OQ* is bought, the maximum worth of *OQ* units to society is given by the trapezoid area *ODRQ*. Now the quantity *OQ* is bought by the market at price *OP*. Total expenditure by the buyers is, therefore, represented by the area *OPRQ* (price *OP* times quantity *OQ*). Subtracting from the maximum worth of buyers (*ODRQ*) what they have to pay (*OPRQ*) leaves us with a total consumers surplus equal to triangle *DRP*.

If an entirely new good *x* is introduced into the economy and is made available to all and sundry free of charge, the area under the resulting demand curve, *ODE* (given that prices of all other goods are unaffected), is a good enough measure of the gain to the community in its capacity as consumer. The services provided by a new bridge or a new park would be familiar examples. Again, however, if a price *OP* for the service is introduced, the amount *OQ* will be bought, leaving the triangular area *PDR* in Figure 4.2 as the consumer surplus. Estimates of consumer

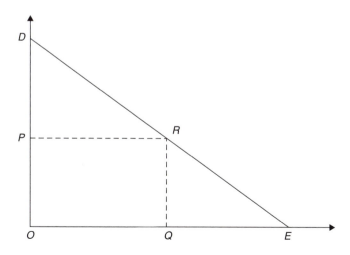

Figure 4.2

surplus, it need hardly be said, are to be entered as benefits in all cost–benefit calculations. Alternatively, it represents a welfare gain from consumption.

4   Any investment with the object of reducing the cost of a product or service is deemed to confer a benefit on the community, which benefit is often referred to as a 'cost-difference' or a 'cost-saving'. The benefit of a new motorway or flyover is estimated by reference to the expected savings in time and in the cost of fuel by all motorists who will make use of the new road or flyover. As already indicated, however, the concept of cost-saving is derived directly from the concept of consumer surplus, as shown in Figure 4.3. Thus, prior to the introduction of, say, the new flyover in question, the consumer surplus from using this particular route (being the maximum sum motorists are willing to pay above the amount they currently spend on the journey – an average of OP per journey) is the triangle PDR. If the flyover halves the cost of the journey to them, from OP to OP_1, at which lower cost the number of journeys undertaken is increased from OQ to OQ_1, the consumer surplus increases from PDR to P_1DR_1, an increase equal to the shaded strip PP_1R_1R.

This increase in consumer surplus can be split up into two parts. There is, first, the cost-saving component, the rectangle PP_1SR, which is calculated as the savings per journey, PP_1, multiplied by the original number of journeys made, OQ. The other component, represented by the triangle SRR_1, is the consumer surplus made on the additional journeys undertaken, QQ_1, either by the same motorists or by additional motorists. The cost-saving item that enters a cost–benefit calculation is, as indicated, no more than a portion of the increment of consumer surplus from a fall in the cost of the good. Since it takes no account of the additional goods that will be bought in response to the fall in cost, the cost-saving rectangle alone can be accepted as a *minimum* estimate of the benefit.

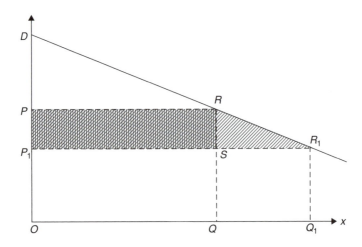

Figure 4.3

We might call this explanation a casual account of the matter, though not a misleading one. Nothing need be said about *utility*, as we are not going to translate our money magnitudes into utility terms: the area under the market demand curve, that is, does not become translated into a sum of individual utilities, but remains simply as a sum of their valuations. The extent of the collective improvement from the introduction of a good is, then, expressed in terms of a sum of money which is measured by a triangle of consumer surplus, such as *PDR* in Figure 4.2. Its interpretation is simply the maximum amount of money the group as a whole would offer in order to be able to buy *OQ* of this new good at price *P*. The extent of the collective improvement from a reduction in its price, however, is expressed as an increment of consumer surplus, as for example the strip PP_1R_1R in Figure 4.3. The strip can be interpreted as the maximum amount of money the group as a whole would offer in order to have the price reduced from *OP* to OP_1.

5 So far, the consumer surplus analysis has had reference to the demand for a final good, say a clock, although it can also be extended to the derived demand for some input or intermediate good, such as the steel that is used in the manufacture of clocks.

The appropriate consumers surplus measure for steel, or steel of a particular kind, is obtained from the correctly *derived* demand curves for steel. Thus, the short-run demand curve for steel derived from the clock industry is obtained by subtracting from the marginal valuation of the first clock produced, that of the second clock and so on until that of the *n*th clock, the combined cost of all the *a* inputs other than steel that enter into the production of each successive clock produced – assuming the prices of all inputs other than steel to be fixed and assuming also that they are combined efficiently.[3] We are also to take care not to violate the *ceteris paribus assumption* for the demand curves for steel derived from all other steel-using goods, which requires that such demand curves be introduced in sequence, as will be explained in the following chapter.

6 Something more must now be said about this relationship between price and quantity. Beginning from a general equilibrium system, we could deduce that the amount of a good *x* that is bought depends not only on its own price but, in general, on the prices of all other goods and factors; also on tastes, on technical knowledge and on the distribution of resource endowments. In statistical estimates of the price demand curve for *x*, the relationship is much more restricted. We might, for example, try to gather enough data so as to derive a specific equation from the relationship $X = F(P_x, P_y, P_z, M)$, where X is the maximum amount of good *x* demanded, P_x, P_y, P_z are the prices respectively of the goods x, y and z, and

---

3 The first-order conditions for productive efficiency require that input rates of substitution be inverse to the ratio of input prices. The elasticity of the derived demand for an intermediate good such as steel varies *inter alia* with the elasticity of substitution between this intermediate good and others, and also with the elasticity of the demand for the final goods using the intermediate good.

M is the aggregate real income. Goods y and z could be chosen as being close and important substitutes for x, or else y could be a close substitute and z a close complement of x, the relative prices of all other goods being ignored. Sometimes the price of one or more factors is to be included in the function. If, for example, the good x is taken as being farm tractors, the income of the farm population would obviously be a significant variable in the demand for tractors. In any statistical estimate of the price–demand curve for x, the *ceteris paribus* clause will operate to hold constant only those variables, other than P_x, that are included in function F. All those variables that are not included in function F – an almost unlimited number of goods and factor prices – are assumed, provisionally at least, to be of negligible importance.

In cost–benefit analysis, however, the emphasis in the *ceteris paribus* clause of the market demand curve for good x is on the constancy of the *prices* of goods closely related to good x. So although the *amounts* bought of all the other goods in the economy, including the amounts of closely related goods y and z, are likely to alter in response to a change in the price of good x, the measure of the consumer surplus arising from the change in the price of x is not thereby affected.[4] Only if, for any reason, alterations in the *prices* of related goods y and z take place following a fall or a rise in the price of good x does the measure of consumer surplus from the initial change in the price of x have to be qualified, as we shall see in the next chapter.

7   This injunction to ignore consequent shifts in the *ceteris paribus* demand curves for other goods does not, however, preclude an interpretation of the resulting areas under such demand curves. Assuming provisionally constant costs in the production of all goods in the economy, a fall in the price of x will cause a shift to the left of the *ceteris paribus* demand curve for good y, which is, we assume, an important substitute for x. The now smaller area under this demand curve for y is the consumer surplus enjoyed from the availability of y, at the unchanged price of y, when the price of x is lower than before. This smaller area of consumers surplus for y accords with common sense, for with the fall in the price of its close substitute x, the existing level of welfare will depend less on good y than before. Thus, if y were now to be totally withdrawn from the market, the welfare loss suffered by society would be smaller, simply because the substitute x has become available at a lower price than before.

To illustrate, in Figures 4.4 and 4.5, the initial *ceteris paribus* demand curve for each good is the solid line. D_xE_x is the demand curve for x (when the price of good

---

4 If the demand curve for x has an elasticity greater than unity along the relevant range, the expenditure on all other goods taken together will fall, and (assuming full employment) some of the factors released will move into the production of good x, the converse being true if the elasticity of demand for x is below unity.

In the limiting case of unity elasticity of the demand for x, there will be no change in the total cost of producing the additional amount of x and no change in the total expenditure on good x. Consequently, there is no change in the total expenditure on all other goods taken together.

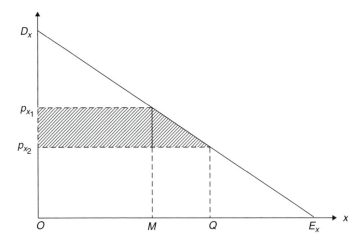

Figure 4.4

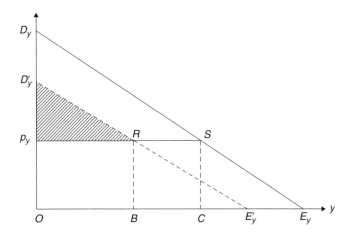

Figure 4.5

y is held constant at p_y); $D_y E_y$ is the demand curve for y (when the price of good x is held constant at p_{x_1}). If now, as a result of some improved method of production, the price of x falls from p_{x_1} to p_{x_2}, the demand curve for y falls from $D_y E_y$ to $D_y' E_y'$, as shown in Figure 4.5. At the unchanged price p_y, the smaller quantity of y (OB) is demanded instead of the quantity OC that was demanded before the fall in the price of x.

With a lower price of x, consumers are obviously better off. They would, of course, be better off even if they had to buy exactly the same amounts of x and y as they did before the fall in the price of x. But they further improve their welfare by buying more of x and buying less of y. Once they have made these changes in their purchases of x and y, how do we interpret these consumers surpluses? First, the measure of the gain in consumers surplus is represented wholly by the shaded strip in Figure 4.4 between the original price p_{x_1} and the new price p_{x_2}. Provided all other goods prices remain unchanged – and in particular that of the close substitute y – this shaded strip measures the most that consumers will pay to have the reduction in the price of x.

Second, the shaded triangle shown in Figure 4.5 represents the consumer surplus in having a price p_y when the price of x is now p_{x_2}. (This triangle is the difference between the most they would pay for OB of y (OD'_yRB) when x is priced at p_{x_2} and what they have to pay for OB of y (OP_yRB).)

Note particularly the interpretation of this reduced triangle of consumer surplus – that where the demand curve for y shifts inward in response to a fall in the price of x. The reduction of the *initial* area of consumer surplus p_yD_yS (corresponding to the original price of x, p_{x_1}) to this smaller area of consumer surplus $p_yD'_yR$ (corresponding to the lower price of x, p_{x_2}) – a reduction in area equal to D'_yD_ySR – *is* not to be regarded as a loss of consumer surplus consequent upon the fall in the price of x from p_{x_1} to p_{x_2}. This reduction in area is simply the consequence of consumers' bettering themselves by switching from good y to the new lower-priced good x. Provided supply prices are constant, and we assume they are, the *ceteris paribus* conditions are met, and the partial analysis depicts the consumers' gains wholly within the area of the demand curve of the good, the price of which has fallen – irrespective, that is, of the resulting magnitude and direction of the shifts in demand for all other goods in the economy.

It follows that, if we are focusing our attention on the consumer surplus of the good x, and it appears to increase in response to a rise in the price of the substitute good y, this larger area under the demand curve for x is to be interpreted as the maximum amount of money that people are now willing to pay for having x available at its unchanged price when all other prices are given and the price of the substitute good y is higher.

8   No exception to this analysis occurs if the rise in the price of a good y, or of any other good related to x, is a result of direct government intervention. If the government levies an excise tax on y or adopts a policy of withdrawing y from the market, the economist is always at liberty to point out the lack of economic justification for such policies, and the consequences that are likely to follow from their implementation. But assuming these policies are to prevail over the relevant time period, he has no choice but to measure the changes in the consumer surpluses of good x in the usual way.

Only if the economist is engaged in a cost–benefit study that encompasses a number of closely related goods is he in a position to pronounce on actions to change other relevant prices from some generally acceptable pattern, say from that corresponding to marginal social costs. A transport economist, for example, would wish to point out that the apparent increase in the consumer surplus of private traffic, which *seems* to warrant investment in road-widening schemes, is the result simply of a reduction in the availability of public transport, a reduction that is itself the result of traffic congestion on existing roads. The imposition of a toll on traffic designed to produce an *optimal* flow of vehicles on the existing road will, of itself, also increase the efficiency along it of public transport. Moreover, with such a toll in place, the resulting consumer surplus may no longer warrant investment in road-widening. Such a solution is clearly the more efficient, and that which, in the circumstances, the economist will propose.[5] In contrast, if the economist is required to advise on road-widening schemes but is allowed no control whatsoever on the existing volume of private traffic (which may well be greatly in excess of an optimal flow), he has no choice but to accept such political constraints and to calculate the benefits of a road-widening scheme under the existing conditions.

9　We have stated that, in the construction of the demand curve for a good x, the comprehensive *ceteris paribus* pound contains all other product prices, all factor prices, tastes, technology and resource endowments. Since changes in resource endowments can imply changes in distribution or in the size of population, and changes in technology can imply changes in real income per capita, the *ceteris paribus* clause can be expressed in an alternative form that requires constancy of product prices, population, per capita income, distribution and tastes. We shall now go on to consider the treatment of consumer surplus when each of these items is no longer held constant, beginning in the next chapter with the treatment of consumer surplus when the prices of related goods are altered.

5　This analysis is used by Mishan (1967a) in connection with the misuse of consumer surplus in road-building proposals.

5 Consumer surplus when several prices change

1 This chapter is a simple exercise in partial equilibrium analysis: in the adding and subtracting of consumer surpluses arising from sequential or simultaneous changes in the prices of two or more related goods.

2 Hicks (1956) has shown how the consumer surplus on two or more substitute goods, say gas and electricity, that are introduced simultaneously can be measured. Suppose that gas is introduced at a given price p_g into an area that has no electricity. The shaded triangle of Figure 5.1 can be taken as a measure of the resulting consumer surplus. If, following this event, electricity is introduced at a price p_e, the demand curve for electricity D_eE_e, is obviously smaller when gas is available at a fixed price p_g than it would be in the absence of gas, for the consumers already derive much benefit from gas, and the introduction of a fairly close substitute is not so great a boon as it would be if, instead, there had been no gas in the first place.

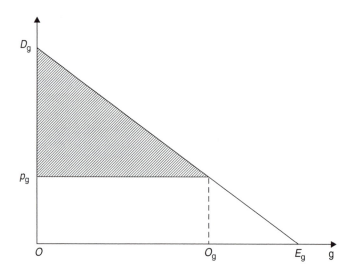

Figure 5.1

The additional gain to consumers from introducing electricity into a gas-using area is given by the shaded triangle in Figure 5.2. The sum of these two triangles together measures the consumer surplus from providing both gas and electricity at prices p_g and p_e, respectively.

Should the economist elect to measure the simultaneous introduction of gas and electricity using the same sequential device but in the reverse order (that is, first measuring the consumer surplus for introducing electricity when gas is assumed to be unavailable, and then measuring the consumer surplus for gas on the assumption that electricity is already available), the sum of these two component surpluses should, theoretically, be exactly the same.

This method of adding consumer surpluses can, of course, be extended to three or more goods, and is just as valid if the goods in question are complements rather than substitutes. If, for example, gas and electricity were complements – as they would be if the only use of electricity were the heating of electric pokers for lighting gas fires – a fall in the price of gas would raise the demand curve for electricity.

The analysis is, of course, symmetrical for simultaneous *withdrawal* of two or more goods. Thus, assuming again that gas and electricity are close substitutes, if electricity is first withdrawn from the market while gas remains as readily available at its old price p_g the loss of consumer surplus is given by the shaded triangle in Figure 5.2. Since gas is a substitute, the demand curve for gas shifts to the right following the withdrawal of electricity. The resulting or final consumer surplus for gas then becomes the shaded triangle in Figure 5.1, and is the measure of the loss sustained if gas, previously available at p_g, is also withdrawn from the market.

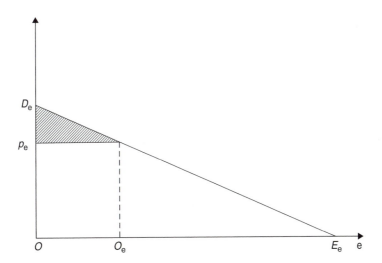

Figure 5.2

3   The further extension of the method to simultaneous *price* changes poses no problems. Suppose once more that electricity and gas are close substitutes and that the prices of both rise. The loss of consumer surplus arising from the rise in the price of gas from p_{g_1} to p_{g_2}, the price of electricity being (provisionally) unchanged, is shown by the shaded strip in Figure 5.3. As a direct result of the rise in the price of gas, the demand curve for electricity now moves outward from $D_e E_e$ to $D'_e E'_e$ in Figure 5.4. If, following this adjustment, the price of electricity rises from p_{e_1} to p_{e_2}, the further loss of consumer surplus is given by the shaded area in Figure 5.4. It is hardly surprising, after all, that the loss of consumer surplus from a rise in the price of electricity becomes greater when the price of its substitute good has become higher. The less available or the more expensive substitute goods are, the more it matters if the price of the good in question rises, and vice versa.

If, instead, gas and electricity happen to be complementary goods, a rise in the price of gas causes an inward shift of the demand curve for electricity. The additional loss of consumer surplus of any concomitant rise in the price of electricity is then smaller than if the price of gas had not risen in the first place. This also makes good sense, as an initial rise in the price of gas makes electricity *less* useful when it is complementary to gas – and not more useful as it will be when it is a substitute for gas.

4   The reader can soon convince himself that the analysis is symmetric for a sequential or simultaneous fall in the prices of two or more goods. A brief caveat is called for in this context because of the much-touted 'path-dependence' problem which, when applied to the adding of consumer surplus, has it that the aggregate of consumer surpluses from several price changes will differ in general according to the order in which they are taken. Although the mathematical theorem is

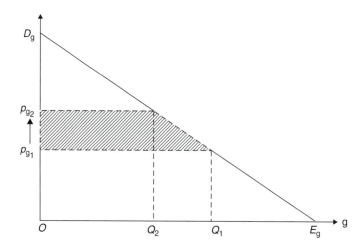

Figure 5.3

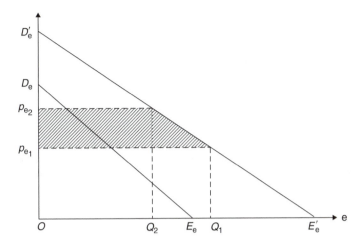

Figure 5.4

itself a valid one, it has no relevance to this particular economic exercise. The economist is obliged to take the number of price changes in a particular order only because he finds it convenient for calculation purposes to portray them within a partial equilibrium setting. These price changes are, however, deemed to occur simultaneously.

The imaginative reader may be able to picture a set of concave indifference surfaces in three-dimensional space, the vertical axis *y* being (real) income, the two horizontal axes being, respectively, goods *x* and *z*. A shift of the individual's budget plane, arising from a simultaneous change in the prices of *x* and *z*, will touch only one of the indifference surfaces – a higher, lower, or the same one – at only one point. In consequence, there is a unique measure for any definition of consumer surplus.[1]

Were it possible, then, to imagine a set of *n*-dimensional indifference surfaces, a simultaneous change in any or all of the goods prices, represented now by a change in the *n*-dimensional plane, would again reveal a unique equilibrium and, therefore, a unique consumer surplus.

5   For expositional purposes, we have so far held supply prices of all goods constant. By now removing this simplification, we can see that the above analysis is applicable also to cases in which supply curves slope upward or downward. For,

---

1   Although, as affirmed in the text, the theorem is without application to the simultaneous change in a number of goods prices, it is of passing interest to remark that the necessary and sufficient condition for path *in*dependence with respect to any pair of prices p_i and p_j is that $\partial q_j / \partial p_i = \partial q_i / \partial p_j$ (where q_i and q_j are the corresponding quantities), a condition that is explicit in the Hicksian system (see Hicks, 1939: Appendix).

if any good y is related to good x, the equilibrium price of y will also be affected if, in the first instance, there is an exogenous change in the price of x.

Let us restrict our attention to the two-good case, in which the good that has an exogenous fall in price, say electricity, has constant costs and the related good, say gas, which is a substitute for electricity, does not have constant costs.

Again, using the device of taking the price changes in sequence, the exogenous fall in the price of electricity from p_{e_1} to p_{e_2} first increases consumer surplus in electricity by the shaded area in Figure 5.5. But this fall in the price of electricity induces a leftward shift of the demand curve for gas from DD to $D'D'$ in Figure 5.6. If we assume first that, as in Figure 5.6, gas has an upward-sloping supply curve, there will be a fall in the equilibrium price of gas from p_g to p'_g. In consequence, there will also be a small leftward shift in the downward curve for electricity which, however, we provisionally ignore.

The total increment of welfare arising from the initial fall in the price of electricity *plus* the further induced fall in the equilibrium price of gas is calculated by adding the shaded strip in Figure 5.6 to the shaded strip in Figure 5.5. The interpretation of this procedure is straightforward enough.

First, the shaded strip in Figure 5.5 represents the increment of consumer surplus arising from the fall in the price of electricity *with the price of gas at* p_g. Second, the shaded strip in Figure 5.6 represents the further increment of consumer surplus for a fall in the equilibrium price of gas from p_g to p'_g *with the price of electricity remaining at* p_{e_2}. The sum of these two areas is then a measure of the amount that consumers are willing to pay for reducing the price of electricity from p_{e_1} to p_{e_2} when, as a result, the price of gas to them will also fall from p_g *to* p'_g. An extension of the analysis reveals that if gas has, instead, a *downward*-sloping supply curve, the leftward shift in its demand curve which is associated with the fall in the price of electricity results in a higher equilibrium price for gas and therefore entails

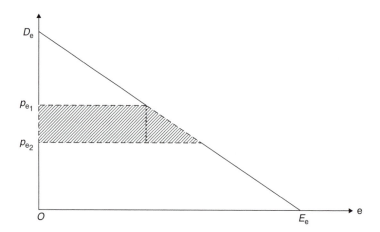

Figure 5.5

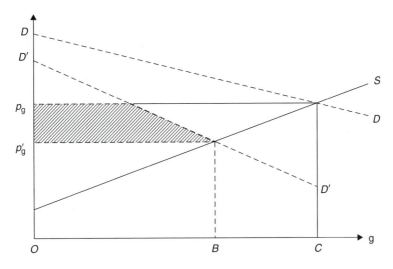

Figure 5.6

the loss of a strip of consumers surplus – consequently a *subtraction* of that strip from the shaded area in Figure 5.5. The resulting difference between the two areas is then a measure of the amount consumers are willing to pay when the price of electricity falls from p_{e_1} to p_{e_2} and, as a result, the price of gas is increased.[2]

2 The measure of simultaneous changes, whether of prices or availabilities, can have particular importance when measuring the community's loss or benefit from alterations in the amounts of collective goods or bads. To illustrate with a case of related sources of disamenity, say two chief sources of noise in a given area, that from cars and that from aircraft.

For each source of noise, we have an *individual*'s downward-sloping marginal valuation curve which measures the maximum sum he would pay to be rid of successive units of noise, beginning with some almost unbearable volume of noise, given – and this is critical – the existing large volume of noise from the other source.

With this sort of *ceteris paribus*, consider the marginal valuation curve for reducing car noise. Since there is not that much benefit to the individual from reducing car noise while aircraft noise continues at its high level, such a marginal valuation curve would not be very high. The same is true of the marginal valuation curve for reductions in aircraft noise.

Obviously, the benefit to the individual of a simultaneous reduction in the noise of both would be considerable: certainly more than the sum of the valuation as measured by the areas under the two *ceteris paribus* marginal valuation curves.

The correct measure of the benefit of removing both sources of noise is derived by adding to the benefit (or consumer surplus) as measured under the marginal valuation curve for car-noise riddance *given the existing high volume of aircraft noise*, the subsequent benefit (or consumer surplus) as measured by the area under the now much higher marginal valuation curve for aircraft-noise reduction. This latter curve is now much higher, simply because the relevant *ceteris paribus* contains the information that all car noise has been removed. Consequently, removal of aircraft noise now does make a real difference to the individual's amenity.

Symmetrical reasoning applies also to goods that are complements. If, for example, gas were now complementary with electricity, a fall in the price of electricity would cause an *outward* shift in the demand curve for gas. First, assume the supply curve of gas to be upward sloping. The outward shift in its demand curve increases the equilibrium output and price of gas. This rise in the price of gas entails a consumer loss which must be subtracted from the consumer gain arising from the initial fall in the price of electricity.

If, conversely, the supply curve of gas is downward sloping, the outward shift in its demand curve, arising from the initial fall in the price of electricity, results in a fall in the output and equilibrium price of gas. To that extent, there is now an additional consumer surplus in gas to be added to the increase in consumer surplus from the fall in the price of electricity.

6   To introduce a little more complication, let the supply curves slope upward both for electricity and gas. It now follows that the induced fall in the price of gas (from the inward shift of its demand curve resulting from the reduced price of electricity) will itself induce an inward shift in the demand curve for electricity, and therefore a *fall* in its price. Some further correction in consumer surplus is therefore necessary.

One may continue in this way indefinitely, although under plausible assumptions (related to *familiar* stability conditions) these mutually induced shifts in the two demand curves become smaller and converge to new equilibrium prices for both gas and electricity.

However, since the errors in estimating the relevant demand curves – in the above example, the initial demand curve for electricity and the inwardly shifted demand curve for gas, following a fall in the price of electricity – are likely to be large enough to swamp the refinements from further mutually induced shifts in the demand curves, some attempted corrections are best ignored. They would be worthwhile only if the initial price change was unusually large.

6 Consumer surplus when other things change

1 We now consider the treatment and interpretation of consumer surplus when there are changes in population size and in per capita real income, when enterprises producing similar goods already exist, and when there are changes in people's taste over time.

2 When estimating the demand curves over the future for goods to be provided by new investment projects we must make allowance for the growth in aggregate real income and its distribution.

Ignoring considerations of military or political power, a rise in population without any rise in real per capita income is not generally thought of today as conferring an increase in social welfare. Nonetheless, the resulting rise in demand for goods does operate to increase consumer surplus as defined and, consequently, may eventually make economically feasible particular projects that would, in the absence of population growth, remain economically unfeasible.

In fact, population growth and growth of per capita real income are the two components of aggregate economic growth and, together, contribute over time to the apparent growth of social benefits arising from any investment project that is currently undertaken. Clearly, the expectations of such growth-induced benefits must be taken into account by the economist, who is required to declare in advance the average rate or future pattern of aggregate economic growth on which his calculations are to be predicated. Having adopted some acceptable pattern over time of aggregate economic growth, he must then determine the way in which this economic growth will affect the magnitude of the benefits conferred by the goods that are to be produced by the investment project(s) under examination.

For example, in the *absence* of any expected growth in the economy, a hypothetical investment of 100 this year is expected to yield an annual stream of real benefits of 10, 10, 10, . . . , 10, ignoring the question of uncertainty. Allowing for an annual average growth rate of aggregate real income of 4 per cent, and assuming an income elasticity of unity for the goods produced by this investment, it becomes necessary to revise the annual stream of benefits to something like 10.4, 10.8, . . . , $10 \, (1.04)^n$, the nth year being the terminal year. Indeed, as indicated, the investment may prove to be economically unacceptable in the absence of such a rate of growth of aggregate demand.

This appears to be straightforward enough wherever a unique project is at issue such as a tunnel under the Severn river, a bridge over the Channel or a new national park. For such projects will not, over the foreseeable future, be 'threatened' by rival projects of a like nature. In such cases, growth in population alone (ignoring, that is, any increase in per capita income) will act to increase the demand for the services of such projects. The value of such services will grow, then, simply because the same service is being provided to more people. The bridge or tunnel or national park will accommodate an increasing number of travellers or visitors per annum – up to some point without an increase in current costs of upkeep.[1]

As for growth in per capita income in the absence of population growth, the increase in the usage of such newly created assets is less certain. For example, it may be the case that very few people will demand more park visits in response to a continuing rise in their incomes. Nevertheless, even if a person pays no more visits to a national park as he becomes richer, the value he places on the same number of visits will 'normally' – that is, if his income (or welfare) effect is positive – increase over time. This is not because his annual visits to the national park necessarily provide him with more utility as he becomes richer, but simply because the maximum sum he is prepared to pay for the same number of visits is higher when his real income is higher. Making our calculations on the basis of constant money prices over time, any rise in the value of benefits over time for all such reasons must be entered into the calculations.

3   Consider now the situation when one or more enterprises are similar to that being contemplated. The demand for the goods from, and the returns to, the existing enterprise(s) will be diminished by the introduction of the project in question. In what way should we allow for this?

Suppose the issue is that of building a bridge A now, bearing in mind that another such bridge B may be built a few years hence. If this later bridge B is built in response only to the growth in traffic – itself a result of the growth in population and in per capita real income – no problem arises. But if bridge B is to some extent competitive with the original bridge A, two questions must be faced: first, whether bridge A should be built at all if it is expected that a competitive, and possibly superior, bridge B will be built at a later date. Second, if it does appear economically feasible to build bridge A today, notwithstanding the later introduction of bridge B, when should bridge B be introduced?

Concerning the first question, the alternatives to be considered are those of introducing bridge A today and of building bridge B at some later date, where the sizes or construction of the two bridges can be varied, as can also the date at which the chosen bridge B is to be introduced. If the number of discrete variations in the timing and the size of the bridges are large, so also will be the alternative

---

1 We are ignoring the eventual costs of congestion as numbers increase. These are adverse spillover effects or external diseconomies that fall on the users themselves of tunnels, bridges and national parks, and they are discussed in some detail in Part III.

combinations, each such combination being regarded as a distinct and separate investment project. The object of the exercise – obviously, a somewhat tedious and time-consuming business – is to choose that combination which, on a net benefit criterion, is ranked above all others.

As for the second question, once bridge A is already in existence, the building of bridge B can be justified only when the benefits over time from building it – as measured by the expected consumer surplus of its users – exceeds its capital costs. And it does not matter whether the traffic expected to make use of the new bridge B is so great as to leave bridge A devoid of traffic. In economics, bygones are bygones. Bridge A has already been built; the capital sunk into its construction is irrecoverable. What matters now is whether the variable costs of bridge A could still be covered, otherwise bridge A should close. We need compare only the capital cost of building a new bridge B with the expected benefits over time, given that bridge A is still available.

The demand schedule for the use of bridge B is that which provides us with a measure of the community's benefit to be reaped by incurring the required capital expenditure. The area under the relevant demand curve that is above the variable cost of maintaining the bridge can be taken as a measure of the consumer surplus conferred by bridge B – being interpreted as the maximum sum above this variable cost that users of the bridge are ready to pay when they already have bridge A at their disposal.

4   Let us now move on to consider shifts in demand, and therefore of consumer surpluses, when there is a movement over time from one area to another, say from London to the Brighton area. Clearly, an increase in the investment in social capital, especially in public utilities, *will* be required in the Brighton area at the same time as existing social capital in London falls into disuse. If we suppose that, prior to the exodus, the amount of social capital was just right in both places, a prospective shortage of 100,000 houses in Brighton would be matched by a prospective vacancy of 100,000 houses in London. There would also be a need to extend schools, build roads, invest more in transport, electricity, gas, water and telephones, and provide additional distributional services in Brighton, all of which would require additional capital, while the equivalent capital investment in London would become superfluous. Clearly, it would have been more economical of society's scarce resources if the desire to move to Brighton had not occurred, for then the existing social capital stock would have sufficed.

But, once this change has occurred, the economist is concerned only with ways of meeting it efficiently.

Once social capital is irretrievably sunk in the London area, nothing can be done about it. In the light of existing demands, unwanted capital facilities become useless. All that matters now is the economic feasibility of building a new social capital in Brighton, where it is wanted. We must, therefore, compare only the additional capital outlays in Brighton with the magnitude of the expected benefits over the future as measured by the demand schedules for the extra services in question.

However, what the migrants into the Brighton area are willing to pay for the services will depend, among other things, on what they are compelled to pay for them in the London area. Only if they had to pay more than the marginal costs of public services in London could the amounts they would be willing to pay in Brighton be accepted as a correct measure of the benefits there. Indeed, an ideal allocative procedure would require that the managers of these service industries (public utilities and the like) be ready at all times to reduce the charges for such services to no more than the current marginal costs of providing them, rather than lose a customer. If the economy actually worked in this way, the services of the economist could be dispensed with in such circumstances. But as it is difficult to discriminate between customers in this way, and as extending a reduction in charges made on behalf of one customer to all other customers involves the company in losses of revenue – such losses being, in effect, transfer payments from the company to its customers – the customary charges (which are generally in excess of marginal cost) are generally maintained.

If this is so, however, it follows that the choice of moving from London to Brighton is being made on the wrong terms, for if, by reducing the charges of one or more of such public services until it is nearer to the marginal cost of its provision, a number of such 'emigrant' families can be induced to stay on in London, then a potential Pareto improvement can be effected: everyone concerned can be made better off as compared with the alternative situation in which such families move to Brighton.[2] The ideal experiment is not to allow any family to move from London to Brighton without first offering it the option of buying all such existing services at their marginal running costs. If, when such terms are offered to potential migrants, they are still willing to move and to pay for all newly required public services prices which cover their inclusive costs, all well and good.

Unless marginal cost pricing is already established in the public utility sector, such an ideal experiment – call it option 1 – is likely to run into administrative and political objections. For the costs of discovering potential migrants and of offering them special marginal cost terms without arousing the suspicion and hostility of other households can be prohibitive. If, however, option 1 is adopted, and all potential emigrants from the London area are presented with special permits enabling them to buy public utility services at their marginal costs, their demand schedules for any such service, say electricity, in Brighton will be based on a *ceteris paribus* clause that includes a price for electricity in London equal to its marginal cost.

If this condition can be met, the installation of an (additional) electricity plant in Brighton can be justified only if (measured, say, on an annual basis) the total

---

2 If the price per unit of electricity charged by the London supplier yielded an excess over its variable cost of $100 for the amount used by family A, an effective bribe of less than $100 that induced family A to remain in London would make both parties better off than they would be if family A moved to Brighton.

revenue from the sale of the additional electricity along with the consumer surplus exceeds in total both current and overhead costs.

The economist, however, may well have to accept as a political constraint the existing prices set by public utilities in London and to calculate the benefits from extending them in Brighton by reference only to the resulting demand schedules.

5 Life would be less trying for the economist if people did not change their tastes so often over even short periods of time, as they habitually do in a modern economy. Such changes are not always rational: they may spring from trivial causes or be inspired by ignoble motives – greed, envy, the desire for attention or for being in fashion. It is no part of the economist's brief, however, to uncover or to judge people's motives in this respect. He has perforce to accept as basic data the individual's choices or revealed preferences at any particular time.

As already indicated, allowance can be made for a growth in benefits over time arising from increases in population and per capital real income and also for the introduction or withdrawal (when they can be foreseen) of goods or bads associated with the operation of subsequent enterprises. Tastes may also change spontaneously or in response to advertising campaigns.

In so far as he cannot foretell such changes, the economist, if he is to make estimates at all, *has perforce to project current valuations* into the future in the knowledge that (to that extent) they are vulnerable. However, for public projects designed to improve the environment, to reduce pollution or to increase amenity, the valuation of their benefits is not likely to change significantly – at least not to fall significantly – with the passage of time. What is more, the economist's confidence in his findings will grow if his calculations of the criterion $\Sigma V > 0$ is met in a so-called sensitivity analysis that involves variation in the magnitude of key parameters.

6 Although there can be justification for a programme that spreads accurate and useful information within the community, it is doubtful whether such justification can be extended to campaigns designed to change people's tastes for no good reason. Part, at least, of the expenses of a commercial advertising agency is directed into an attempt to alter the existing patterns of tastes among potential buyers so as to favour the sale of goods supplied by their clients. Can there be any benefit to society of employing resources for this purpose?

If purely spontaneous changes in people's tastes that are in no way related to dependable information necessarily incur wastage of resources, so *a fortiori* do commercially induced changes. And if, under existing political institutions, society permits scarce resources to be used expressly for the purpose of inducing changes in taste, then society is indeed countenancing the incurring of avoidable waste. In a dynamic economy where tastes are being manipulated by agencies, success in shifting the demand for a good x to that for good y, then from y to z, then from z to w and, possibly, from w back to the original good x – which changes, we can suppose, would not have occurred in the absence of advertising expenditures – then idle capacity is prematurely brought about in the production of each of these goods. An unnecessary rate of obsolescence is created. The economist who remains neutral in the matter of people's tastes may properly conclude that avoidable waste is the price paid for the acceptance of persuasive advertising. This wastage of resources is, of course, passed on to the community at large through the higher prices needed to cover the higher cost of more rapid obsolescence.

7 Introduction to the compensating variation

1   So far, we have used a single value V to be the measure of a good or bad. But following the Hicksian definition of consumer surplus (Hicks, 1939), we must recognize that, in general, there can be two useful ways of valuing a good or bad. First, there is a compensating variation (CV), which measures the largest sum a person is willing to pay for a good (or for the removal of a bad). Then there is what Hicks called an equivalent variation (EV), which measures the smallest sum a person will accept to forego a good (or to accept a bad).

The CV or EV measure can, however, be used as a measure either of a gain or a loss of the individual's welfare. And it transpires that the so-called EV measure is, in fact, no more than the CV measure for the reverse movement. That is to say, if CV^{12} measures the individual's compensatory sum, as in the change from state 1 to state 2, then EV^{12} is exactly equal, in fact, to CV^{21}, the compensating variation for the movement from state 2 to state 1.

2   In more general terms, we can define CV^{12} as the sum of money (or numeraire) paid or received by the individual following the movement from state 1 to state 2 (according to whether it raises or lowers his welfare, respectively) that would exactly maintain that individual's original level of welfare – the state 1 level of welfare. We can then define the CV^{21} measure as the sum of money paid or received by the individual that, in a movement from state 2 to state 1, would maintain his welfare at the state 2 level. To illustrate, if the change to state 2 is a fall in price of a good (or alternatively a rise in the price of his services) *ceteris paribus*, and therefore a rise in the individual's welfare, his CV^{12} is *positive*, being the most he would pay for this movement from state 1 to state 2 – which, if paid, would restore his to his original or state 1 level of welfare. *Per contra*, if the change to state 2 is a rise in the price of a good (or alternatively a fall in the price of his services), *ceteris paribus*, and, therefore a fall in his level of welfare, his CV is *negative*, being the minimum sum he would have to receive in this movement to state 2 – which sum, if received, would restore him to his original or state 1 level of welfare.

To be tedious about it, if we now go on to suppose that, having moved to state 2, the individual is to contemplate a return to state 1, the relevant measure is the CV^{21}. And if the original movement to state 2 raised his welfare, this movement back to state 1 must lower it. Consequently, his CV^{21} is *negative*, being the minimum sum he must receive if he is to maintain his state 2 level of welfare. It follows that if, instead, the movement from state 2 to state 1 raises the individual's welfare, his CV^{21} is *positive*, being the most he would pay for the movement.

3   Is the most an individual would pay for a good always less than the smallest sum he will accept to go without it? The short answer is almost always.[1]

To be more precise, it is so for what is sometimes called a *normal* good – one of which more is bought when the individual's real income, or more generally his welfare, is increased. The so-called *inferior* good, of which less is bought when his welfare is increased, is exceptional (a favourite example is margarine, at least when it is regarded as a poor man's substitute for butter) and, unless otherwise stated, we may consider only normal goods, which will, of course, include collective goods.

Why this must be so can be understood if we bear in mind that the CV^{12} is the maximum a person would pay for a good that would increase his welfare, say, from his original indifference curve I_1 to a higher indifference curve I_2. This maximum sum he would pay will therefore be such as to return him to his original indifference curve I_1. Conversely, his CV^{21} is the minimum sum he must receive, this being the (larger) sum that will maintain him on his I_2 indifference curve.

Now, if the welfare effect is normal (as posited), then whatever the price of the good x, the individual buys more of it the higher his real income, which – on a diagram with real income y on the vertical axis and good x on the horizontal axis – would show that, for a given slope of the indifference curves, the amount of x taken on the higher indifference curve is larger. Therefore for the *same* amount of good x taken, the slope on the I_2 curve is steeper than that on the I_1 curve.

It follows that if, with respect to each of these two indifference curves in turn, we were to plot the increments of y, or real income, that have to be given up for successive and equal increments of x, the resulting 'marginal indifference curve' or what we may call the marginal valuation curve MV_2, that is derived from the I_2 indifference curve will at all points be above the MV_1 curve derived, that is, from the I_1 indifference curve.

The area below the MV_2 curve in Figure 7.1 is, of course, the measure of the minimum sum a person would accept for having to part with the x_2 amount of

---

1 Recently, much has been written on the divergence between willingness to pay and willingness to accept measures. There appears to be considerable empirical evidence which suggests that individuals' demand for money compensation to give up goods in their possession or enjoyment is greater than their willingness to pay to acquire the same goods. This endowment effect or loss aversion is important for CBA, depending on whether a proposed project takes away existing goods and/or services (as in state 1) or introduces or adds new goods and/or services (as in state 2). For an in-depth discussion on loss aversion, see Knetsch (1989, 1995, 2003); also see Kahneman and Tversky (1979) and Hanemann (1991).

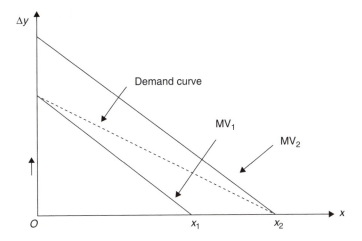

Figure 7.1

x, the corresponding smaller area below the MV_1 curve being the measure of the largest sum he would pay for the x_1 amount of x.

This figure can also be used to trace the locus of amounts of x a person would buy as the price of x, from being so high that no x at all is bought, is gradually lowered to zero. This price–quantity locus is clearly that of the individual's demand curve and, for all normal goods, it will lie diagonally between two marginal valuation curves, as shown: the higher MV_2 curve being appropriate to the level of welfare reached when a person has, at the zero price, taken all the x that he wants; the lower MV_1 curve being appropriate to his welfare before he buys any x at all.

4   In the light of the above, the measurement of consumer surplus we have been using in the previous two chapters – the area under the demand curve that is above the price line – is seen to be an overstatement of the maximum sum the buyers will pay to be able to buy a good x at the market price. It is also an understatement of the minimum sum required to compensate them if that price is no longer available.

Such refinement of the measure of consumer surplus that emerges from the implications of CV^{12} and CV^{21} might be of some use if we were able to obtain exact measures of individual and collective demand curves. Alas, the errors in any actual statistical estimates of demand curves are such as are more than likely to swamp these theoretical refinements we would seek to impose on a (hypothetically) perfect estimate of a demand curve. For all practical purposes, then, the economist perforce continues to measure the consumer surplus from the area under these unavoidably imperfect estimates of demand curves (sometimes called the ordinary or Marshallian demand curve).

Yet, our treatment of the measures of compensating variation has more than an academic value, albeit a heuristic one. In particular, the differences between CV^{12} and CV^{21} measures can be important in other cost–benefit measurements, chiefly in connection with the measurement of spillover effects, as we shall see in Part III.

8   Measurements of rent

1   Rent may be defined as the difference between what the owner of factors of production – say, a worker or a landowner – earns by employing his factors in producing some current good(s) and the minimum sum he would accept to keep them there.[1] It is then a measure of the resource-owner's gain from the opportunity he has of placing his factors in this chosen occupation – given, of course, the opportunity of placing them in any other occupation.

It is the proper counterpart for the gain to factor-owners of a consumer surplus, the latter being regarded as the measure of gain to the consumer from the opportunity of buying some good(s) at the existing price(s). In general, then, rent is in tandem with consumer surplus in as much as it is a measure of his change in welfare when the relevant prices or opportunities facing him are changed. The only distinction between the two is that, whereas an increase in consumer surplus is a measure of gain in welfare for a fall in one or more prices of goods, an increase in rent is the measure of his gain in welfare for a rise in one or more of his factors of production. In both cases, however, the introduction of new opportunities in place of, or in addition to, favourable price changes will also raise his welfare and is measured by an increase in consumer surplus or rent.

This much understood, it has now also to be said that the area below the demand curve provides a good enough measure of consumer surplus (indeed, the only practicable measure), we cannot go on to suppose that the area above the supply curve of factors, say the supply curve of labour, offers a good measure of the labourer's rent. Let us see why.

2   It is usual to draw a person's price–demand curve as sloping downward from left to right and his supply curve for labour or other services sloping upward. If his welfare effect (or 'income effect') is normal, the individual's demand curve has to be downward sloping. (It can slope upward only if the welfare effect is negative and is large relative to the substitution effect – the characteristics of the so-called Giffen good.) Analogous remarks apply to the individual's supply curve.

---

1 A more detailed elaboration of the measurement of the concept of rent will be found in Appendix 5, again employing the CV^{12} and CV^{21} measures.

If the 'welfare effect'[2] is zero, the individual supply curve must slope upward: it can slope downward or become 'backward-bending' only if the welfare effect is positive and large relative to the substitution effect.[3]

In general, the smaller these welfare effects that accompany price changes, the more accurate as an estimate of consumer surplus or rent will be the relevant area derived, respectively, from the individual's demand or supply schedule. In the case of a person's demand curve, there is a presumption that the welfare effects are small, for a man's current expenditure is commonly spread over a wide variety of goods each of which – with, perhaps, the exception of housing – absorbs only a small proportion of his total income. Indeed, as living standards rise, the variety of goods offered by the market increases along with the increase in a man's real income. One might surmise, therefore, that the welfare effect will become less important an ingredient in his price–demand curve for any single good.

The case is otherwise for the individual's supply curve, in particular for his supply of productive services, say the supply of labour, skilled or unskilled. If he supplies to the market only one sort of labour, the impact of the welfare effect arising from a change in the price of this labour falls entirely on the amount of it supplied. It then exerts a preponderant effect. Backward-bending supply curves for individual workers are not regarded as curiosa, a fact which would seem to make the measurement of economic rent rather awkward.

But there is a countervailing feature in connection with individual supply curves, which tends to restore measurability. Notwithstanding the mathematical convenience in postulating an economy in which each individual contributes, in general, to all goods in the economy, spreading his total effort among them – as he spreads his income among all goods – on the equi-marginal principle, this postulate is recognized as unrealistic. Nor is it a necessary condition for the model of perfect competition, which model is quite consistent with the more realistic assumption

2 Assuming that his money income is constant, a fall in the price of a good which makes a person better off can be regarded as an increase in his real income, for there is some rise in his money income which (given all other prices constant) will be accepted by him as equivalent to a fall in the price of that good. Here, no difficulty arises in identifying the increase in his welfare with the income effect so measured.

In the case of his supplying a service to the market, however, his money income cannot be assumed constant, as, obviously, it varies with the amount of the service he elects to supply at the price offered. What is more, a rise or fall in the resulting money income does not necessarily correspond to a rise or fall in his welfare (or 'real' income). A rise in the wage rate, for instance, may result in the worker's choosing so to reduce hours as to maintain money income constant, notwithstanding which his welfare has increased: for his income is the same, while he enjoys additional leisure. A positive welfare effect, that is, can be associated with no change in his money income or even with a reduction of his money income. For this reason, it is more sensible to talk of the 'welfare effect', resulting from a change in the supply price.

3 An increase of welfare has a 'normal', or positive, welfare effect if the person offers *less* at any given price – if, that is, he keeps more of the good he is offering for himself. A worker who came into an inheritance would supply less labour (or take more leisure). Hence, if the price of the good a person supplies is raised, the substitution effect induces him to supply more, while a positive welfare effect causes him to supply less. As distinct, then, from the 'welfare effect' on the demand side, the 'welfare effect' on the supply side, if it is positive or 'normal', works *against* the substitution effect.

that the worker is constrained in his chosen employment to work a given number of hours, and between stated times. (He may, of course, be offered overtime work, though again it will be subject to constraints on the days and times.) For this reason, there is little point in conceiving of the worker's rent from his employment in precisely analogous terms as his consumer surplus.

3   In depicting any consumer surplus for a good x in terms of the CV^{12}, we may derive an MV_1 curve, as in Figure 8.1 to show the excess of marginal valuation over price of the first unit of x bought, of the second unit of x bought, and so on until, with the purchase of the nth unit of x, this excess valuation is zero. By again explicitly ignoring welfare effects, the analogous way of measuring rent is by reference to an upward-sloping MV curve, and would amount to the excess of the price offered for the factor over its marginal valuation for all the factors supplied at that price: for a worker, these marginal valuations are now the minimum sums acceptable to him for successive units of labour provided. Clearly, the amount of labour he chooses to provide will be that at which the (rising) marginal valuation of his labour is equal to the prevailing wage rate. This measure of the resulting rent – the area above his MV_1 supply curve of labour and below the wage rate – is to be interpreted as the maximum sum he would pay to remain in this chosen occupation at the prevailing wage rate, given the existing pattern of prices and wages.

As mentioned above, however, the worker does not choose to spread his hours of work among different firms and occupations on the equi-marginal principle. If the contrary were the case or if, at least, the worker were free to set the hours he would choose to work in a given enterprise, he would, given his rising MV_1 supply curve VV in Figure 8.1, choose to work 32 hours only each week, the amount of time for which his VV curve intersects the horizontal W line, measuring the wage rate. His rent would then be equal to the shaded area above the VV curve. But if, as is likely, the working day were fixed and he had to work, say, a 40-hour week

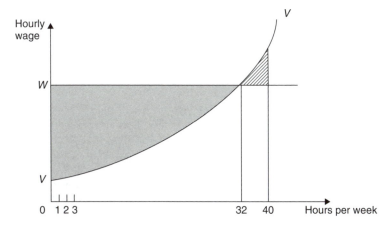

Figure 8.1

to get the job, he would be obliged to work eight hours longer than the 32 hours that he himself would choose. For each of these additional hours he has to work, the wage he receives is below his successive marginal valuations. On these eight extra unwanted hours, he suffers a loss equal to the striped triangle. His net rent is therefore the shaded area minus the striped area. And, as he is offered the job as an all-or-nothing proposition, he will accept the job only if the difference between these two areas is positive.

As all workers finding employment in this occupation will be obliged to work the 40-hour week, irrespective of whether they would prefer to work fewer or more hours, the net rent from working the 40-hour week is, for any one of them, the first area less the second area (if any). Letting the worker's weekly (disposable) pay be represented as the area of a unit column with height equal to this weekly wage, as in Figure 8.2, the rent is the shaded rectangle measured from the top of the column.[4] By gradually raising the weekly wage and observing the numbers that enter the industry in response to the higher wage, a supply curve of labour to the industry is generated, and from this we are able to identify the rent of those employed. Thus in Figure 8.3, if at the lowest wage, W_1 seven men just agreed to work, they make no rent. If now the wage rises to W_2, and, in response, another ten men are just willing to enter industry, the first seven enjoy between them a rent equal to the shaded rectangle (W_2-W_1) *times* the distance 0–7. If the wage rises to

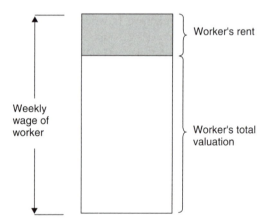

Figure 8.2

---

4 This minimal wage necessary to attract the worker into the industry or project will be greater, by the costs of movement (pecuniary and psychic), than the hypothetical minimum wage where movement costs are zero. *Per contra*, once the worker has moved into the industry, the minimal wage he will accept to remain there is equal to this hypothetical minimum wage *less* the full costs of movement.

In considering a possible introduction of a new project, however, it is the former minimal wage that is relevant.

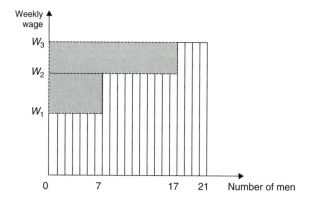

Figure 8.3

W_3, and four more men enter, the first seven men between them make a rent equal to (W_3-W_1) *times* the distance 0–7, and the next ten men between them make a rent equal to (W_3-W_2) *times* the distance 7–17, and so on. We are able to do this simply because no worker is allowed to alter the number of hours he works in that occupation.

As the number of workers grows, the stepped supply curve becomes closer to a smooth curve, the corresponding area above it being the measure of the aggregate of rents enjoyed by the workers employed in that occupation. And this aggregate rent is to be interpreted as the largest sum they would, in aggregate, be willing to pay to remain in this occupation at the prevailing wage rate, given all other prices and opportunities open to them.

To be sure, it is virtually impossibly to construct an MV supply curve for the individual worker. His actual supply curve of labour could perhaps be discovered, but such a curve would not serve as a tolerable proxy for the MV_1 curve in view of the operation of a relatively strong positive welfare effect, one that may result (as indicated earlier) in a backward-sloping supply curve.

Without recourse to the worker's actual supply curve, however, the difficulty can be overcome if we can somehow discover the least sum the worker is willing to accept to remain in his chosen occupation on an all-or-nothing basis; accepting, that is, the required number of hours per day and per week along with all the other constraints that go with the job. Such a sum may then be represented as equal to the area of the lower (blank) part of the column in Figure 8.2, which becomes a unit in the construction of the stepped supply curve of Figure 8.3, which, again, becomes a smooth supply curve as the number of workers grows.[5]

---

5 In calculating the rent to the aggregate number of workers from such a supply curve, it is not necessary that all workers be equally efficient. If additional workers that are hired were less efficient than the original ones, the cost of production would indeed rise. But the measure of workers' rent would not thereby be affected.

4   This workers' rent as measured by the area above the aggregate supply curve of labour is one thing. The rent that is sometimes measured as the area above the supply curve of a good x for a firm or an industry is another. This latter may be accepted as valid only in either of two cases.

First, there is what we may call Ricardian rent, in which labour and capital, both of them available in any amounts at constant prices, are applied in fixed proportions to a given quantity of land. The supply curve of the resulting product, say corn, rises, not because of any changes in the supply prices of the variable factors, labour and capital, since, as just stated, their supply prices remain unchanged. The supply curve of corn rises simply because the best land is limited in supply, and, as the price of corn rises with an expanding demand, it becomes worthwhile to bring inferior land into cultivation. Even if there is only one quality of land, though limited in amount relative to demand, rent will accrue to it once the marginal cost of a bushel of corn rises above its average cost – as it eventually will, because of diminishing average returns to additional 'doses' of labour and capital. In these circumstances, the area between such a supply curve and the price of the product provides a measure of the rent accruing to the owner of the fixed factor, land. Increases in such rents arising from the introduction of an investment project are accordingly entered on the benefit side of the analysis.

Second, there is the case in which the area above the supply, or cost, curve has to be identified as what Marshall (1925) called *quasi-rent*. For over a short period, during which the capital employed by the industry or firm is in the specific form of plant or machinery, it is deemed to be fixed in amount and to have no alternative use. In this short period, then, it partakes of the nature of land, and all its earnings *above* those necessary to induce it to remain in the occupation (zero in the strict Marshallian quasi-rent concept) are to be regarded as rent. In this short period, then, if the price of the product rises above the per unit variable cost of the product, the resulting excess receipts over the total of these variable costs are quasi-rents; such positive sums make a contribution to the industry's or firm's overheads or capital costs.

The above two instances are clear examples of economic rent to a scarce factor. They enter as part of the benefit of producing a given amount of goods during either a short or a long period. Thus, if a given piece of land is used to grow a new crop or to site some new project, any rise in the rent of the land is to be entered on the benefit side of the scheme. If, within a short period, some investment in the industry or firm causes its variable costs to fall, the additional quasi-rents that result are also to be entered on the benefit side.

9   Is producer surplus a rent?

1   Given a fully employed economy in which the supplies of the various factors are fixed, the long-period supply curve for a good x is generally conceived to be upward sloping. Indeed, if production functions are homogeneous and linear,[1] and each good combines factors in different proportions, upward-sloping supply curves for all goods become a necessary implication.

The question is then whether the area above such an upward-sloping long-period supply price for a good, often referred to as a producer surplus, can be interpreted as a gain to some members of society, being then on a par with such measures of gain to society members as those discussed in the preceding chapters on rents and consumer surplus. The short answer is no.

2   In order to appreciate the difference between the valid measures of gain such as consumer surplus or rent, and the spurious measure of gain, producer surplus, let us follow standard textbook procedure and assume, first, that all firms in the particular industry are of equal size and efficiency. In that case, the rising supply price of the industry's output of good x has to be attributed to the growing scarcity of the factor that is intensively used in the production of good x. In an economy with only two factors, say capital and labour, we may suppose that good x uses a larger proportion of capital to labour than does the only other good y. If the amount of good x produced is increased at the expense of good y, an initial shortage of capital in the economy relative to labour will result in a rise in the price of capital and fall in the price of labour. The cost of a unit of x, being capital intensive, will therefore rise as more of x is produced and that of a unit of y, which is labour intensive, will fall as less of y is produced.[2]

Any point along this rising supply price for the product indicates the minimum average (inclusive) cost for each of the firms in the industry and, therefore, the

---

1 A homogenous linear production function is one where the output x increases by the proportion c, if each of the inputs is increased by c.

2 Only in a full-employment economy in which all goods (with homogeneous production functions of degree one) use factors in the same proportion as their availability will the long-period supply curves of goods be horizontal.

minimum average (inclusive) cost for that output. Thus, at output Ox_1 in Figure 9.1, the minimum average inclusive cost for all firms is given by x_1m_1. A typical long-period envelope curve for such a firm is represented as S_1S_1. At the larger output Ox_2, the minimum average inclusive cost for the industry is given by x_2m_2, and the typical long-period envelope curve for the firm is represented by S_2S_2. Clearly then, this long-period industry supply curve cannot be interpreted as a net gain by the producers of this particular good, as each of them makes zero (Knightian) profit[3] in long-period equilibrium. It is, in fact, a curve of average cost *including* rent.

Since real rentals (the price of units of capital) rise and – unless there are increasing returns to scale – real wages fall as the output of x is expanded, we are able, under particular monetary assumptions, to calculate the rise in money rentals and the fall in money wages corresponding to increased amounts of capital and labour required by some given increase in the quantity of the product x. We can then associate the increase in the area above the supply curve of x with the increased amounts of the two factors employed in the x industry when each factor is multiplied by the increase or decrease in its income. More specifically, the addition to the area above the supply curve for x is made up of the gains of *only* those units of capital now employed in x *less* the losses of only those workers now employed there. These gains and losses in x alone are clearly only a small part of

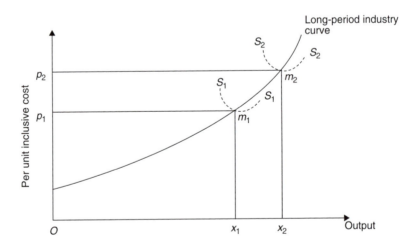

Figure 9.1

3 Normal return on capital is not 'profit' any more than normal return on labour. In the long-period equilibrium, at any point on the industry supply curve, expenditure on factors (both labour and capital) is deemed to be just covered by revenue, leaving no profit, positive or negative, to induce firms to move into or out of the industry.

the total gains and losses accruing to the factor classes as a whole, since they are also employed in other industries.

It is certain, therefore, that any increase in the area above the supply curve for x is *not* to be associated with a net gain by either factor or by both factors taken together or by the producers.[4]

Thus, so far as shifts of demand curves are concerned, say from product y to product x, attempts to measure net benefits arising in the x industry – or, to be more ambitious, net benefits arising in all industries that use the two (or more) factors – are hardly practicable, especially where, as is likely, a larger number of factors are involved. Indeed, such a shift in production implies no more than a movement from one part of the production boundary to another. It is a movement that, in general, raises the earnings of some factor classes and lowers those of others. But one cannot infer that there are net gains to society as a whole.

If, however, the area above the supply curve of x were to increase solely in consequence of a downward shift in this curve, the result, say, of an improvement in technology, it need have no effect on factor prices. In this technically 'neutral' case, the increased area does indeed count as a benefit. In so far as the reduction in the cost of producing x is wholly passed on to consumers, the gain will be measured as an increase in consumer surplus. In so far as some part of this gain is withheld by the producer, for a time at least, it partakes of monopoly rent.

---

4 This long-period supply curve cannot, that is, be regarded as an average cost curve that includes the rent of a *fixed* factor, for in that case the curve would also be one that is a marginal cost of the good x excluding rent – as, say, in Ricardian rent or Marshallian quasi-rent.

It might seem, however, that this long-period supply curve for a good x, arising as it does from varying combinations of two or more factors, could be treated as a marginal curve by a perfectly discriminating monopsonist. For, by paying more only to any additional factors he may require in expanding production, he would be able to appropriate a sum equal to the area above the supply curve.

Such a discriminating monopsonist would, however, have to be the sole buyer of the factors he employed, else he would be unable to employ them at prices lower than those prevailing in the rest of the economy.

So singular a case may hardly be considered seriously as a possible exception. We are justified, therefore, in treating the long-period supply curve for a good as no more than an average cost to the one or more firms producing it.

Part III

Shadow prices and transfer payments

10 Introductory remarks

1 Broadly speaking, a 'shadow' or 'accounting' price – the terms are interchangeable – is the price the economist attributes to a good or factor on the argument that it is more appropriate for the purpose of economic calculation than its existing price, if any. There is nothing very special about the notion of a shadow price. In evaluating any project, the economist may effectively 'correct' a number of market prices and also attribute prices to unpriced gains and losses that it is expected to generate. He will, for example, add to the cost of a factor or subtract from the cost of a good in making allowance for some external diseconomy. Wherever the amounts of a good to be added to or subtracted from the existing consumption are large enough, the economist will substitute for price the more discriminating measure of benefit, consumer surplus. Certain gains or losses to an enterprise he will value as zero, because, for the economy at large, they are only transfer payments. The cost of labour he must value at its opportunity cost, not at its wage, and so on.

Nonetheless, the term has been used more specifically in a number of connections, and it will, perhaps, avoid confusion if these are briefly indicated.

2 First, the term has long been used in mathematical programming, a technique in which the value, at given prices, of an 'objective function' is, say, maximized, subject to certain amounts of inputs and a number of technologically feasible factor combinations. From this 'primal' problem, a 'dual' problem can be derived, with a corresponding objective function which is to be minimized. It transpires that, for a wide class of problems, the variables in the dual solution can be interpreted as shadow prices or accounting prices, inasmuch as they are the 'correct' input prices – being consistent with the maximum value of the primal objective function.[1]

---

1 When these shadow prices are imputed to the given inputs, the value of the dual objective function is minimized. It can then be interpreted as the minimum input cost, subject to the constraints and to the requirement that no profits (excess revenues) be made. These shadow prices are, therefore, no different from the factor prices that would emerge in a perfectly competitive equilibrium in which product prices are exogenously determined. An unusually clear introduction to the uses of mathematical programming is provided in Throsby's book (1970). See also Takayama (1994) and Sydsaeter and Hammond (2005).

We shall not, however, be using the term shadow price in connection with this technique.

Second, the term has been extended to estimates of social benefits or social losses that are either unpriced or not satisfactorily priced. Unpriced or inadequately priced benefits or losses may be valued by (i) adopting the prices of similar things elsewhere or (ii) calculating the price for a good or a 'bad' that is *implicit* in government decisions to undertake particular projects or (iii) calculating the spillover effects by reference to market prices, or by some other method. Consider each method in turn.

(i) The price adopted for some public good, or service, may be based on that at which it is sold in some other region of the country. Thus, the value of a public amenity such as a beach, a park, or a museum, to be established, say, in New York may be estimated by reference to the prices charged for similar beaches, parks or museums, in other parts of the United States. Such prices, even when attempts are made to allow for differences in circumstances, are not very satisfactory. The prices that are set elsewhere for such things are not likely to be optimal prices, and are sometimes set arbitrarily or, rather, by reference only to political considerations. Since a correct measure of the benefit is the maximum that people would pay for the service rather than go without, one cannot hope for much from this device. At any rate, no generalization that is useful, and also not obvious, can be made with respect to this practice, and we need say no more about it here.

(ii) Wherever there is an uncalculated benefit B associated with an authorized public project which, on a CBA that is confined to *measurable* benefits, reveals an excess of costs over benefits ΔK, it can be argued that the implicit value, or shadow price, of this uncalculated benefit B is equal to ΔK or, rather, that it is at least equal to ΔK.[2] One of the difficulties of this argument is that one cannot hope for a deliberate and systematic criterion to be invoked in such a case. There can be, and there usually are, the widest discrepancies between these implicit valuations, though, even if this were not the case, the validity of this procedure is open to methodological criticism.[3]

(iii) The existence of spillover effects requires that market prices be corrected *inter alia* for incidental losses and gains falling on persons other than the producers or users of goods. These incidental social losses or gains can sometimes be valued by reference to market prices, though not without difficulty. Prices of such goods, once corrected for the spillover effects they produce, are also spoken of as shadow prices. However, we shall defer the discussion of

---

2 If, instead, there happens to be an *uncalculated* social loss D, arising from an authorized public project which shows an excess of measured benefit over measured cost ΔB, then, on the same argument, the implicit value, or shadow price, of this uncalculated loss D can be taken to equal ΔB – or, rather, as not greater then ΔB.

3 For arguments tending to reject the validity of this procedure for deriving implicit valuations, the reader is referred to the chapter 'The value of life' in Part VI.

spillover effects to Part IV. Finally, and most commonly in a CBA, shadow prices are associated with the calculation of opportunity costs of the materials or productive factors used in the building and operation of the project in question, whether they are transferred from domestic sources or from abroad. It is in this latter opportunity-cost sense that we shall discuss them, and with particular reference to the opportunity cost of labour and the opportunity cost of imports.

11 Opportunity cost of labour

1   So far, we have been using the abbreviated notation ΣV to denote the aggregate of the valuations created by the project over time to its terminal period T, omitting, for the time being, the discounting or compounding procedure necessary to reduce the ΣV to a single figure.

However, we may write $V_t = (v_t^b - v_t^c)$, where V_t is the *net* benefit in the year t (which could be positive or negative), v_t^b is the valuation of the benefit in year t, while v_t^c is the valuation of the cost in the year.[1]

The calculation of v_t^b presents no problem, at least in so far as the goods produced by the project are marketable. In the earlier chapters in Part II, we perforce had to adopt, as an adequate measure of consumer surplus, the area under the demand curve for a good x *less* the amount the consumers have to pay for the amount, OQ, they buy. Thus, the *full* valuation for the total value OQ amount of x is the area under the demand curve (without any subtraction of the sum paid by the consumers). And it is from this valuation v_t^b of the benefit of the project's output of the good x that we now have to subtract the real cost, the v_t^c.

In a cost–benefit calculation, however, costs are not, in general, equal to the costs of the materials and productive factors used by the project in the ordinary sense; say, as they would be calculated by a private enterprise from their market prices. The relevant costs in a CBA are what are known as 'opportunity' costs – a term which serves to indicate the valuations forgone when the materials or factors are transferred from other employments.

2   In general, then, this key concept of opportunity cost to the project is the worth of that particular input in some alternative use. Yet, so defined, there will be ambiguity wherever there is more than one alternative use. In such cases, the definition adopted may refer to the alternative use that yields the highest value.

---

1 It will be convenient, nonetheless, to continue to use ΣV as shorthand for the aggregate of valuations (both positive and negative to the end of the period T), although it is more revealing to use notation ΣV_t or $\Sigma (v_t^b - v_t^c)$. In either case, if the aggregate is positive – at least when reduced by discounting to a present sum – it must be concluded that all the factors and materials used in the project over time have a higher value in aggregate than the value they created in the uses from which they are transferred.

And were the economist at liberty to choose from which use the material or factor should be transferred, such a definition would be valid. In so far as the economist is, in this respect, subject to political constraints, he has no choice but to calculate the opportunity cost of anything as the value it created in that particular (politically determined) use from which it is to be transferred. It will simplify the exposition if, henceforth, we think of opportunity cost in terms of a particular designated alternative use.

Although the concept of opportunity cost, using this definition, can be extended to any material or productive factor that is to be used in a project, either for its initial construction or for its operation upto some terminal year T, nothing is lost in our understanding of its nature and method of calculation if, in the main, we confine our treatment of it to labour or to labour of a particular skill.

In respect of labour, however, we should be aware that the calculation of its opportunity cost must also take into account any occupational preference the worker has when comparing the employment conditions offered by the project and those in his existing occupation. We may also have to take account of any costs of movement the worker may have to incur in moving from his present employment to employment in the new project.

In the absence of either of these, however, the opportunity cost of a unit of labour – say, a 40-hour working week of that labour – to the project is no more than the value it can create in the production of the amount of a good x from which it is to be transferred. In more familiar jargon, its opportunity cost is equal to the value of its marginal product in x, abbreviated to VMP_x, this being the value forgone when the unit of labour is moved from producing x to producing alternative goods – say, y and/or z – in the project.

In a cost–benefit calculation, this VMP_x figure must, in general, be adjusted to make allowance for any externalities associated with the production or consumption of the amount of good produced by the unit of labour. If, in that labour's unit of production of good x, a positive externality of $50 is conferred on the community, this $50 is added to the VMP_x. Conversely, if the community suffers a loss valued at $80, that much has to be subtracted from VMP_x. The adjusted VMP_x may be referred to as the *social* value of the marginal product of labour in producing the good x, or $SVMP_x$, and is therefore the appropriate opportunity cost of that labour to the project.

3   In order to fix our ideas, we may suppose that a unit of labour is to be transferred from the production of good x to producing something else in the project. If this unit of labour produces 10 units of x during a week, each unit of x having a social value of $50, its $SVMP_x$ is $500, which is then the appropriate opportunity cost per week to the project – *provided* the worker is indifferent between producing good x and working in the project and provided also there are no costs of movement when he transfers his labour from producing good x to working for the project.

If the worker is not indifferent between occupations; if, say, he would require no less than $75 per week additional to his wage in x to induce him to work for the project, the opportunity cost of his labour to the project becomes $575 or SVMP$_x$ plus *op* (*op* being shorthand for the occupational preference premium of the worker). Were the reverse to be the case, the opportunity cost, SVMP$_x$ *minus op*, becomes $425 per week.

A further adjustment to the opportunity cost is required if the worker incurs costs in moving from the production of *x* into the project, where the costs include both the money costs of relocation and the less tangible 'psychic' costs experienced by him, his family and friends, when he departs from an area in which he had settled. Although the physical costs of the relocation are easily ascertained, the 'psychic' costs can be estimated only from the worker himself. Consequently, there can be difficulties in eliciting the true figure. Whatever the total of these costs is, however, they will occur only once and they are, therefore, to be spread over the entire period of the worker's employment in the project.

It will be noticed that, in the above examples, no mention has been made of the wage rate or the worker's rent either in the production of *x* or in the project. Calculation of their magnitudes is unnecessary in estimating the opportunity cost, for the wage paid and the worker's rent are properly conceived as transfer payments from the rest of the community to the worker.

4   Calculating the opportunity cost of the entire output produced by all the factors during a period of, say, a year, is a straightforward business. If the only factor used during the year in project *w* were 2,000 workers transferred from *x*, their opportunity cost to project *w* would be equal to the social value of the amount of the good *x* they produce in a year, say $25 million, corrected, however, for their occupational preference for working in *x* rather than in *w* (which we may suppose to be measured by an average of $75 a week). The full opportunity cost is therefore equal to this $25 million *plus* the measure of occupational preference, which is equal to (2,000 × 50 × $75) for a 50-week working year.

This social value of *x*, assumed above to be $25 million is, of course, equal to the most the community is willing to pay for it, adjusted for externalities in its production or consumption. And the most people are willing to pay for that annual amount is adequately measured by the area under the demand curve for *x*. Nor is there any difficulty if the workers employed in project *w* are transferred from the production of a number of different goods. If, say, 1,200 workers are transferred from producing good *x* and the remaining 800 from producing good *y*, the social value forgone is simply the sum of the area under the demand curve for the amount of *x* produced by 1,200 workers over the year *plus* the area under the demand curve for the amount of *y* produced by the 800 workers over the year – again, adjusted for any incidental externalities.[2]

---

2 No problem arises if the economist wishes to calculate opportunity costs in terms of goods rather than in terms of factors. For example, the opportunity cost of a good *w* is simply equal to the opportunity cost of a unit of of labour (or other *x*-producing factor) divided by the number of *w* goods it produces.

5 Nor is any revision required if the inputs required by the project are materials imported from abroad (as we shall see in Chapter 14) or materials that have to be transferred from a domestic non-augmentable stock.

An example of a non-augmentable stock would be the total oil reserves in a country that has no prospect of increasing the amount of oil at home or abroad in the forseeable future. The opportunity cost of the amount of oil required by the project is equal to the domestic social value of the oil currently being used in the economy.

As for the opportunity costs of other inputs such as plant, equipment and machinery, their calculation follows that of labour. They are not, that is, the prices that are paid for them, but calculated by reference to the social value forgone when they are transferred to the project in question.

If, for example, some particular equipment has to be produced specifically for the project, its opportunity cost, say it comes to $10,000, is calculated by reference to the opportunity cost of labour and other inputs required, whether imported or not. Investment in such a piece of equipment would, of course, be made in anticipation of its contributing to the social value of the project's annual product.

However, the required equipment may not be specific to the project, but one that currently has a social value of other goods being produced in the economy. Its opportunity cost is then calculated as the social value it contributes annually in producing these other goods. This opportunity cost could, for example, be $1,500 per annum for for ten consecutive years.

6 As for the opportunity cost of a significant area of land required by the project, this is sometimes entered as the DPV of the expected net benefits over the future that would otherwise accrue to this area of land if it remained in its current use; or sometimes, and this is worth, simply as the market value of the land.

It may then seem that its opportunity cost may be properly calculated as the DPV or, rather, the compounded terminal value (CTV),[3] of the net contribution of the land to the annual social value since these annual contributions have to be forgone when the land is transferred to the project. However, the contribution made to the social value of the product by the land itself may not be possible where it is combined in fixed proportion with the other inputs. In addition, transferring the land from its current use to the project entails a dismantling of the whole of the existing concern and also, therefore, the disposal of the various sorts of labour, machinery and equipment used in producing its goods. Such losses must also be counted. Yet, it would be erroneous to cost such losses arising, say, from the disposal of labour or machines once used by the concern as equal to their resulting opportunity costs. For it may well be that the machines have only scrap value, and the discarded labour has no use, or little use, elsewhere.

---

3 As will be indicated in Part V on 'Investment Criteria', our critique of the popular DPV for evaluating net benefit streams is a prelude to our proposal that it be supplanted by our proposed CTV.

On such a reckoning, the cost to the project of taking over the land, and therefore the consequent disposal of the labour and machinery involved, would be understated. For these other factors would, if the land remained in its original use, continue to contribute to the full social value there.

It must be concluded that, wherever a significant area of land is involved (significant in that the area of land has value in some other use), it is virtually impossible to assign to it an opportunity cost. The only valid procedure then available to the economist entrusted with the cost–benefit analysis of a project is that of comparing the social value of the land in its current use with its use in the proposed project.

In each of the two alternative uses to be considered, the fixed factor, land, is combined with other factors to yield a stream of net social benefits – the social value of the annual benefits *less* the opportunity costs of the other inputs required. The project meets the economist's criterion if the DPV, or preferably the CTV, of the net social benefits from using the land for the project exceeds that from continuing the current use of the land.

In the particular case where the project being mooted is that of restoring an area of land to its original wilderness state or creating a designed wilderness area, additional costs may be incurred if demolition has to be employed; apart, that is, from the opportunity costs of labour and other inputs required initially in restoring or designing a wilderness area and, subsequently, in maintaining and monitoring the area.

12 Opportunity cost of unemployed labour

1   The method of calculating opportunity cost continues, in the main, to be serviceable when extended to unemployed labour. In a less than fully employed economy, that is, the opportunity cost of such labour to the project is, again, equal to the social value of a worker's labour in its existing use, allowance also being made for the worker's occupational preference.

Should the worker place some value on the leisure perforce available to him while unemployed, which value has to be forgone when he takes up employment, that is indeed the value which must be attributed by society to his being in the unemployed state, as he himself is a member of society. Thus, if the minimum sum he would accept to move into employment generally were $50, this $50 has to be accepted as the appropriate opportunity cost. If, however, he is not indifferent to the occupation and to the organization that offers him employment, an adjustment will again have to be made for occupational preference. In other words, this minimal sum acceptable to him will vary with the sort of work he will be required to do and the organization with which he will have to work. For the work he is required to perform in project w, for example, it may be as high as $80.

However, his enforced leisure may be burdensome to him, so much so that he is prepared to pay to be employed even where no wage at all is offered to him. If he would pay as much as $20 a week – from his assets or from sums borrowed – to be employed in project w, even where he receives nothing in return, the opportunity cost to the project is equal to *minus* $20, This can be regarded as a benefit to the community of $20, even if he produces nothing of value. By his being no worse off when he pays the rest of the community $20, and their being better off by the $20 he pays them, the *net* benefit V to the community is $20.

More generally, to the value the worker attaches to his enforced leisure[1] must be added the value of the externalities consequent upon his leisure activities and

---

1 What we call his leisure may be complete idleness or it may be, wholly or in part, recreational, educational or productive (the production of some goods that brings him in some income). But whatever he chooses to do with this 'leisure', the economist has to accept the worker's own valuation of it in calculating his opportunity cost.

behaviour, in particular the effects on his friends (or enemies) and members of his family. If, on balance, these externalities are positive in value, this value must be added to the $80 minimum he would accept to work in the project in calculating his opportunity cost.

2   Let us disregard these externalities, however, and therefore continue to calculate his opportunity cost to the project as equal to $80. If we now introduce unemployment benefit, say $100 a week, then by taking up employment in the project, he will have to forgo this sum. The minimal sum he will then accept to agree to work in the project must now be $180. Does the introduction of unemployment benefit make any difference to the opportunity cost, calculated above as $80? The answer is no. The opportunity cost is still no more than the $80 value he places on the 'leisure' of being unemployed.

Thus, if working in the project he produces goods worth exactly $80, the net gain to society V, equal to $(v^b - v^c)$ – equal therefore to $80 *minus* $80 – is zero. Let us check this carefully.

To employ the worker, the project must transfer $180 to him. Of this amount, $100 represents the transfer to him of the unemployment benefit – originally assumed by the rest of society but, when employed, undertaken by the project. So far as this $100 of payment to the worker is at issue, there is neither gain nor loss to society as a whole: the $100 gain to the worker is offset by the $100 loss to the rest of society. But the project pays the worker $180. The additional $80 received by the worker represents a net loss to the project (and to society as a whole) in as much as the $80 received by the worker is no gain at all: simply a compensation for his work that leaves him no better off then he was when unemployed. But this net loss of $80 to society is exactly offset if the worker produces goods worth $80, leaving the net gain to society equal to zero.

It is much more likely, however, that the worker will produce goods worth more than $80. If he produces goods valued at $500, V becomes equal to $500 - $80, or $420.

3   However, the calculation of opportunity cost of labour in conditions of what is sometimes called 'disguised unemployment' is no different from that of labour when employed in creating goods of value to the community, as in the preceding chapter. The fact, then, that the marginal product of labour in, say, agriculture in some parts of Africa or Asia is zero may well warrant its opportunity cost to the project being equal to zero.

We may suppose that the worker values his leisure when unemployed at $2 a week when the alternative is that of working in agriculture; this $2 being the opportunity cost of his labour to agriculture. But working in a commune of village workers, he receives $3 a week, this being the *average* product of labour when it happens that the *marginal* product of labour is zero. Our worker therefore enjoys a rent of $3 minus $2, or $1 a week. If he has no occupational preference or costs of movement, he will not move out of the commune to take up employment in the project unless he receives more than $3 a week there.

Since his opportunity cost, equal to the value of his marginal product in agriculture, is zero, it follows that were he to move to the project but again produces nothing of value, society would neither lose nor gain from his employment in the project; V is equal to zero. This is so, no matter what wage the project pays him, but it will be easier to check this result if we assume that he receives exactly $3 in the project, the same as he received in agriculture.

Bear in mind that the worker himself is no better off (or worse off) with the $3 wage that he receives from the project than with the $3 he receives from the agricultural commune. The agricultural commune, however, is made better off by the $3 a week, since it no longer has to pay, for his departure does not reduce the amount of the crop produced. The project, on the other hand, is worse off by the $3 a week it now pays the worker who produces nothing of value. Taken together, society as a whole is neither better nor worse off.

Put otherwise, the $3 a week received by the worker continues to be a transfer from the rest of society, whether from the agricultural community or from the project so that, for society as a whole (including the worker), there is neither a gain nor a loss. And, since he works either in agriculture or in the project, the worker produces nothing of value, the conclusion that the net gain V to society is zero remains.

Should the worker indeed produce some social value when working in the project, say $5, then $5 becomes the net gain V to society.

We may therefore confidently conclude that the calculation of the opportunity cost to the project of labour moving from *disguised* unemployment – from some economic activity where his output is either zero or some low figure (less than his wage there) – is the same as that if, instead, he moves from an activity in which he is profitably employed; equal, that is, to his SVMP$_x$ where x is the good in whose production he was employed before moving to the project in question (adjusted for occupational preference and costs of moving, if necessary).

13 The additional benefits of using unemployed labour

1   In times of low unemployment, there is obviously a stronger case to be made for implementing public projects, since they act not only to absorb otherwise idle resources, but also generate additional income and employment. It follows that public projects that would not be economically feasible under conditions of high employment may be economically feasible under conditions of low employment. In this chapter, we explore the effect of such benefits on the calculation of the opportunity cost of labour.

In the preceding two chapters, we addressed the calculation of the opportunity cost of labour to the project, first, within a fully employed economy and, second, when the labour required is drawn entirely from the unemployed – the latter being calculated, however, without any reference to the additional benefits arising from the multiplier effects generated.

In the more general case, of course, a proportion of the workers required by the project will be drawn from the ranks of the unemployed, the remainder from those already productively employed. This presents no difficulty. It should be manifest that the total opportunity cost of the labour required by the project is simply the sum of two parts: the opportunity cost of those workers productively employed elsewhere in the economy and that of the unemployed workers.

To illustrate a case where the opportunity cost of a construction worker drawn from his existing employment is calculated to be, on average, $12,000 per annum and that calculated for a construction worker from the unemployment pool to be, on average, $4,000 per annum, the total opportunity cost to the project of employing 1,000 workers, of which 625 are drawn from their existing employment and the remaining 375 from the unemployment pool, is – provisionally ignoring multiplier effects – equal to ($12,000 × 625) *plus* ($4,000 × 375); that is $7.5 million plus $1.5 million, or $9 million in total.

2   However, before adjusting this opportunity cost for multiplier effects, we may as well recognize the existence of a self-evident relationship between, on the one hand, the proportion of unemployed workers likely to be found among the total required by the project and, on the other hand, the extent of the unemployment in the economy as a whole. Although this relationship will differ somewhat for each particular skill, in every case, the greater the degree of unemployment in the economy, the larger the likelihood that the worker will be drawn from the unemployment pool.

Such a relationship can be plotted on a diagram in which the probability of the worker's coming from the unemployment pool is measured along the vertical axis and the percentage unemployment in the economy along the horizontal axis, as in Figure 13.1.

Although an attempt has been made to establish such a relationship for a number of different skills,[1] it is uncertain how useful the results would be to an economist engaged in CBA. The amount of empirical work to be undertaken in plotting such a relationship for even a small number of skills could be justified only if it could be assumed that they would remain constant over the years, which is highly unlikely in a modern economy. In any case, the economist should be able, without undue effort, to ascertain at the time the likely number of workers of a particular skill that the project will be drawing from the unemployment pool.

3 This much said, we may finally address ourselves to the additional benefits to society conferred by a project that uses labour from the ranks of the unemployed, bearing in mind that, for additional income and unemployment to be generated, additional money must be activated or otherwise made available. Put otherwise, in order to create additional aggregate expenditure in the economy, there must be no offsetting reduction of expenditure elsewhere. Should the funds necessary to finance the project be raised by a loan, say by an issue of bonds floated on the stock market, hitherto idle bank balances are directly or indirectly activated. Alternatively, the money required may be created by the banking system: the

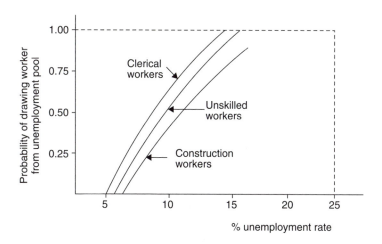

Figure 13.1

1 See Haveman and Krutilla (1968).

government may, for instance, choose to finance the public project, not from revenues raised by additional taxes,[2] but by borrowing from the central bank which creates the additional money required.

If an additional $1 billion is created, or activated, to be spent on bringing into employment hitherto unemployed workers – therefore without reducing income and employment elsewhere in the economy – the expenditure of the newly employed on currently produced domestic goods (equal to $1 billion *times* their marginal propensity to consume *domestic* goods) adds further to the increase in aggregate income, and so on. With a Keynesian multiplier of 5, the eventual increase in aggregate income becomes $5 billion.[3]

4   Let us now return to the example used in section 1 above, in which, of the total opportunity cost to the project of $9 million, $1.5 million was that of the 375 workers drawn from the unemployment pool. The effect on the calculation of the latter part of this opportunity cost – and, therefore, on the total opportunity cost – of the multiplier-generated increase in aggregate income must now be considered.

If the wage paid by the project is $20,000 per annum to each of the 1,000 construction workers it employs, the 375 workers drawn from the unemployment pool will together receive an income of 375 *times* $20,000, or $7.5 million.[4] With a multiplier of 5, this initial increase of $7.5 million will go on to add an *additional* increase in aggregate income equal to 4 *times* $7.5 million, or $30 million, this sum being the additional benefit to society created by the initial employment of the 375 construction workers drawn from the unemployment pool.

5   In so far as the opportunity cost to the project of employing the 1,000 construction workers was calculated in the absence of this $30 million of additional benefit to society, arising from the expenditure of the 375 workers newly employed, its inclusion will constitute a subtraction from the original calculation of $9 million.[5] The properly corrected opportunity cost of the 1,000 construction workers is therefore $9 million less $30 million, or minus $21 million.

2 Were the government to raise an additional $1 billion in taxes in order to spend it entirely on the public project, the additional aggregate income generated would just be $1 billion, irrespective of the multiplier, a result that follows from the so-called balanced-budget multiplier.

3 A multiplier of 5 assumes that of an additional $1 of income, 80 cents is spent on domestically produced goods, and the remaining 20 cents on saving, on imports and taxes.

4 To be sure, if the unemployed construction worker received $100 dole/charity money each week, his *net* income when employed is reduced by this $100 per week. But the $100 he forgoes when employed is transferred back to the rest of the community, whose disposable income is increased to that extent, the multiplier of 5 being unaffected.

5 Regarding the additional benefit of $30 million as equal to the addition of $30 million to aggregate income is warranted in as much as the additional expenditure on *all* goods – including personal savings (expenditure on additional bonds or equities), imported goods and additional taxes for (hopefully) additional government services – is also equal to $30 million.

Although it comes to the same thing, it is obviously easier to leave the original calculation of opportunity cost at $9 million, leaving the additional benefit of $30 million to be added to the benefit side of the project.[6]

6   It may first be thought that an addition to this benefit should be made in the belief that an additional $30 million of expenditure generates a consumer surplus on the goods bought. But any attempt to measure additional consumer surplus in these circumstances is misguided in view of the accepted definitions of consumer surplus. As indicated in the chapter on consumer surplus, an economic surplus (positive or negative) to the individual can be calculated only for a *change* in his situation. Thus the CV^{12} is a measure of his gain, or loss, from moving from an initial state 1 to an alternative state 2; the reverse being true for the CV^{21}.

Were we to ask what consumer surplus a person derives from his existing income, the only sense one can make of the question is by a comparison of two situations: a state 1, in which the individual has no income at all, and a state 2, in which the individual has his existing income. The CV^{12} measure is calculated by asking what is the most that the individual would offer for a movement from the zero-income state 1 to the full-income state 2. And the answer is unambiguously, the whole of his income. And the CV^{21} measure gives the same answer, since the question is now: what is the smallest sum the individual would accept to induce he to move from state 2, in which he enjoys his full income, to state 1 in which he would have nothing.

The same reasoning applies to a consumer surplus of an addition to his income, say from, $4,000 per annum to $12,000 per annum. Accepting the $4,000 as state 1, the CV^{12} measures the most he would pay for moving from $4,000 per annum to $12,000 per annum, which is obviously equal to $8,000 per annum, The CV^{21} is also equal to $8,000 per annum being the minimum annual sum he would accept to forgo $8,000 per annum.

We may conclude, then, that the only conceivable measure of a consumer surplus of the benefit of the $30 million additional aggregate expenditure is no less than the $30 million itself.

---

6 It may be as well to remind the reader that the rent enjoyed by each of the 625 construction workers (on average equal to $20,000 *less* $12,000, or $8,000 per annum) and the rent enjoyed by each of the 375 newly employed construction workers (on average equal to $20,000 *less* $4,000, or $16,000 per annum) are *not* net benefits to the community but only transfers from the rest of the community to the 1,000 workers.

14　The opportunity costs of imports

1　In the literature on project evaluation, it is common enough to present formulae for calculating the shadow price, or opportunity cost, of any imports to be used in the construction or operation of the project. We shall, however, continue to adhere to our method of using simple examples to illustrate the basic logic that informs a valid formula for the opportunity cost to the project of the required imports in particular circumstances or, for that matter, a more general one for all circumstances.[1]

Before embarking, it will make for smoother sailing if first we make a number of easily removed assumptions which in no way affect the basic logic

(i)　that the exchange rate between trading countries remain constant, so enabling us to use a common currency, say the US dollar, in all transactions;

(ii)　that the amounts of the additional imports or exports to be considered are such as not to affect the prevailing prices;

(iii)　that no spillovers are present, which assumption allows us to equate the social value of any goods with its market price;

(iv)　that the foreign prices which the country has to pay for its imported goods include the costs of freight, insurance, loading and unloading, etc.

It should be manifest that the removal, later, of the first three assumptions adds something to the workload of the economists, though without in any way modifying the principle ideas. If, for instance, exchange rates are likely to vary over time, the economist must evidently adopt the exchange rate that is expected to prevail at the time the project will require the imports. Clearly, he can only guess what the exchange rate will be in future years[2] and perhaps his best stratagem will be to set upper and lower limits to the expected exchange rate, these limits being farther apart for farther years. Recourse to this stratagem produces a lower and a higher opportunity cost of the goods to be imported by the project in any year t.

1　A good example of the latter can be found in Dasgupta *et al.* (1972: 216) and Boardman *et al.* (2006).

2　The opportunities for hedging against adverse movements of the exchange rate, by selling or buying currencies in the forward exchange market, are limited to a couple of years at most.

Again, if the amounts of the goods to be imported or exported are large enough to affect their market prices, the valuations of such goods are taken to equal the relevant areas under the downward-sloping demand curves.

Finally, adjustment for possible positive or negative spillovers, discussed in detail in Part IV, although time-consuming, requires us to add or subtract from existing market prices in order to produce the *social* valuation of the relevant goods.

2 It may be thought that matters could be greatly simplified by ignoring domestic prices in the importing country by restricting ourselves instead to world prices of all traded goods, which prices may then serve as opportunity costs. Grounds offered for recourse to this expedient include:

(i) that everything produced and consumed domestically has an effect (via the availabilities argument) on the balance of payments;
(ii) that, because of substitution possibilities, we can compare one thing with another and, in particular, we can conveniently compare any good with foreign exchange;
(iii) because world prices express their real cost or benefit to a country in terms of foreign exchange; and
(iv) free foreign exchange is a good yardstick, as it can be used to satisfy almost any need.[3]

These arguments are far from compelling. The employment of world prices, where they do exist, as a proxy for the opportunity costs to a country of its imports could be valid only in exceptional cases. They are certainly not valid for an importing country in which the production of some goods is taxed or subsidized or in which some imports are regulated by quotas or subjected to tariffs, or where goods exported are regulated by quotas or subjected to taxes or subsidies.

In general, that is, the economist must accept the effect on all prices of government policies, and to accept also any constraints imposed by the government in any operations involved in the paying for goods or materials required by the project.

Bearing this in mind, let us consider the calculation of the opportunity cost of the import of an additional 100 tons of copper for a project in India, the copper being supplied by some foreign country at a price of $1,000 a ton. We shall do so under the assumed existence of two limiting circumstances: first, that India cannot increase the value of its exports, or else does not wish to do so; and second, that India is, indeed, willing to increase its exports, at least to the extent necessary to pay for the additional imports required by the project.

Before we start, however, it is as well for the student to be aware of a familiar microeconomic proposition, namely, the equivalence of a quota and a tax or tariff

---

3 Such reasons are those given by Little and Mirrlees (1968).

in respect of their impact on the price and quantity demanded of the good in question.

If, for instance, there is a 200 per cent *ad valorem* tariff on the imports of copper, which has the effect of reducing the annual amount imported by India to, say, 1,500 tons, an annual import quota of 1,500 tons of copper will also have the effect of raising the domestic equilibrium price by 200 per cent.

In either case, a transfer payment takes place within the Indian economy. A 200 per cent rise in the initial price of $1,000 per ton of copper will yield the government a revenue of 2 *times* ($1,000 × 1,500 tons), or $3 million. And this is the sum that is, in the new equilibrium, transferred from the consumers of copper-containing goods to the government, in the first instance, whether the government uses a tariff or a quota system to limit the imports of copper to 1,500 tons – provided that the government charges $2,000 for a licence to buy a ton of copper or else auctions such licences in a competitive market.

Should the government distribute such licences as a sort of perk among particular firms for political reasons, the additional profits made by these favoured firms would also amount to $3 million, being now a transfer to them of $3 million from the consumers of copper-containing goods.

This much granted, we may confine ourselves to assuming a tariff, regardless of whether the government uses a tariff or an equivalent quota – at least in so far as we are addressing ourselves to the calculation of the opportunity costs of imports. For what is essential to our understanding is a recognition that, when the government receives an *additional* revenue of $200,000 on the additional 100 tons of copper that is imported, the transfer of this sum is, itself, of no consequence to the calculation. What one segment of society (the government) gains is equal to the loss sustained by another segment (the consumers of goods containing copper). The economy as a whole is no better or worse off.

What is of consequence, whether the government uses a tariff or the equivalent quota, is the rise in the scarcity value of the copper resulting from the imposition of the tariff or quota. In our example, the resulting rise in the market price of a ton of copper to $3,000 is the social value that is now placed on it by the Indian community.

If, therefore, the *additional* 100 tons of copper required by the project were, in fact, *not imported* but instead bought from the domestic market at the prevailing price or, indeed, appropriated without compensation by a tyrannical government, the opportunity cost to the project would have to be $300,000, this being the value of the 100 tons of copper that would be lost to the rest of the economy when it was transferred to the project.

3   Once we return to our initial assumption, that the value of India's exports cannot be increased, the only way we can now *import* the 100 tons of copper from abroad at the foreign supply price of $1,000 a ton is by reducing the amounts of other imported goods that could be bought from abroad for $100,000. Were the government to decree that the $100,000 needed for the 100 tons of copper become available by a reduction only in its imports of manganese, all we have to know is the value on the domestic market in India of the amount of it, say 200 tons, that can be bought abroad for $100,000. If the domestic market value of these 200 tons of manganese is $200,000 (this $200,000 that has to be forgone in order to make the 100 tons of copper available to the project), then $200,000 is the opportunity cost to the project of the 100 tons of copper.

True, if the economist were permitted to choose the amounts of imported goods to be reduced so as to make available the $100,000 of foreign exchange required to buy the additional copper, we should expect him to choose those imports that have the lowest value on the domestic market, so minimizing the opportunity cost of the 100 tons of copper. This could be as low as $100,000. And it could, indeed, be lower if some goods in India were subsidized.

Nor is it entirely inconceivable that, for political reasons of its own, the government should decree that the $100,000 needed for the import of an additional 100 tons of copper be made available by reducing the required amount of some goods on which it pays a subsidy, say, of 40 per cent. The domestic value of this amount of imports (which saves the country $100,000 of foreign exchange) would therefore be no more than $60,000. Again, the transfer – this time from the government to the consumers of this good – is immaterial to the calculation. What is material is the $60,000 that is the value lost in that market, notwithstanding that the scarcity value of the good in question has been depressed by an expansion of its consumption consequent upon the subsidy. In these circumstances, the opportunity cost of the 100 tons of copper to the project is equal to $60,000.[4]

4   We now remove the restriction on exports. The additional imports of our 100 tons of copper can be paid for by exporting domestically produced goods that will fetch $100,000 on the world market or, to be more precise, will fetch $100,000 in the foreign country that is prepared to buy them.

From what has been said above, the reader will immediately appreciate that the opportunity cost of the 100 tons of copper to the project is now equal to the domestic value of the goods that are exported to pay for it. True, in the real world, there may be some difficulty in determining which are those particular exports. But the economist should at least know just what he is after – what, ideally, he should be calculating if all the relevant data were available.

If the economist is not permitted to select the batch of goods to be exported to pay for the copper (that having the lowest domestic value), he will discover, if he can, the domestically produced goods that the government has elected to export. In our example of the additional 100 tons of copper, the government may decide to export Indian jute worth $100,000 to the foreign importer. At, say, $4 per pound

---

4 It may be unnecessary to remind the reader that, although the prevalence of taxes, tariffs, quotas, subsidies and any other regulation, in addition to the prevalence of monopolies, are associated with a sub-optimal position for the economy as a whole, a CBA is an exercise in partial economic analysis. The economist has to calculate gains and losses starting from the prevailing sub-optimal position that is reflected in the resulting prices. See Appendix 4.

of jute to the foreign buyer, $25,000 pounds of it has to be exported to pay for the 100 tons of copper. And if, for any reason – for instance, a tax on its production or a monopoly that controls the sale of jute – the domestic price in India is $6 per pound, the opportunity cost of the 100 tons of copper is equal to $150,000.

Clearly, if the Indian government were to export, instead, an amount of jute that could be sold to the foreigner for $60,000, the remaining $40,000 needed by selling cotton, the opportunity cost of the 100 tons of copper becomes equal to the domestic value of the jute exported *plus* the domestic value of the cotton exported, and so on for three or more goods exported.

More generally yet, the 100 tons of copper required by the project may be made available by both reducing some imports and expanding some exports. Where this is the case, the calculation of the relevant opportunity cost becomes somewhat more tedious but, in essence, it comes to no more than an addition of sub-calculations.

5   It remains to deal briefly with the social value of any good exported by the project itself. If the project sells one of its goods, say w, to a foreign country for $5, so enabling the country to use the $5 of foreign exchange to import an additional $5 of goods from abroad, such imported goods are to be valued by the project at their domestic value in India. Assuming the goods sell at $8 in India, then that is their value to the project.

In sum, the social value *to the project* of the goods that it exports during a given year is equal to the domestic value of the additional goods such exports enable it to import.

15 Transfer payments and double counting

1   So far, the transfer payments discussed have been of the (disguised) unemployment benefits received by workers in connection with the calculation of the opportunity costs of labour. We now turn our attention to the other sorts of transfer payments.

2   The obverse of the benefits or direct subsidies received by unemployed persons are the direct taxes paid by employed persons. While a private firm properly calculates profit as *net* of all taxes it has to pay, the economist interested in social net benefit properly values such benefits as *gross* of tax. If, out of $100,000 annual net benefit from the operation of a dam, $35,000 is paid as tax to the government, this amount is to be regarded as a transfer to other nationals via the government, not as a loss to society as a whole; in effect, a form of redistribution of the net social gain of $100,000.

Similarly, tariffs that have to be paid by citizens on imported goods – or subsidies on them received by citizens – are also no more than inter-community transfer payments.

There is, however, a caveat to be made if foreigners are involved. If, for instance, the project in question is financed by an issue of shares on which shareholders receive a dividend, although the amount of tax paid to the home government is, as indicated, a transfer payment (from shareholders to other nationals), any *additional* tax paid by foreign shareholders to their own government is obviously *not* a transfer to nationals: it is a transfer abroad of part of the annual benefit produced by the project. Hence, the tax paid by resident foreigners to their own government constitutes a loss to the home economy and must therefore be subtracted in that year from the value of the project's benefits.

3   Are transfers involved in a shift in the demand for goods from area A to area B consequent upon a shift in population from the former to the latter area? We need not enquire into the reasons for the movement of people from A to B. If we discovered that they moved because they thought the climate in area B was more salubrious or that the tap water tasted better, the benefit would be calculated as the CV[12] of those who chose to move over and above their costs of movement, but for the rest, the consequent increase in the demand for goods in area B does not of itself produce a benefit. Allowing that the additional goods bought in area B after people moved there are no different from those they bought in area A, *qua* consumers, nothing is gained or lost.

Existing storekeepers in area B will, of course, gain, but such gains will be offset by the losses suffered by storekeepers in area A. Yet this may not be a simple transfer of gain from one area to another. Over time, costs may arise. Service personnel may be willing enough to move from area A where they are no longer needed to area B where they are needed, notwithstanding which costs are incurred in their moving. Again, extended store capacity will have to be built in area B while such capacity has to be reduced in area A. But it would be a rare coincidence if, in the very year that, say, $1 million was to be spent in extending store capacity in area B, $1 million was no longer needed to be spent in area A to replace obsolete store capacity. Chances are that the $1 million of additional store capacity needed in area B will be spent soon, and only some years later will area A save $1 million from not having to replace that much store capacity. The resulting cost being equal to the potential return lost in delaying the recoupment of the $1 million spent in extending store capacity. In other words, the $1 million spent in area B may not be exactly offset by the reduction in expenditure in area A, owing to this lagged effect.

4   A caveat may now be entered against the possibility of counting a project's benefits twice.

Consider, first, the proposed construction of a railway linking a suburban area A with a big city, one that will offer an hourly service from six in the morning to midnight. The social value of the rail link is to be calculated, as usual, by the most potential users are willing to pay for it *less* any negative externalities the construction and service may incur. From this figure, the value of the net benefits is obtained by subtracting the opportunity costs of its construction and operation.

In consideration of the variety of advantages conferred by the rail link on the residents of area A, house prices there are apt to rise, the increase in the price of any particular house being, possibly, an indicator of the benefits expected to accrue to those occupying it: in effect, the capitalized value of the expected benefits. But only under special conditions may the rise in house prices in the area be accepted as a valid measure of the benefits over time from the introduction of the rail service. One of these conditions is that the size of area A be large – large enough to accommodate residents that are so far distant from the location of the railway station that the rail link offers them no advantages at all. The houses of such residents will therefore not rise at all in consequence of the rail link to the city. For the remaining houses, the closer to the railway station, the greater the benefit of the railway service and the greater the rise in the house price. Yet even were this condition met, people's uncertainty about the future usefulness of the rail link in view of possible later developments, to say nothing of the possible irrelevance of the implicit rates of discount involved, make it apparent that the differential rise in house prices in the area that may be attributed to the introduction of the rail link is a poor indicator of the extent of the benefits conferred.

This is particularly so when area A is such that all residents find the rail link to be an advantage. And this is likely to be the case. Even for a resident that will continue to drive into the city, the existence of a rail connection to the city has a contingent or insurance value; his automobile may be damaged, the weather may make driving risky, he may have damaged his wrists or otherwise feel disinclined to drive.

When all residents derive some benefit from the introduction of a rail link, a zero increase in the price of a house cannot be taken to mean that the residents derive zero benefit from the rail link. Indeed, the limiting case is where area A is such that, irrespective of the location of the house, accessibility to the railway station is much the same for everyone. For in that case, there can be no differential rise in house prices. In fact, house prices do not increase at all in consequence of the introduction of the rail link, no matter how advantageous.

One can only conclude that the only accurate way of measuring the social benefits of the rail link is by direct calculation of the magnitudes: that is, by calculating the CV[12] for every one affected by the change. On an annual basis, this amounts to ascertaining the largest sum the residents of area A are willing to pay for the rail services *less* the costs of any unwanted spillovers, and subtracting from this figure the annual opportunity costs of constructing and servicing the railway.

5   Although, in the above example of a rail link, there is no risk that the economist engaged in evaluating a project will double-count benefits, once as a flow of benefits and again as a capitalized value of expected benefits, there is a possibility that a double-counting of the flow of benefits may occur in some circumstances.

For example, consider an irrigation project that reduces the costs of grain production over the area of cultivation. The value of the benefit created by the project is to be reckoned, ultimately, as a consumer surplus – as a 'cost-saving' to the consumer arising from a reduction in the price of the grain. There will also be, initially, a rise in the profits of the cultivators or farmers, a rise in the profits of grain merchants, a rise in the profits of bankers, and so on. But these gains, no matter how long they continue, are not to be entered as benefits to the project – at least not as benefits *additional* to the cost-saving of the consumers of grain. Such extra profits are to be conceived as transfer of a part of this benefit to consumers of grain to the farmers, grain-merchants, banks and other middle men – at least during the period of adjustment in a competitive economy. Put more generally, the total benefit of the project which, as mentioned, is equal to no more than the gain to consumers from a lower price of grain, is distributed over a varying period of time among consumers, farmers and middlemen according to the operation of market forces and institutions.

Clearly, double-counting would be involved if, to this 'cost-saving' to consumers, we were also to add (temporary) gains by middlemen.

Part IV
External effects

16 Introduction to external effects

1 External effects, an abbreviation for external economies and diseconomies – sometimes referred to as 'externalities', more picturesquely as 'neighbour-hood effects', somewhat vapidly as 'side effects', and more suggestively as 'spillover effects', or briefly, 'spillovers' – first appear as 'external economies' in Alfred Marshall's *Principles* (1925) in connection with a competitive indus-try's downward-sloping supply curve. Marshall's argument is that, as industry expands by, say, an additional firm, any resulting reduction in the average costs of production accrues to all the firms in the industry. The total reduction in costs experienced by all the intra-marginal firms is to be attributed to the entry of the additional firm. The true or 'social' cost of the additional output produced by this marginal firm is not the total cost of it as calculated by that firm, but this cost *less* the total savings in costs by all the intra-marginal firms. This proposition is important in determining the 'correct' or 'optimal' output of the industry. For in practice, the additional firm makes no allowance for the savings in costs it contributes to the rest of the industry. If, therefore, firms continue to enter the competitive industry until, at the going price of the product, the total cost of the firm is equal to its total revenue, the equilibrium size of the industry will be that at which the market demand price is equal to the average (inclusive) cost of the good in question. But the marginal cost, or total cost of the incremental firm, will be below average cost by the amount of the total cost-savings it confers on the intra-marginal firms. Therefore, marginal cost will, to the same extent, be below the market price and, abiding by the marginal-cost pricing rule, output should be extended beyond the competitive equilibrium until marginal cost is equal to price. The existence of external economies in a competitive industry, Marshall concludes, entails an equilibrium output that is below optimal.

Constructing a curve marginal to the industry's downward-sloping supply curve, the point at which this marginal curve cuts the demand curve identifies the 'ideal' or optimal output. This concept, and its corresponding construction, was extended in a symmetrical manner to external diseconomies, to reveal that the optimal output of a competitive industry was below the equilibrium output.

When such externalities first appeared in the literature, they tended to be regarded, if not quite as curiosa, as in the nature of a refinement of economic analysis, one having limited applications. For among the older textbooks, at least, as among the population at large, there was a tacit presumption in favour of the spread of industry, the prevailing conviction being that, although the establishment of additional plant and equipment might cause some local inconvenience, the growth of industry would, on balance, confer economic benefits to society as a whole.

With the passage of time, it was realized that externalities had wide application, not simply as between firms in connection with the optimal size of an industry – which may be referred to as external effects *internal* to the industry – but also as between industries themselves or, more generally, as between different economic activities in which the gains of one or more groups are at the expense of others.

2　Familiar examples of negative spillovers include the manifold adverse ecological repercussions on flora and fauna, and on the climate and soil, in clearing the trees of forest land.[1]

Other examples within urban areas include the traffic congestion suffered by all drivers along roads and highways, the noise or pollution suffered by people in the vicinity from the operation of industry or of its products, and the consequent effects on people's health and longevity. Even the offence to citizens given by the erection of some tasteless or incongruous building or other structure may properly be regarded as a spillover – as, indeed, would the reverse of this, the pleasure in a beautiful building enjoyed by citizens being properly regarded as a positive spillover.

From a little reflection on examples such as these, it emerges that one characteristic common to all of them is the incidental or unintentional nature of the effect produced. The person or industrial concern engaged, say, in logging may or may not have any idea of the consequences on the profits or welfare of others. But it is certain that they do not enter into his calculations. The factory owners, whose plant produces smoke as well as other things, are concerned only to produce the other things that can be sold on the market. They have no interest in producing the smoke, even though they may be fully aware of it. But so long as their own productivity does not suffer thereby, and they themselves are not penalized in any way, they will regard the smoke as an unfortunate by-product.

If these external effects are not deliberately produced, however, neither are they willingly absorbed by others. Such effects may add to the enjoyment of life, as does the smell of fresh-cut grass, or else add to life's vexations as does the noise, stench and danger of increasing car traffic. But they are not within the control of the persons who are absorbing them – at least not without their incurring expenses.[2]

1　Again, the adverse spillovers from creating a dam or artificial lake, include the erosion of fertile soil, the reduction of fish in the river, the silting of the river or canal, the spread of water-borne diseases and of breeding grounds for mosquitoes and locusts.

2　If an adverse spillover effect could be avoided without incurring any costs, it could hardly be called an adverse spillover. Certainly, no problem would arise.

However, a definition of external effects that gives prominence to these aspects – that a person's welfare or a firm's profits depends upon things that are initially outside his control, which things are incidental to the activity of others – is by itself insufficient and may, indeed, lead to confusion. Let us see how.

3 The statement that a firm's or industry's outputs or profits or a person's welfare can be influenced by the activities of others is true, apparently, within the context of any general equilibrium system. In particular, it is true within a general equilibrium system that has no external effects of the sort illustrated above.[3] The familiar interdependent system of Leon Walras is a case in point. Among the set of equations posited are those for individuals regarded as consumers and owners of productive services. All the *variables* in each person's utility function – whether they refer to the amounts of finished goods bought or the amounts of productive services offered – are deemed to be entirely within his control. The parameters within each person's utility function, however, are the set of prices; and these are determined by the system as a whole.

Thus, for each person, the quantities of the things that he is willing to buy or to sell depend, *inter alia*, on the set of market prices of these things. The amounts of goods supplied by perfectly competing firms also depends upon the market prices. These sets of market prices can, in general, be altered by any changes in technology, in people's tastes, or in the accumulation and redistribution of assets. It follows that the activities of persons and firms, in response to these sorts of changes, also have incidental effects on the welfare of others. If, to take a simple example, people start changing from tea to coffee, the price of tea will at first tend to fall and that of coffee to rise. The producers of tea will initially suffer and those of coffee benefit, while the consumers of tea will be better off and the consumers of coffee worse off.

But in this general equilibrium system, in the absence of all external effects as commonly understood, such interdependence operates *indirectly* through changes in market prices. Each and every exogenous change mentioned – a change in techniques, in tastes or in factor endowment – entails a corresponding change in the equilibrium set of prices. Since, in general, every price is affected, every person's welfare is affected also, and this can be very important.[4] Nevertheless, given perfectly competitive markets and no external effects, each general equilibrium position meets the requirement of a Pareto optimum, i.e. one in which it is not possible to make one or more persons better off without making at least one person worse off.[5] In contrast, the concern with external effects arises just because their

---

3 This system is, of course, a theoretical construct only. Engineers affirm that in all input–output activities there is wastage, and therefore waste material is absorbed into the air, the earth or its waters, so creating the potential for external effects.

4 For instance in appraising welfare criteria. See Mishan (1957).

5 If every relevant effect in the economy is properly priced, the economy is in an optimal position. The reverse, however, is not true, since optimality can be consistent with unpriced spillovers. See the example in Chapter 17.

existence implies that, unless special arrangements are made, the equilibrium solutions attainable may *not* be Pareto optimal.

We may, then, infer that external effects are effects on others that are conveyed directly and not indirectly through prices. If we allow that these effects on people's welfare matter in principle no less than do the priced products and services, it follows that it is just because these external effects, these by-products of the activities of others, are not properly priced or not priced at all, that the equilibrium solution is not Pareto optimal. To illustrate, the competitive equilibrium price of steel spades is $10, price being equal to long-run average and marginal cost. In their production, however, noise is produced, this being the only external effect in the economy. The noise created in producing the marginal spade would be tolerated without complaint only on receipt of, say, $7 by those disturbed by the noise. The social cost of the marginal spade is, therefore, $10 plus $7, or $17 altogether.

If we produced one spade less to start with, the factors released would, assuming universal perfect competition, create $10 of goods elsewhere. But the accompanying removal of noise is tantamount to a gain of $7. Society as a whole is better off to the extent of $7. The original output is then clearly in excess of the optimal output.

If all external effects, both positive and negative, could somehow be properly priced by a universal system of property rights,[6] then any perfectly competitive equilibrium would, indeed, be optimal. In fact, if every external effect, positive or negative were to be properly priced within a competitive market along with other goods and bads, it would cease to be an external effect: it would have been 'internalized' into the competitive economic system – as expressed, say, in the Walrasian system of equations. This will be fully appreciated once we have satisfactorily defined an externality.

4   Let us begin by writing the equation

$$U^1 = U^1(x_1^1, x_2^1, x_3^1, \ldots) \tag{16.1}$$

where U^1 is the utility, or welfare, of person 1, and, x_1^1, x_2^1, x_3^1, are the amounts he has (flows or stocks, according to the problem) of three of the goods, x_1, x_2, x_3, on which his utility or welfare depends. Equation (16.1) is no more than the statement that person 1's utility or welfare depends on the quantities he has of those goods: no external effects are implied by the equation. If, instead, we write the equation as

$$U^1 = U^1(x_1^2; x_1^1, x_2^1, x_3^1) \tag{16.2}$$

6 A proposition initially stated by Coase (1960), one that apparently gave immense satisfaction to the business community in as much as it was assumed that such a system was feasible enough to vindicate unfettered free enterprise. The sobering fact, however, is that a universal system of property rights is far from being feasible. Were it otherwise, there would certainly be no need for CBAs. In this connection, see Appendix 7.

the possibility of an external effect is implied. The term x_1^2 gives the additional information that person 1's utility, U^1, depends not only on his own quantities of a number of goods, but also on x_1^2, on person 2's quantity of x_1. If x_1 were flowers, then person 1's welfare would be affected not only by the flowers in his own garden, but also by those in his neighbour's garden. We could also interpret equation (16.2) as a production function, U^1 being the output of good 1, and the xs as the inputs used in the production of good 1. Equation (16.2) is now interpreted as saying that the amount of good 1 depends directly on the inputs x_1, x_2, x_3, etc., used directly in the production of good 1, and depends also on the amount of input l used in the production of good 2. The amount of the ith input used in the production of good 2 (this amount being under the control of the producers of good 2, *not* of the producers of good 1) is therefore regarded as imposing external effects on the output of good 1 and also, therefore, on the price of good 1 and the profits of the producers of good 1.

Such notational definitions are common enough in the literature. Another would be $\delta U^1 / \delta x_i^2 \neq 0$, which can be interpreted as saying that a small change in person 2's quantity of good i will *not* leave person 1's utility unchanged. For the external effect to *exist*, however, we should have to add the information that $x_i^2 \neq 0$. Thus, $x_i^2 > 0$ implies that person 2 purchases some of the ith good; $x_i^2 < 0$ implies that he sells some of the ith good. If we write $\delta U^1 / \delta x_i^2 > 0$, then person 2's external effect is one that raises person 1's welfare, the converse being true for a reversal of the inequality sign. Notation of this sort is helpful, but there are limitations. Thus, if x_i^2 refers to person 2's purchase of, say, a lawnmower, it is not possible to infer from the notation alone whether person 1's welfare is reduced (a) by his envy of person 2's new lawnmower, (b) by its being a noise nuisance, (c) by the extra smoke suffered by person 1 among others (including person 2) in consequence of the factory's production of an extra lawnmower or (d) by a combination of any or all of these. We return to these possibilities in the following section.

Again, the fact that person 1 reacts to the amount of good i taken or produced by person 2, without his being able to control person 2's consumption or production of good i – which information is imparted by the notation above – does not suffice to define an external effect in the economist's sense. My wealthy aunt's welfare (as well as my own) depends unambiguously on the amount of arsenic I put into her tea. If it was discovered that, in my impatience to inherit her fortune, I had used arsenic to accelerate the natural process of ageing, the coroner would be unlikely to refer to the results of my enterprise as an external effect. Yet, if person 1 is my aunt, person 2 is myself, x_i^2 is the amount of arsenic that I use, $\delta U^1 / \delta x_i^2 < 0$ expresses the proposition that my aunt's welfare varies inversely with the amount of arsenic that I use. It would therefore fit the situation just depicted. In contrast, an alternative interpretation of the external effect indicated by the same term, $\delta U^1 / \delta x_i^2 < 0$, would be that of my good aunt suffering at the thought of my injudicious consumption of arsenic, in small doses, as a stimulant. In order, therefore, to comply with the conventional meaning of external effect, the x_i^2 notation is to be interpreted strictly as person 2's consumption or production of good x_i which is determined solely by reference to his immediate interest, and in disregard of the effects it may have on the welfare of others.

5   Once the reader has a clear idea of what an externality is,[7] a little reflection will convince him that the number of external effects in the real world is virtually unlimited. If my wife is envious of her friend's new fur coat, her friend's wearing it in my wife's presence has an adverse external effect on at least one person. A cigar smoked in the presence of non-smokers has adverse external effects. Attractive short-skirted women may generate adverse external effects on other women and favourable external effects on men. A's promotion causes B to rejoice and C to curse. And so one could go on.

But should they all be taken into account by the economist? No, for there are at least two qualifications to consider.

First, there must obviously be a very large number of spillover effects that, if not trivial, would certainly be uneconomic to correct: the administrative costs and other expenses necessary to ensure compliance would exceed the social benefit of correcting the spillover effect. Because of the incidence of such 'transactions' costs, however, it may also appear uneconomic to correct even significant spillover! It may, nonetheless, transpire that some adverse spillovers may be eliminated or reduced either by alteration in the mode of production or in the use of the good in question or else by the employment of some technical device (which we discuss in later chapters).

Second, the question of the 'legitimacy' of certain spillovers has to be faced. For among all those spillovers that could, in fact, be economically corrected by one means or another, not all may be worthy of social recognition. Economists, and society at large, might wish to distinguish and, in practice, do distinguish, between external effects that are a source of 'legitimate' satisfaction or grievance, and those that are not. Among the latter is the resentment or envy felt by some people at the achievement or possessions of others.[8] But though such reactions may elicit sympathy and qualify for psychiatry, they are unlikely to command moral approval. Once ethics are bought into external effects in this way, the question of which effects are to count and which are not must, in the last resort, depend upon a consensus in the particular society. Since ethical distinctions of this sort are consistently made and acted by society, the economist is justified in following suit. Though perhaps not formally embodied in legal documents, no economic policy that caters to these 'negative feelings' of people has ever been introduced.

---

7 There are quite a number of economic phenomena – all, perhaps, relevant to considerations of optimality – masquerading in the literature as external effects that cannot be admitted on the interpretation in the text. Common among these are such developments as the pooling of risks, improved training facilities and other cost-saving arrangements. Such arbitrary extensions of the original concept, and the consequent ambiguity generated, are discussed in Mishan (1965a).

8 This is all-too-common phenomenon, envy of the greater income or wealth of others, is often referred to in the literature as the 'Jones' effect' (the obsession with 'keeping up with the Joneses'). The more prevalent it is, the less can economic growth be held to increase society's welfare.

In contrast, there is no lack of evidence that society does take seriously all tangible damage inflicted on people in the pursuit by others of pleasure or profit. As adverse environmental effects provide, today, the most important instances of damage inadvertently inflicted on other people, they will feature prominently in our discussion of methods of evaluating them.

17 Adverse spillovers
The complacent view

1   We now turn to a more detailed consideration of adverse environmental spillovers. The warrant for doing so does not derive simply from their rapid growth, especially in the post-war period, nor simply from their frequent neglect, but from the evaluative problems that arise whenever an adverse spillover effect has a large effect on the welfare of a number of people. If the judgement that adverse environmental spillovers have become more important since the war than favourable spillovers is questioned by the reader, he need not complain of bias.

The analysis of favourable spillovers is quite symmetrical, and economy in exposition suggests that a thorough treatment of either type of spillover alone, favourable or unfavourable, will suffice to demonstrate the principles.

2   We have taken it for granted that spillovers have to be evaluated, ultimately, by reference to the subjective estimates of the victims of spillover effects. One can go further. One can argue for these compensatory sums being actually paid to the victims in the event of a project being introduced that generates adverse spillovers. Indeed, this view of the matter would seem to follow from the classical liberal doctrines as expounded by John Stuart Mill, in contradistinction to a Pareto economic decision based simply on the determination of a net balance of gain or loss, one in which the question of actual compensation is disregarded. *A fortiori*, the liberal doctrine would reject the 'social engineering' approach to the spillover problem, an approach that seeks to formulate 'tolerance levels' for society. True, the upper limit of the tolerable degree of, say, noise may be so chosen as to preclude ascertainable, physical damage or bodily hurt, given our present knowledge of the effects of noise on people and property. Yet, noise below that limit can be highly irritating to a lot of people. If a man were subjected at regular intervals to the gentlest tap on the back of his head, his subsequent exasperation would hardly surprise us. Neither the fact that he emerged from the treatment without bruises nor the affirmation that this head-tapping business was, in some mysterious way, an unavoidable by-product of the operation of modern industry and, indeed, could be counted on to promote exports, would assure us about its moral justification. And if the occasional or frequent bombarding of a man's ears with noise, as a consequence of other people's pursuit of pleasure or profit, can be said to differ from this imaginary case, it is not so much that, over time, people become less physically sensitive to its incidence but rather that, of necessity, we have learned to curb our desire to give expression to our annoyance, in the belief that there is little we can do to prevent or reduce its omnipresence.

Yet, granted that the growing incidence of noise does reduce people's well-being, if the true liberal would reject the adoption of some maximum tolerable levels of noise at different times of the day, it is not merely because such a policy is necessarily arbitrary. It is because the adoption, of such tolerance norms runs counter to the doctrine that each man is to be deemed the best judge of his own interests – no less so in matters that affect him directly and intimately.

3 It must be acknowledged, however, that economists are seen as more eager to defend men's interests in cases where they are beneficiaries of privately pro-duced goods than when they are the victims of those adverse spillovers created by the production or consumption of privately produced goods. The proposal by high-minded members of society that, say, provocative lace underwear should be withdrawn from production, or at least not advertised in the media, would be sure to provoke condemnation by free-enterprise economists, notwithstanding that provocative lace underwear is not a requisite of the good life. Yet, when it comes to the distress that many people suffer in consequence of the destruction of envi-ronmental amenity – something, it can be argued, that is indeed a prerequisite of the good life – the response, until very recently, has not been impressive. At all events, for decades, citizens had submitted to being continually robbed of choice in respect of amenities such as clean air, quietude, green space and other collec-tive goods that vitally enhance their sense of well-being. They tended to accept the spoliation of the physical environment in which they were immersed much as they might accept climatic changes, as a phenomenon to which they can perhaps adapt, but which, in itself, is outside the control of men.

Such an attitude, however, is not justifiable. Some framework of law is necessary if markets are to function in an orderly fashion, and if trade and enterprise are to flourish. But not all laws are equally effective in harmonizing the search for commercial gain with the welfare of society. The economist's interest in social welfare or, more simply, in extending the citizen's area of choice, can do more than offer suggestions to promote a smoother functioning of the existing economic mechanisms. At a time of rapid deterioration of the environment, he can propose alterations in the legal framework itself as something that can make significant contributions to social welfare.

Prior to such proposals, however, let us summarize three aspects of the approach to adverse spillovers still popular among those economists who argue for a presumption in favour of competitive enterprise.

4 (i) First, granted that, for any good x that incidentally also creates measurable adverse spillovers that vary with the output of x, there exists a uniquely determined optimal output, which is that at which the price of x is equal to its social marginal cost (the latter term being the sum of the private marginal cost of x and the marginal cost of its spillovers).

It is easily demonstrated that this optimal output can just as well be reached by levying an excise tax on good x as by offering an excise subsidy for reducing the output of x – for the purpose, in either case, of inducing producers to supply the optimal output of good x. This same optimal output can also be reached either by compelling the producers of x to compensate all those who suffer from the incidental adverse spillovers or else by such victims themselves bribing the producers of x to reduce its output.

One is supposed to conclude that the question of responsibility for the reduction of the spillover – the question of who compensates whom – in these cases of manifest conflict of interest has no bearing on the allocative problem of determining the optimal output. From such a conclusion, it follows that differences in the ways by which this optimal output may be reached affect only the distribution of welfare in the community.

(ii) Nor, apparently, can this question of which party should compensate the other, be settled by considerations of equity. To be sure, it may be argued that, although the smoke produced by a soap factory does indeed damage the welfare of many of the inhabitants living in the vicinity, so also can the required curtailment of the smoke-producing output (or the required installation of anti-smoke devices) be said to damage the interests of the manufacturers. The fact is simply that the interests of the two groups – the soap manufacturers (or beneficiaries from soap production), on the one hand, and the victims of their smoke pollution, on the other – are mutually opposed, and only a misuse of language can detract from the essential symmetry in respect of equity.[1]

(iii) Finally, whatever the institutional framework, the party suffering from the spillovers in question has a clear interest in bribing the other party to reduce the initial (uncorrected) output in the direction of the optimal output. But recognition of the opportunity for mutual gain in moving to an optimal output leads to a consideration of the costs of negotiating an agreement between the two parties.

For instance, *in the absence of such negotiating costs*, the potential gain in reducing the output of x by successive units can be reckoned as the excess of the most the inhabitants will pay for the reduction of that particular unit of x less the minimum sum the manufacturer will accept for agreeing to the reduction. And if this potential gain is, say, $100, its division between the two parties will depend upon their respective bargaining power.[2]

If, now, negotiating costs amount to $120, they will exceed the $100 of potential mutual gain. The contemplated reduction in the output of x is, therefore, no longer mutually advantageous. With this consideration in mind, an observed absence of negotiation to reduce the particular spillover is explained by the argument that the

---

1 This proposition gathers plausibility from habitual attention given to the spillovers generated between two firms or industries.

2 The loss to the manufacturer from reducing the output of x by a unit is calculated as the profit forgone. Where, however, we are thinking in terms of the long-period supply curve of a competitive industry and ignore the costs of adjustment, the loss is calculated as that of a consumer surplus.

potential mutual gain in the movement towards an optimal output must be smaller than the costs of negotiating it. Since these negotiating costs are real enough, involving as they do the use of scarce resources, they may be supposed frequently to swamp the (costless) mutual gains of a movement toward an optimum position.

By such reasoning, some economists found themselves perilously close to an ultra-conservative doctrine that, in respect of spillovers at least, what is already in existence is best. And for the rest, one can do no more than await the advent of innovations, technical or institutional, that reduce the costs of preventive devices or the costs of negotiation and administration.

5   This complacent, though fairly widespread, doctrine has been challenged in the literature on externalities.[3] But it must also be challenged in the cost–benefit literature. It may be thought that, whereas the externality literature is concerned primarily with optimal outputs, CBA addresses itself, in the main, to the question of the economic justification of a specific project taken as a whole (or the selection of several from a large number of technically feasible projects) and only in a secondary way to the question of optimal outputs of projects once they are established. But the arguments about optimal outputs summarized above, dealing as they do with compensatory payments, with equity and with negotiation costs – or transactions costs as they are more generally called – can just as well be extended to the issue of the acceptance or rejection of specific project.

Having said this much to affirm the relevance of considerations (i), (ii) and (iii) to CBA, a brief word on each is appropriate before concluding the chapter.

(i)   The alleged uniqueness of the optimal solution rests on the implied assumption of zero welfare effects. Once the assumption is removed, as it has to be wherever the project in question has significant effects on welfare, optimality becomes ambiguous. This aspect of the problem is treated in some detail in Chapter 20.

(ii)   The freedom of one group to pursue its own interests or enjoyment, it is alleged, necessarily interferes with that of the other group once the externality situation is created. For example, the inhabitants of an area being polluted by the smoke emitted from a soap-works suffer accordingly, but so also does the soap-works (and its beneficiaries) if its operations are curtailed. The question, then, of which of the two parties should have the property rights in the airshed over the area – in effect, the question of which party has legally to compensate the other for forgoing some of the advantages it enjoyed before the externality appeared – may be settled by reference to the alternative distributional implications.

To be sure, distributional considerations ought properly to be taken into account in a social decision. But they are not the only considerations. Although such externality situations are indeed Pareto-symmetric, as

---

3 Mishan (1967b, 1971b); Cropper and Oates (1992).

described above, they are not, in general, symmetric with respect to ethical merit. In accordance with the classical liberal dictum, the freedom of a man to pursue his own interests has to be qualified in so far as it reduces the freedom or welfare of others. And the freedom of the soap manufacturer to spread smoke over the inhabitants of the area will conflict with the freedom of the inhabitants to continue to enjoy unpolluted air. For the mere action of the inhabitants in enjoying the unpolluted air does not *of itself* cause any damage to the soap works beneficiaries, whereas the action of the soap works – the emission of smoke – does *of itself* reduce the welfare of the inhabitants. The conflict, that is, is initiated directly by the action of the soap works: it is not initiated by the inhabitants breathing the unpolluted air. To take an extreme example, a conflict of interests between a householder A and a burglar B is indeed Pareto-symmetric and, of course, an optimal solution is possible. But the conflict of interests is clearly not ethically symmetric. The conflict is initiated by B's action and is manifestly culpable.

(iii) The argument that the existence of negotiating costs, or transaction costs as they are sometimes called, act to support the *status quo*, or at least the presumption in favour of unconstrained private enterprise, may be valid under existing legal institutions. But in the light of the ethical considerations discussed above, it is manifest that transaction costs are more justly to be borne by the party that inflicts the damage on others. Once the law clearly recognizes this, the existence of transaction costs no longer acts to strengthen the *status quo* in so far as it favours unconstrained private enterprise but, instead, must act to strengthen the *status quo ante* – the original state that was free of smoke or noise nuisance or other adverse spillover, prior to the introduction of the enterprise in question.

18 Internalizing externalities

1 The verbal description of an external effect – that is, a direct effect on another's profit or welfare arising as an incidental by-product of some other person's or firm's legitimate activity – would seem adequate to convey its meaning. Its nature is made yet clearer, however, by examining the notion of 'internalizing' the external effect. The basic idea is that of transforming the incidental by-product into a joint product that is priced on the market. I have been told by a number of Argentinians that, before the turn of the century, cattle were slain on the ranches for their leather only. Their flayed carcasses were left to rot but, if found in time, they could be used as fresh meat by the poor peasants. Apparently, only the leather had a market price, the meat being a by-product, or external effect, of leather production – a favourable spillover of the leather industry for those peasants who happened to be in the vicinity.[1]

Suppose, however, that the human population began to multiply more rapidly than the cattle population, that the taste for meat grew, that meat began to be stored in refrigerators and that, most important of all perhaps, the meat could be exported to distant markets. Domestic meat would become scarce and, therefore, a market for it would come into being. It would then cease to be a spillover, an unintended by-product in the process of obtaining hides for leather. It would take its place as a good in its own right, a joint product with leather. Whatever the separate demands for meat and leather are like, the long-run competitive equilibrium output is optimal, as the cattle population is expanded to the point at which the sum of the market prices are equal to the marginal cost of cattle production. The external effect has been internalized into the pricing system.[2]

1 Notwithstanding which the number of cattle slain could be optimal if, at the margin, the value of the meat was zero. We discuss this point further in the next chapter in terms of 'allocative significance'.
2 It may seem unnecessary to remark that the possibility of internalizing an external effect (or, in the absence of internalization, correcting for optimal outputs) does not mean that the creation of an *adverse* external effect need not make things worse. Yet, students do sometimes argue as though this is so; as though, so long as optimizing by one method or another takes place, the creation of adverse external effects may be viewed with equanimity. The introduction of an adverse external effect into the economy is a bad thing no matter how the economy adapts to it. By internalizing the bad, or by optimizing the output that produces the bad, we are doing no more than making the best of a bad job. We are certainly not as well off as we should be if this bad had not appeared on the economic scene.

Internalizing spillover effects arises also in the case of external diseconomies that are internal to the industry. Common examples of the latter category are deep-sea fishing, in which any additional fishing boat above a certain number reduces the catch of each of the existing fishing boats in the fishing grounds, or traffic congestion, in which every additional vehicle above a certain number causes delay to each of the existing number of vehicles using a given highway system. Internalizing this sort of spillover would require that a positive market price be imputed to the currently unpriced though scarce resource – the area of the sea in the first case, the highway in the second. Once such a resource is priced, it will be used more economically. The analogy of scarce land used in the production of, say, corn is exact. If priced correctly, which implies that in a competitive industry the rent of this scarce resource be maximized, the competitive equilibrium output that emerges is also the optimal output.[3]

Another example, though one in which internal accounting prices are substituted for market prices, is that of two separately owned but adjacent factories, A and B. Factory A produces shoes and is powered by an old-fashioned coal engine, which emits so much smoke as to seriously affect the output of factory B, which produces chocolate bars. The manager of factory B remonstrates with manager A, but to no effect. The daughter of the owner of factory A and the son of the owner of factory B decide to get married, in consequence of which the two factories come under common ownership and control, and the couple live together happily ever after. The cost of the smoke, reckoned in terms of the damage inflicted on the output of factory B, is no longer a spillover generated by A and suffered by B. It is now unambiguously a cost to the joint A–B enterprise and, as such, ways and means of reducing it will be sought. Either anti-smoke devices will be installed in factory A, or else, if cheaper (and assuming the smoke damage to B's output varies directly with A's output), A's output will be reduced to the point at which the value of the marginal damage to B's output, added to the marginal cost of shoe production in A, is equal to the market price of A's shoes. Thus, the smoke ceases to become a spillover effect, but becomes a properly costed item that is internalized into the costing system of the A–B merger.

2   The number of spillover effects that can be internalized into the pricing mechanism or into the costing systems of firms is, however, limited. Among those that cannot easily be internalized through the market are many of the by-products of modern industry and of the hardware it produces. One thinks, in this connection, of traffic noise and various forms of pollution arising from the spread of sewage,

---

3 Assuming a period during which there is one scarce fixed factor and one factor that is variable in supply at a constant price, the average cost curve eventually slopes upward. A curve drawn marginal to this average cost curve cuts the demand curve at the optimal output. At this output, the difference between average cost and marginal cost *times* output gives the amount of the rent to the fixed factor – the maximum rent possible in a perfectly competitive market in which the price of the product is treated as a parameter.

garbage and radioactive wastes; also of the post-war phenomenal growth of diseases of the nerves, heart and stomach, caused by high-tension living, the most ubiquitous by-product of sustained technological advance. Why cannot such spillovers be so internalized? The answer is simple: in order for a competitive market for such spillovers to emerge, certain conditions have to be met which, in the nature of the physical universe, cannot be met. First, the potential victim of these adverse spillover effects must have legal 'property rights' in, say, their ownership of some quantum of quiet and clean air which, if such rights were enjoyed, they could choose to sell to others. Second, in order for such rights to be enforceable, it would be necessary to demarcate a three-dimensional 'territory' about the person of each potential victim in order to identify the intrusions of others and take appropriate legal action. Third, in order for a monopolistic situation not to arise, each of these three-dimensional properties within a given area, which can be rented for particular purposes (say, to accommodate the noise or pollution of someone's activity), must be a close substitute for the others.

The first condition could, of course, be met in the sense that all forms of pollution could be outlawed in the absence of specific agreements between the parties concerned. But because the second condition cannot be met in the world we inhabit, there is difficulty in demarcating each person's property, and a consequent difficulty in identifying the trespasser and the extent of the trespass. Nor can the third condition be met, for, in this hypothetical scheme of things, the right to use one man's 'territory', within some given area, is no substitute for that of another man. Each man within the area has his own three-dimensional territory and, since the noise to be created by the new activity enters in some degree into all of such territories, the enterprise has to reach agreement with each one of them. None can substitute for the other. Unless all agree, the permission of those who do is worthless.

If it were otherwise, if one territory could be substituted freely for another, as could plots of land in an agricultural area, an appropriate market price would arise from the competition of the sellers. The physical universe being what it is, however, each potential seller is in a completely monopolistic position for, without his particular consent, the necessary arrangement for the whole of the affected area cannot be concluded. The reader will detect a similarity between this hypothetical problem, posed by the third condition, and that facing a railroad company having to buy every mile of land through which the track has to run. The cost of acquiring rights where a large number of landowners are involved could be prohibitive were it not for legislation compelling the sale of rights on terms which the courts decide are reasonable. Another instance, occasionally reported by the press, is that of a single householder or small business holding out against a property company that is attempting to buy up a specific area of land as part of some new development scheme.

We must, then, resign ourselves to the prospect of never being able to internalize these important environmental spillovers within the market economy; that is, of not being able to create a market for them – which is, of course, one of the reasons why cost–benefit methods are required to evaluate them.

3   Some further light is cast on the nature of spillover effects by briefly observing the connection between them and collective or public goods. Environmental spillovers usually affect a large number of people within an area. But whereas the positive spillover has been defined as an unintended beneficial effect on others arising from some legitimate economic activity, the benefits conferred on the community by a collective good are those that are deliberately created. It may be noted, moreover, that the collective good may be optional for members of the community, an example being a public park which allows each person to choose how many hours, if any, he wishes to spend there.[4] A non-optional collective good, in contrast is one in which each person perforce receives some amount of it, an example being the rainfall over a certain area that is caused by 'seeding' the clouds above it. In such a case, the amount of rain falling on the land of each person can be more or less than he would prefer. It may even be so large an amount that, on balance, it becomes a net loss to the recipient – an adverse spillover.[5]

4   It is not to be supposed, however, that the evaluation of positive spillovers in a cost–benefit calculation is confined to collective goods. What are often referred to as public goods – whether or not they are publicly financed – need not also be a collective good as defined. A hospital or a railroad is not, strictly speaking, a collective good: once constructed, the services produced by either can be separately allocated to each of a number of persons for their own particular use.

For the collective good, the benefit in any period of any one unit of the good is equal to the aggregate of the benefits enjoyed by all affected by it. If, therefore, the amount of the collective good is variable, the net benefit to the community is maximized by increasing the amount of it until its marginal (aggregate) benefit is equal to its opportunity cost.

The same is true if, instead, we are initially addressing ourselves to the construction of some public good that is not, strictly speaking, a collective good. For instance, if we are to determine the longest distance to be covered by a proposed rail link that would connect a number of towns and villages over the time span contemplated, we have to aggregate the benefits of each potential passenger over that time span for each alternative length of the railroad – adequately measured in each case by the areas under the expected future demand curves – and compare them with their relevant opportunity costs.

Once the chosen rail link has been established, however, the service it provides has to be treated as a private good. Hence, in operating the service, net benefits are maximized if every person pays the marginal cost he incurs which, in the absence

---

4 There can, however, be a problem of congestion if the number of people increases relative to the number, or the size, of the facilities provided.
5 Among those who on balance gain from the given artificial rainfall, there can be those farmers whose crops receive too much rain, in the sense that the benefit to them of the marginal inch of rain is negative. The optimal condition, however, requires that rain be increased until the sum of the benefits and losses of the marginal inch of rain is equal to the cost of producing it.

of congestion, could be zero, provided that the daily or weekly overheads are covered by the consumer surplus.

In the case of a public good such as a hospital, in contrast, once the optimal size of the hospital has been constructed, the marginal cost of each patient is positive and will generally vary between one patient and another.

19 Evaluating spillovers

1 In principle, the method of evaluating spillovers arising from the construction or operation of a project is straightforward enough. For the given amount of any spillovers created by a project during a specified period, either everyone affected by it benefits (unambiguously a positive spillover) or everyone affected loses (unambiguously a negative spillover) or else some gain by it and some lose. In the last case, the net effect of the spillover is, of course, the algebraic sum of all the individual valuations and can, therefore be, on balance, either positive or negative. There will be instances when part or all of a community's valuation of a spillover can properly be calculated by reference to prevailing market prices. The cost of any person's additional laundry bill arising from industrial smoke in the vicinity is a good example. So also is the cost of the damage resulting from cattle straying onto adjacent farmland. But in the last resort, there may be no alternative but to value the spillover as equal to the subjective valuations of those who suffer or benefit from its effects. In terms of the Kaldor–Hicks criterion, the relevant subjective measure is conceived as that sum of money (to be paid by the individual if the spillover raises his welfare; to be received by him if it lowers his welfare) that would restore his welfare to its original pre-spillover level.

Thus, an algebraic aggregate of all the individual valuations of a spillover that is positive is one that meets the Kaldor–Hicks criterion for the community. It may then be inferred that a costless distribution of the gains could make everyone in the community better off, the reverse being true for an algebraic aggregate that is negative.

If, for instance, the building of a dam for irrigational purposes creates only two spillovers: (i) the creation of an artificial lake in which people can swim or boat, and (ii) a body of stagnant water which causes a vast increase in the insect population, each spillover is to be evaluated in the manner stated above and then added, to result in either an excess of benefits or an excess of costs attributable to the project.

2 A common proposal for dealing with the conflict of interest arising, say, from the proposed use of some natural resource is that of auctioning the property rights, a solution that does not comport with our adopted potential Pareto-improvement criterion. This can be illustrated by a proposal to build a dye-works that pours its effluent into the otherwise clear waters of a lake along which it is to be situated. People living close to the lake shore are incensed, as the resulting effluent would ruin their customary recreations that depend upon the lake's pristine waters.

True, it can be argued that, of the two conflicting parties (the owners of the dye-works and the lake-shore community), the one offering the highest sum for use of the lake should be assigned the property rights to it. Such a solution meets the principle that any scarce resource should be allocated to the organization that can use it to produce the greatest value for society.

Yet, it is also true that the auctioning method is one that may not be able to meet the potential Pareto criterion. In our example, we can suppose that the expectant owners of the dye-works are able to offer, at most, $45 million, whereas the lake-side community could manage, at most, but $35 million, in consequence of which the dye-works is given the go-ahead. But it may also transpire that the smallest sum that would reconcile the lake-side inhabitants to the establishing of the dye-works by the lake far exceeds the $45 million that the dye-works' owners can afford. If, say, the smallest acceptable sum were $65 million, then certainly the use of the lake by the dye-works would fail the Kaldor–Hicks test: the loss to society as a whole (including the dye-works' owners) would be such that a costless distribution of the $20 million loss could make everyone in society worse off.

3   In evaluating the costs of adverse spillover effects, the economist engaged in a cost–benefit calculation also has a duty to seek ways of minimizing their costs by proposing recourse to whatever technology is currently available. This search to reduce spillover costs is of the highest importance, as it can make all the difference to whether the project in question meets the cost–benefit criterion.

Whether the adverse spillover is, so to speak, an overhead in the productive process – an example being the power required to drive the machinery in a weaving shed, where the volume of noise created by it is quite independent of the number of looms, if any, in operation – or whether, instead, the amount of the spillover effect varies directly with the amount of the goods produced will make little difference to the analysis. But the exposition is simplified by addressing ourselves, first, to the latter case and also by provisionally assuming that the cost suffered by the community from the unit of spillover generated is uniquely determined. Thus, in Figure 19.1, the cost of the spillovers created by successive units of the good x being produced is measured by the height of the EE_1 curve increasing from left to right. The figure also shows that, *in the absence of all spillovers*, there is an excess (consumer) benefit-over-cost curve BB_1 that slopes downward from left to right so that the optimal output (again, in the absence of all spillover effects) is seen to be equal to OB_1, the amount of this excess benefit being measured as the area of the triangle OBB_1.

We must now consider ways of dealing with the cost of the spillovers, represented in the figure as the area under the EE_1 slope. Let us first illustrate three alternative methods.

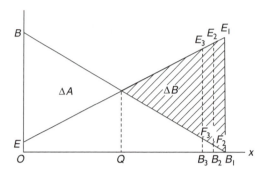

Figure 19.1

4   *Method I*: If the only available method of reducing the spillover is to reduce the output of good x, we should want to reduce that output to OQ as, beyond output OQ, each additional unit of x produced results in an excess benefit that is, increasingly, below the cost of the concomitant spillover.

In other words, we may start with the output OB_1. On this last unit of x produced, the spillover cost is equal to B_1E_1, whereas the consumer gain is zero, leaving a net social loss equal to B_1E_1. Proceeding in this way, moving toward the left, as we cease to produce successive units of x, we reduce ever smaller amounts of net social loss until we reach output OQ. It follows that the measure of net gain to society from reducing output of x from OB_1 to OQ is equal to the striped triangle area indicated by ΔB in Figure 19.1.

It also follows that if, instead, we begin with zero output of x and then start producing x, the net social gain of successive units of x produced can be measured as the excess of the height of the BB_1 curve above the corresponding height of the EE_1 curve, which excess height is zero at output OQ. Thus, by producing, the output OQ of x, we secure the maximum social net gain, one equal to the area of triangle ΔA.

Whichever way we look at it – whether we begin with the commercially deter-mined output OB_1 of x, or whether we begin with zero output of x – the net social gain can be maximized by producing output OQ of x.

5   *Method II*: Using the same sort of figure (Figure 19.2), we again measure the excess benefit curve and the corresponding EE_1 curve that measures the cost of the spillovers created by successive units of x.

But now, rather than reducing the spillovers by reducing the market output of x by B_1Q, we begin by maintaining the market output OB_1 and reduce the spillover effects by the employment of some technical device, say the fitting of some anti-noise device to aircraft, where OB_1 is to measure the number of flights per annum to some given destination.

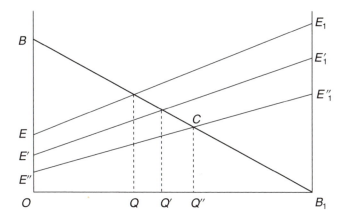

Figure 19.2

Suppose that an initial expenditure of $100,000 per annum in muffling the noise on all the aircraft to that destination reduces the cost of the noise to people living within the relevant area by $180,000, the original curve EE_1 has to be lowered, say to $E'E_1'$. Each of the OB_1 flights, that is, now inflicts less noise on the community, the reduction in cost for any one flight being measured by the vertical distance at that point between the original EE_1 curve and the $E'E_1'$ curve. The area or the strip between the two curves, $EE'E'E_1'$ is, therefore, equal to the benefit of $180,000 (or reduced cost) from the resulting reduction in noise.

A further expenditure of $100,000 on muffling aircraft noise has the effect of reducing the cost of noise by, say an additional $140,000, lowering the cost curve to $E''E_1''$. Clearly, we can continue in this way until the value to people of a further reduction in aircraft noise is no greater than the expenditure required to produce that reduction.

If we assume that the curve $E''E_1''$ is as far as we can go in increasing the net social gain by the method of noise muffling, it will be observed that there are still a number of flights, measured as the number from Q'' to B_1, that will continue to create noise whose cost is above the excess benefit from the flights. Therefore, by eliminating $Q''B_1$ flights per annum, we can secure a further net social gain which can be measured as equal to the area of the triangle $E_1''CB_1$.

It may be concluded that the more effective is this second method of muffling aircraft noise, the greater will be the reduction of the cost-of-noise curve EE_1. Consequently, the fewer will be the number of flights that have to be eliminated in order to reach an optimal reduction in aircraft noise when using both methods I and II.

6   Now it need hardly be remarked that these two methods, among others that are possible, are available to be used at the same time, that is, in combination.

This being the general case, we have devised a method for determining an optimal combination of all methods that are feasible.

The diagram by which the optimal solution, using only method II, can be more neatly exhibited is that shown in Figure 19.3. Along the horizontal axis, we measure, from left to right, successive units of pollution. Along the vertical axis, we measure two things: (i) the social value (or cost) of any unit of pollution and (ii) the opportunity cost of eliminating that unit of pollution.

This (i) value (or cost) of pollution curve, which we may more suggestively refer to as the marginal social damage curve, rises with the amount of pollution generated. Up to OV' units of pollution that are generated by the production of the good, or goods, in question, no perceptible effect on people's welfare is registered, after which it is shown that successive units of pollution entail increasing social loss – each being measured, say, by the maximum sum people affected are willing to pay to eliminate that unit of pollution. Thus the Nth unit of pollution suffered is valued, or costed, at NV.

The total amount of pollution created by the production of the goods in question being equal to ON, the opportunity cost of removing successive units of pollution can be measured from right to left along the rising CC' curve.

Figure 19.3 clearly suggests that the net social gain from reducing pollution is maximized by a reduction of NR pollution units, at which point the (falling) marginal gain from pollution reduction is equal to the (rising) marginal cost of pollution reduction. A tax of TN per unit of pollution would therefore be 'optimal', as without knowledge of, or reference to, the VV' curve, the levying of such a tax will impel the industry to reduce pollution by NR. For up to the first NR units of pollution, it is cheaper to reduce pollution than pay the tax. After NR units, the reverse is true. The optimal amount of pollution remaining is, therefore, equal to

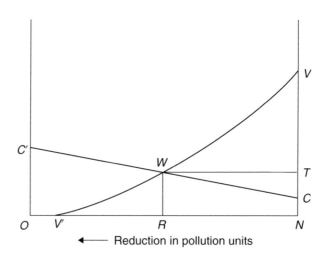

Figure 19.3

OR, and this much pollution has to be borne, inasmuch as the loss sustained, as measured by the area $V'RW$, is well below the opportunity cost of its removal, a cost equal to the area $ORWC'$.

Looking at the matter otherwise, the net social benefit from reducing the initial amount of pollution ON by NR units is the excess of the social gain from reducing NR pollution over the opportunity cost of its removal, this net social gain being equal to the area bounded by CVW.

7   *Method III*: As an alternative method of reducing pollution, we may consider moving a smoky pottery-works away from a populated area. Along the horizontal axis of Figure 19.3, we now measure the distance in miles that the pottery-works can be moved from its initial position N, the CC' curve being the marginal opportunity cost per mile of moving the works[1] and the VV' curve the marginal social gain per mile of moving the works further from its initial location. It may then be concluded that the optimal distance the works should be moved is equal to NR miles.

For direct comparison with method II, it will be convenient to posit a unique transformation of the distance from N in miles into the number of pollution units that are eliminated, for once the number of miles distant from the original location of the works has been transformed into the corresponding number of units of pollution removed that were adopted in method II, we are able to superimpose the resulting CC' and VV' curves of this third method on those resulting from method II.

So much by way of demonstration. We shall now, however, restrict the analysis to a direct comparison of the first three methods of pollution reduction, one that is applicable to any given sort of pollution. Thus, in Figure 19.4, which has the same axes as Figure 19.3 and the same VV' social damage curve, $C_aC'_a$ is the marginal opportunity curve for method I,[2] $C_bC'_b$ is that corresponding to method II, while $C_cC'_c$ is that corresponding to method III.

In general, and as can be seen from Figure 19.4, the optimal level of pollution reduction when any one method is used alone differs from that of the others. In the figure, these three optimal levels of pollution reductions are OR_a, OR_b, OR_c, corresponding to methods I, II and III, respectively. Used alone, their corresponding optimal pollution taxes must also differ. If instead of using only one method singly, all three methods are to be simultaneously employed, economy requires that the amount reduced by each method is such that the marginal cost of each method is the same. This result follows from the idea of reducing the first, second, third, . . ., nth unit of pollution by whichever method is the cheapest for that unit, bearing in

1   The rising CC' curve measures the rising marginal cost of transporting the pottery-works products over an increasing distance to sales outlets in the populated area.
2   The $C_aC'_a$ curve corresponding to method I can be derived from the excess benefit curve $B'B$ in Figure 19.1, as the amount of excess benefit that is forgone increases with successive units of pollution eliminated.

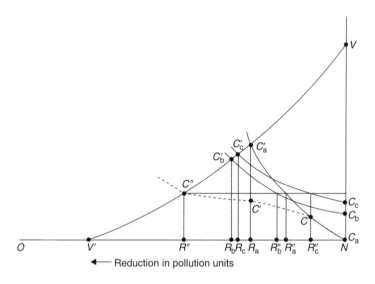

Figure 19.4

mind that, eventually, each of the methods is used increasingly. The succession of lowest incremental costs so derived forms a composite marginal cost curve, and the true optimal pollution-reduction is determined where this curve cuts the VV' curve at R''.

For simplicity of construction, we assume the marginal cost curve of each of our three methods is independent of the costs, if any, incurred by the other two methods (an assumption that is unnecessary but facilitates the geometry). We can then construct the composite marginal cost curve for pollution reduction $C_a CC' C''$ by 'horizontally adding together' the three separate marginal cost curves. From C_a to C on this composite curve, method I alone is used to reduce pollution. From C to C', some reduction is effected by both methods I and II. From C' onward, further reductions receive a contribution from each of the three methods.

The reader will at once observe that the composite optimal pollution $V'R''$ that remains is smaller than the 'optimal' pollution determined by the employment of any one method alone. Consequently, the composite pollution tax $C''R''$ is also smaller than a pollution tax determined by reference to any single method of pollution reduction. Since the magnitude of the composite pollution tax is to be adopted by each of the three methods when they are used together, the pollution reduction contributed by each of the methods when they are used together is smaller than the 'optimal' pollution reduction effected by that method when it is used alone. Thus, of the total pollution reduced jointly, NR'', methods I, II and III are responsible, respectively, for amounts NR''_a, NR''_b and NR''_c. Clearly, each of these amounts is smaller than NR_a, NR_b and NR_c, these being respectively the 'optimal' pollution reductions of methods I, II and III, when each method is used alone.

20 Compensating for environmental damage

1 In demonstrating the determination of an optimal output of a good in the presence of the spillover effects that it generates, economists have seemingly been unaware or, if aware, have failed to make explicit that a conclusion of the uniqueness of the optimal position depends upon the assumption of zero welfare (or income) effects and zero budgetary restrictions.[1] It may, however, also be possible that some economists, although aware of these welfare and budgetary effects, believe that attention to them would serve only to clutter up the analysis without adding anything of much value to the result of the analysis.

There may be cases where the analysis that determines a unique optimal output is valid. But the welfare effects and budgetary restrictions may not be ignored when we are to consider those spillovers that make a substantial difference to people's welfare – substantial enough, at any rate, to make the question of whether the cost–benefit criterion is met depend crucially upon which of the conflicting groups is the one entitled to compensation.

In general, wherever the adverse spillover takes the form of a pollutant that cannot be entirely or economically removed by technological means, the residual amount of the pollutant must be costed by recourse to compensatory payments. Concentrating for the present on this residual amount of pollution that cannot economically be removed by any feasible technology, its pertinent cost can be valued as a compensating variation in either of two alternative ways: as the most that a group B, suffering from the pollutant, is willing to pay for its elimination, or else the smallest sum that this group will accept to bear with it. A comparison of the cost–benefit calculations from using each of these two alternative

---

1 This is certainly the case in the well-known article by Coase (1960), and is illustrated by his initial example of cattle straying into neighbouring agricultural land, the optimal position (whether in terms of the number of cattle admissible or the cost of fencing) being uniquely determined by existing market prices.

ways of evaluating the damage can, not surprisingly, result in contradictory outcomes.[2]

2   Once the reader is familiar with the CV^{12} and CV^{21} measures of benefits and losses, his attention may be drawn to the differences in the application of these alternative measures. In all normal circumstances – those in which welfare effects are positive, as they will almost certainly be for environmental goods or bads – the least sum a person is willing to accept (to forgo a good or to bear with a bad) will, as stated earlier, exceed the largest sum he is willing to pay (to forgo a bad or to enjoy a good). And the difference between the two is magnified when we bring a budgetary constraint into the picture. For, in the absence of any welfare effects, the most a person is able to pay for a good, or for the avoidance of a bad, no matter how important it is for his well-being, is limited by his budget – by his present and expected future income, his assets and by what he can borrow. To illustrate by an extreme example, if he were compelled to undertake a dangerous mission in which his chances of survival were slight, but from which obligation he would be freed if he could offer a large enough sum of money to induce some other person to undertake the mission, the largest sum he could scrape together would be finite and limited. The limit might be, say, \$2.5 million. Conversely, if he were asked to name the smallest sum he would accept for voluntarily accepting to undertake the mission, we would not be surprised if there was no sum large enough to tempt him to do so.

In general, then, the more important to his well-being the item in question, the greater the difference between the most he would pay for it and the smallest sum he would accept to go without it. And it is this phenomenon, the large magnitude of the difference between these two sums that, as we shall see, presents the economist with a problem. For the choice of using the CV^{12} measure or the CV^{21} measure in evaluating the spillovers can determine whether or not the project is able to meet the cost–benefit criterion.

Bearing in mind that the economic activity involved during, say, the operation of the project that unavoidably damages the interests of group B also produces benefits, else it would not be undertaken. And since these benefits, however valued, are reaped by another group, group A, there is clearly a conflict of interest between

---

2 The seeming contradiction that is possible in applying the Kaldor–Hicks criterion first revealed by Scitovsky (1941) arises in a different economic context; that of a general equilibrium analysis in which the distribution of the available goods is related to their market prices. (See Appendix 3, 'The alleged contradiction of the Kaldor–Hicks criterion'.) Also, recent empirical studies seem to find a consistent divergence between the willingness to pay and the willingness to accept measure. While there are good reasons for this disparity of measures, it appears that the consensus has been that, if there is a welfare loss (as in the case of environmental damage), the choice measure is that of willingness to accept (compensation demanded), while if a project results in a welfare gain (as in the case of environmental improvements), the choice measure is that of willingness to pay. For more on this literature, see Knetsch and Sinden (1984) and Hanemann (1991).

the two groups.[3] Therefore, in illustrating the alternative uses of CV^{12} and CV^{21}, we shall compare the value to each of the two groups of that operation of the project producing the damaging spillover effects.

3 The cost–benefit criterion introduced in Part I of this book, that $\Sigma V > 0$, was identified as the Kaldor–Hicks test, sometimes also referred to as a potential Pareto improvement, It may now be more precisely expressed as $\Sigma CV^{12} > 0$. This is properly interpreted as requiring for its fulfilment that everyone in the community could be made better off by a costless distribution of the gains in moving from state 1 to 2.

Yet, it is no less compelling to employ, instead, the alternative criterion, $\Sigma CV^{21} < 0$, which is properly interpreted as requiring for its fulfilment that everyone in the community could be made *worse off* by a costless distribution of the losses that are incurred in moving from state 2 back again to state 1.

Admittedly, a superficial reflection would suggest that, if $\Sigma CV^{12} > 0$, then indeed $\Sigma CV^{21} < 0$ and vice versa. After all, if it is true that everyone can indeed be made better or worse off by a movement from state 1 to state 2, then the return to state 1 must be able, respectively, to make everyone worse or better off. Yet, it is easy to show that having regard now that in *absolute* magnitude, ΣCV^{21} can exceed ΣCV^{12} or vice versa, for each person affected, this superficial reflection referred to is far from certain.

Granted that the choice of the calculation ΣCV^{12} rather than the calculation of the ΣCV^{21} or vice versa can make a crucial difference, the question arises: which of these alternative criteria should the economist adopt? On economic grounds alone, there can be no convincing answer.[4] It follows that if, for any reason, the political decision makers were to require the economist to employ the $\Sigma CV^{12} > 0$ criterion rather than the alternative $\Sigma CV^{21} < 0$ criterion, or the reverse of this, the economist would have no grounds for demurring. He may accept the decision as a valid political constraint.

It is, perhaps, unnecessary to remark that one cannot altogether rule out the possibility that, for every person affected, CV^{12} is (ignoring the sign) exactly equal to the magnitude of CV^{21}, in which case the ΣCV^{12} calculation is exactly equal (save for the sign) to the ΣCV^{21} calculation and, if the one criterion is met, so will be the other. But once the magnitude of ΣCV^{12} and ΣCV^{21} differs for each person, as they generally would, the magnitude of the ΣCV^{12} calculation will differ from that of the ΣCV^{21} and, which is more important, it becomes possible for the $\Sigma CV^{12} > 0$ criterion to fail, while the $\Sigma CV^{21} < 0$ criterion to succeed. It also becomes possible for both $\Sigma CV^{21} < 0$ and $\Sigma CV^{12} < 0$.

---

3 It is not impossible that some people will be in both groups; as a gainer from the good being produced by the project and also a loser from the spillover it generates. This possibility, however, in no way makes any difference to the analysis.

4 Any proposal that we use the ΣCV^{21} calculation for some items and the ΣCV^{12} calculation for others has to be vetoed, as no clear interpretation could be made of the resulting combined calculation.

4   Bearing in mind the conflict between group A and group B for operations of the project that generate environmental spillovers, if we suppose that the movement from a state 1 to a state 2, one that also damages the environment, is one that involves group B in a loss, then the movement from state 2 to state 1 that, instead, *improves* the environment is one that confers a benefit on group B – the opposite being true for group A. Since for each of these four possibilities we can use either the ΣCV^{12} calculation or the ΣCV^{21} calculation, we shall use each case to illustrate a distinct proposition. The four propositions are as follows:

(i) If $\Sigma CV^{12} > 0$, and therefore the project is accepted on that criterion, it necessarily follows that $\Sigma CV^{21} < 0$, which confirms the acceptability of the project.

(ii) If $\Sigma CV^{21} > 0$, and therefore on that criterion, the project is rejected, it necessarily follows that $\Sigma CV^{12} < 0$, which confirms the rejection of the project.

(iii) If $\Sigma CV^{12} < 0$, and therefore the project is rejected on that criterion, it is possible that $\Sigma CV^{21} > 0$, so confirming the rejection of the project. But it is also possible that $\Sigma CV^{21} < 0$, so that, on this latter criterion, the project is *accepted*, contrary to the ΣCV^{12} criterion.

(iv) If $\Sigma CV^{21} < 0$, and therefore on that criterion the project is accepted, again it is possible that $\Sigma CV^{12} > 0$, so confirming the acceptance of the project. But it is also possible that $\Sigma CV^{12} < 0$ which, on that criterion, *rejects* the project, contrary to the acceptance by the ΣCV^{21} criterion.

5   We now use four simple examples that will illustrate the validity of each of these four propositions in the order stated above.

(i) The first example is that of the introduction of a project – the movement from state 1 to state 2 – that eliminates the effluent that hitherto existed in that area, this being a gain to group B while incidentally causing a loss to group A. Using the ΣCV^{12} measure, we shall suppose that the most that group B would pay to move to state 2, one that eliminates the effluent, is (in million dollars) equal to 100, while the smallest amount acceptable to group A which has to suffer a loss in moving to state 2 is equal to 80. The ΣCV^{12} of both groups taken together is then equal to $+100$, -80 or $+20$ (bearing in mind our convention of a plus sign for a payment and a minus sign for a receipt). Since $\Sigma CV^{12} > 0$, the ΣCV^{12} criterion sanctions the project.

If, instead we employ the ΣCV^{21} criterion, which addresses itself to the relevant sums for a return from state 2 to the original state 1, group B will lose in now having to put up with the effluent, while group A will gain. Since the least sum that group B will accept to move back to state 1 must exceed the most it would pay to move to state 2, we may suppose its ΣCV^{21} to be equal to 110. As for group A, which loses in the movement to state 2, it gains if the movement is back to the original state 1. But the most it will pay for the return to state 1 must be less than the least sum it required in moving to state 2. It will therefore be less than 80; say it is equal to 70. The ΣCV^{21} of both groups taken together is then equal to -110, $+70$ or -40. Thus the $\Sigma CV^{21} < 0$ criterion is met and, *a fortiori* the project is accepted. (This example, illustrating proposition (i) is summarized in Table 20.1.)

(ii) In order to illustrate the second proposition in which $\Sigma CV^{21} > 0$ rejects the project, we shall suppose that the movement from state 1 to state 2 is one that creates effluent so that, if the project is adopted, group B will lose and group A will gain.

In order for ΣCV^{21} to be positive, the most that group B is willing to pay for a return to the original (no effluent) state 1, must exceed in magnitude the smallest sum acceptable to group A for this return to state 1. We may therefore suppose these sums to be $+100$ for group B and -80 for group A, taken together equal to $+20$.

The alternative ΣCV^{12} measure for group B, being the smallest sum acceptable for moving to the effluent state 2, must, however, exceed the most it would pay, 100, to avoid the effluent, say it is 110. As for group A, since it would accept no less than 80 to agree to move back to the non-effluent state 1, it would pay less than this to move to the effluent state 2, say 70.

If follows that the total ΣCV^{12} of the two groups comes to -110, $+70$ or -40. Consequently, it transpires that *a fortiori* $\Sigma CV^{12} < 0$, which confirms the initial rejection of the project by $\Sigma CV^{21} > 0$.

This example, which illustrates our second proposition, is summarized in Table 20.2.

6   The two remaining propositions (iii) and (iv) are illustrated in Tables 20.3 and 20.4, respectively, without further explanation, provided the reader bears in mind that the minimum sum acceptable to either group to forgo a good (or to bear with a bad) is always larger than the maximum sum it is willing to pay for the good or

Table 20.1

	A	B	(A+B)	
ΣCV^{12}	−80	100	20	(project accepted)
ΣCV^{21}	70	−110	−40	(project accepted)

Table 20.2

	A	B	(A+B)	
ΣCV^{21}	−80	100	20	(project rejected)
ΣCV^{12}	70	−110	−40	(project rejected)

Table 20.3

		A	B	(A+B)	
(a)	ΣCV^{12}	100	−120	−20	(project rejected)
(b)	ΣCV^{21}	−110	115	5	(project rejected)
(c)	ΣCV^{21}	−130	120	−10	(project accepted)

Table 20.4

		A	B	(A+B)	
(a)	ΣCV^{21}	−120	100	−20	(project accepted)
(b)	ΣCV^{12}	110	−105	5	(project accepted)
(c)	ΣCV^{12}	100	−120	−20	(project rejected)

the removal of the bad. These are the two ambiguous cases, and the ambiguity is revealed in each case by the fact that, in each of these tables, use of the identical criterion in rows (b) and (c) can be shown to confirm and to contradict, respectively, the result of the criterion in row (a).

It may be noted in passing that, when the project in question is one that creates, or increases pollution, the employment of the $\Sigma CV^{12} > 0$ criterion tends to act against adopting the project, as group B has recourse to the larger sum, the minimum acceptable, rather than to the smaller sum, the most it could pay to avoid the pollution. *Per contra*, when the project is one that improves the environment, the $\Sigma CV^{12} > 0$ will tell against group B, because it is the smaller sum, the most it can afford to pay for the improvement, that is to count. In that case, the employment instead of the $\Sigma CV^{21} < 0$ criterion will act to favour group B, because the sum involved becomes the larger one – the least it would accept for returning to the original state 1 (which existed prior to the removal of the pollution).

7   To be sure, those spillovers, positive or negative, that cannot be uniquely priced by reference to the market, and for which, therefore, we have to resort to evaluating by either ΣCV^{12} or ΣCV^{21}, may be a relatively small component of the total effects produced by the project. In such cases, the rejection or acceptance of the project as a whole by either criterion will be unaffected by the evaluation of the spillovers in question. But as the spillover component of the project assumes greater proportions, the choice of the $\Sigma CV^{12} > 0$ or the $\Sigma CV^{21} < 0$ can be the decisive factor in the acceptance or rejection of the project.

Consider, for example a proposal to clear 100,000 acres of forest land in order to use the land for agricultural purposes. The benefits over the future would be reckoned as the discounted sum of the annual excess of the value of crops to the consumers *less* the opportunity costs of producing them for each of the next *m* years. If, however, the farmers were to bid for the land or to be compensated for being denied its use, they would reckon the benefits in terms of expected profits. Conversely, the loss to the community if such a project were implemented would take into account the irrevocable loss for present and future generations arising from the destruction of a variety of species of flora and fauna and the recreational facilities the forest provides.

On the $\Sigma CV^{21} < 0$ criterion that would be used under a ruling or order that requires those who oppose the scheme to recompense those prepared to cultivate the land, producing goods of real value that would augment GNP, it is highly likely that the criterion would be met, and the scheme approved. Yet, as we know from proposition (iv), this result could be contradicted if, instead, we employed the $\Sigma CV^{12} > 0$ criterion, this possible contradiction being that illustrated in row (c) of Table 20.4. For using the $\Sigma CV^{12} > 0$ criterion in this instance, the minimal sum demanded by the community to suffer the loss of this vast forest land is almost sure to be far in excess of any sum the farmers could offer. The scheme, then, could not be vindicated by a CBA.

The same argument would, of course, apply to the activities of logging companies devoted to cutting down many thousands of acres of tropical woodlands each year. For all practical purposes, the loss to society is irrevocable because, given that such trees generally require hundreds of years to reach their full stature, the re-planting of such trees is hardly an attractive economic proposition. Such activities, it may be concluded with confidence, would never be able to meet the ΣCV^{12} criterion.

Finally, in order to illustrate proposition (iii), in particular the possibility exemplified by row (c) in Table 20.3, we may suppose that, two decades ago, a small workshop for producing bicycle tyres was established within a residential area currently inhabited by 5,000 families. The enterprise so prospered that the original small shed gave way to a large factory producing car tyres and housed in an overtowering building, one that was not only an eyesore to the residents, but was also spewing clouds of black smoke from its twin chimneys and creating a foul smell that spread over most of the area.

The residents – desperate to move from the existing pollution state 1 to a non-pollution state 2 – offered as much as $200 million to the factory owner to site his works elsewhere. The latter made it clear, however, that he would require at least $250 million to cover the full costs of such re-siting of his works. The $\Sigma CV^{12} > 0$ criterion cannot therefore be met, as the ΣCV^{12} aggregate amounted to –$50 million.

If, now, on appeal to the courts, the property rights in the ambient air, in and above the residential area, were granted to the residents who, coming together, agreed they would no longer tolerate this blight on their lives unless they received in compensation no less than $500 million – just enough to enable families to move elsewhere – the factory owner would have no choice but to site his works in some other area.

Thus, once the property rights to the ambient air are ceded to the residents, the relevant calculation becomes that of ΣCV^{21} – the sums involved in moving from the proposed non-pollution state 2 back to the original pollution state 1 – which is decidedly negative, being in fact equal to $-\$250$ million. The criterion, $\Sigma CV^{21} < 0$ is met and, therefore, the movement back to the non-pollution state 2 is sanctioned.[5]

The above two examples, both of them highly plausible, should convince the reader of the crucial importance on occasions of the choice between adopting the $\Sigma CV^{12} > 0$ criterion or the $\Sigma CV^{21} < 0$ criterion.

5 Even if, on the one hand, the resident is willing to pay all the costs of movement to another area in order to obtain some relief (that is, some marginal increase in the welfare level pertaining to the existing state 1), the fact that his house is located in the heavily polluted area will have reduced this value of his (possibly) most important asset to virtually nothing, must drastically reduce the most he is able to pay either to persuade the factory to move or to move himself to another area. On the other hand, if he is allowed full compensation for having to remain in the polluted area, the level of welfare which he will have to sacrifice will be that which he would enjoy in the non-polluted state 2 – clearly far above his welfare level in state 1, and reflected therefore in the large minimum compensation acceptable.

Part V
Investment criteria

21 Introduction to investment criteria

1   Investment criteria are the *bêtes noires* of the economist. Although we shall begin by examining the more familiar proposals in the following chapters in order to reveal the particular difficulties inherent in proposals to reduce a flow of values over some time span to a single figure, we may as well mention such difficulties briefly at the start.

First, the data are much harder to gather, or rather to predict, over future years than are currently available data. The unavoidable uncertainty of future benefits, disbenefits, and outlays, may be dealt with in various ways. Yet, they are all somewhat arbitrary inasmuch as none can be anchored in the subjective preferences of those affected by the project being evaluated. Therefore, the treatment used to cope with uncertainty cannot be assumed, strictly speaking, to accord with a potential Pareto criterion.

Second, even if it were the case that all the magnitudes for future benefits, disbenefits, and outlays, were absolutely certain, no investment criterion, no matter how sophisticated, can be sure of meeting a potential Pareto criterion.

What is invariably being suppressed in the popular treatment of such investment criteria as discounted present value, or internal rate of return, is the basic economic rationale involved: what economic meaning can be attached to the magnitude arising from the application of any of these investment criteria?

2   Let us first be quite clear about the nature of these benefits and costs. An investment in, say, a railroad requires an initial outlay of capital to be spread over the first one or two years. These expenditures are clearly costs. So also are the anticipated outlays at future periods of time, whether for repairs, maintenance or for adding equipment, though their magnitudes are usually smaller than the initial outlays. Benefits are understood in the most comprehensive sense to include all additions to social welfare that can, in Pigou's words, 'be brought into relation with the measuring rod of money'.

Benefits should therefore include not only expected *receipts* over time, as the services produced may not, in fact, be sold to the public but provided free, or sold at a price below their cost (underground rail travel could, for instance, be made free). Even if the good produced is sold at a price that covers its cost, the revenue collected is almost always less than the full amounts people would be willing to pay rather than go without. For, as indicated earlier, an estimate of the full benefit to the buyers of the good is roughly equal to the area under the market demand curve.

Again, there are positive and negative spillover effects to be evaluated and added, algebraically, to the benefits of the direct recipients of the goods that are purposely produced by the project. For example, the very existence of the railroad is a form of insurance even to those who use other means of transport, a form of insurance for which they would presumably be willing to pay something. Such sums, the estimated value of indirect benefits, are to be added to the direct benefits. On the other hand, any compensatory sums called for by those people whose assets or whose welfare decline as a result of the noise or pollution, or any other disamenity associated with the railroad service, are to be subtracted from the benefits.

We remind ourselves in passing that if we correct the benefit calculation for all spillover effects in order to come up with a net figure *for social benefits*, we *cannot* also invoke the concept of *social costs* – else we should be entering the same spillover effects *twice*, i.e. on the cost side as well as on the benefit side. By convention, therefore, outlays will be calculated as the actual money disbursements – the sums spent on the project at any time during its life, all the incidental spillover effects on society that arise either in the building or in the operation of the project being added to, or subtracted from, the direct benefits at the time they appear.

3   A distinction is sometimes made between 'capital costs' and 'operating costs', the former being the sums needed to build the project, the plant machinery and the like, the latter being the sums to be disbursed at regular intervals in order to maintain the flow of products or services. Such sums or 'operating costs' can be met from what is sometimes called a revolving fund, which can take the form of a line of credit from a bank which may be drawn upon as needed in order to meet the wage bill, maintenance, repairs, and payments for materials. Indebtedness to the bank or other financial institution, however, may be eliminated altogether or else limited as a result of a stream of cash receipts from the sale of the goods being produced by the project.

In calculating the magnitude of these operating costs, only as a first approximation may they be set to the actual disbursements to be made for repairs, maintenance, and materials. Ideally, however, we should have to calculate the opportunity costs of the resources used for these things by the project – that is, the social benefits that would have occurred if, instead, these resources were left in their current uses. In particular, it is not the wage bill that is to be included in the operating costs but the opportunity costs of the labour employed by the project (as defined and measured in Chapter 11).

Again, if regular borrowings from banks are anticipated, a first approximation to the value of these outlays over the future would be set equal to the interest payments that have to be made in subsequent years. More accurately, however, we should calculate the annual opportunity costs (or net social benefits forgone) whenever the banks lend the required sums to the project managers.

Finally in this connection, it is important to bear in mind that, inasmuch as we are concerned with net *social* benefits, all taxes paid from the revenues of the project are *not* to be subtracted from the value of such benefits. The taxes that are paid from the revenues declared by the project are transferred to the government and have to be valued according to how the government disposes of them.

4   The social benefits, on their own, in each period is to be calculated as the sum of (i) the value of the project's marketable goods (equal to the cash receipts from the sale of those goods *plus* their consumer surplus), (ii) the value of all unpriced benefits conferred on some segment of society, and (iii) the algebraic sum of all externalities, positive and negative, created in each period by the project.

By subtracting the opportunity costs of the factors employed in each period from the value of these social benefits in each period, we derive a stream of *net* social benefits over the relevant time span – some positive, some negative and possibly also some that are zero. And it is to this stream of net social benefits that we can apply our adopted investment criterion.

It is advisable, first, to set out these social benefit figures and their corresponding opportunity costs, period by period – more commonly year by year. For a four-year time span, we might set out our data as in the following example:

Social benefits	0	0	150	260
Opportunity Costs	100	130	135	0

The successive annual *net* social benefits are therefore -100, -130, 15 and 260.

In general, we can summarize the stream of expected gross benefits less their costs as $(b_0 - k_0)$, $(b_1 - k_1)$, $(b_2 - k_2)$, ..., $(b_n - k_n)$, where b_0 and k_0 are the social benefits and opportunity costs, respectively, of the initial period, b_1 and k_1 are the social benefits and opportunity costs of the first period, and so on, the subscript always referring to the period or year. If we now define the *net*, or excess, social benefit in any t^{th} period or year, B_t as equal to $(b_t - k_t)$ we can write the above as a stream of net social benefits: B_0, B_1, B_2, ..., B_n, where the Bs can be negative, zero or positive. This is the stream to which an investment criterion is usually applied.

5   It may sometimes be proposed that the economist himself make available the results of his cost–benefit calculation in the form of an actual stream of net social benefits, B_0, B_1, ..., B_t, thus allowing the decision makers themselves to cast their eyes over the time-profiles of the various projects being mooted, in preference to, or in addition to, their being ranked by the economist on some investment criterion or other.

Yet, in the absence of guidance from the economist, political decision makers cannot be depended upon either to rank alternative projects in a consistent man-ner on any acceptable principle, simply by contemplating their time-profile, or to judge whether any single one is economically acceptable. There is, indeed, no more warrant for decision makers' drawing conclusions about the acceptability or ranking of alternative projects from their study of the relevant time-profiles than there is for their imposing their political judgements on the valuation of the economic data used in a cost–benefit calculation. If it is economic expertise they are requesting, they are implicitly accepting strictly economic methods of calculation.

And in a CBA based on the Pareto criterion, the economist necessarily has to compare alternative investment streams by reducing each to a single figure at a common point of time – the discounted present value (DPV) criterion being currently favoured. Certainly, if we have to use some one rule for the appraisal or ranking of investment streams, this favoured criterion is generally superior to the somewhat crude criteria commonly employed by business concerns.

There is, nonetheless, some pedagogic value in briefly describing the latter, as we do in the following chapter, if only to highlight their weaknesses and so pave the way for an understanding of the standard DPV methods and, later, for more sophisticated investment criteria.

In sum, the search for an investment criterion involves us in a search to discover an answer to the question: what single figure best summarizes the net social benefits of each of the investment streams under consideration? If we are able to find a satisfactory answer to that question, we shall have no difficulty in finding a solution to another common question: given funds that will enable us to finance one, two or more projects, which of these projects, if any, should we choose?

22 Crude investment criteria

1 Suppose we are faced with a choice of four investment options with the net benefits shown in Table 22.1. Which, if any, do we choose if our budget is limited to 100?

If we had to choose *only* one from the four, we could be sure that it would never be A_4, irrespective of the criterion used. For A_3 is as good as, or better than, A_4 period for period. In the jargon, investment option A_3 'dominates' A_4. Thus, if we subtract A_4's net benefit stream from that of A_3, the difference is a series, 0, 20, 0, 0, 10, these figures showing the amounts by which A_3's net benefits exceed those of A_4 in successive periods. In no period is A_3's net benefit less than that of A_4.[1]

Let us now consider three rather crude investment criteria, which, however, are commonly employed in the business sector, especially where the venture contemplated is risky.

2 The *cut-off period* is perhaps the crudest possible criterion that is used in business in order to decide whether or not to invest in a project. A suitable period is chosen over which the money invested must be fully recouped. The period could be ten years, though usually a shorter period such as five years or even less is chosen. Such a criterion may be justified in cases of innovation in products or methods that cannot be protected by a patent, and which innovations are likely to be copied by competing firms within two or three years. A cut-off period of

Table 22.1

	0	1	2	3	4
A_1	−100	115	0	0	0
A_2	−100	20	30	50	170
A_3	−100	100	110	−50	0
A_4	−100	80	110	−50	−10

1 If, however, we had funds enabling us to choose two or more of these investment options, we might choose both A_3 and A_4. But we should never include A_4 while rejecting A_3.

three years, for instance, may be chosen in the belief that, after three years, further profits are uncertain and increasingly unlikely. Glancing down the table, it is clear that a cut-off period of three years *after* the initial outlay would admit the A_1 investment option. Indeed, more than the initial 100 is recouped in the first year after the outlay. The A_2 option only just scrapes home. A_3 would be able to recoup as much as 160 in the three years, while A_4 would recoup 140.

The shortcomings of this criterion are easy to perceive. If the returns were not expected to accrue mainly in the first few years but mainly after the first few years, worthwhile projects would be rejected. A stream –100, 0, 0, 20, 40, 60, 80, 120, ... would be rejected. So also would a stream –100, 20, 20, 20, 20, 20, 20, ...

3   *Pay-off period (or capital recovery method)*: instead of choosing an arbitrary cut-off period, we may rank the investment options according to the number of years necessary to recoup the initial outlay. Clearly, project A_1 would be ranked first, as its pay-off period is less than a year. For project A_2 it is exactly three years. If we ignore subsequent *outlays* in the last two projects, it is one year for A_3 and more than one year for A_4.

The *pay-off period rate of return* is but another way of expressing the above results. It is obtained simply by dividing 100 by the number of years in the pay-off period. Since the A_1 investment option pays off the initial outlay in less than a year; we divide 100 by something less than a year, which yields a pay-off period rate of return of more than 100 per cent. For project A_2, the pay-off period rate of return is equal to 100 divided by three, or 33.33 per cent. For the A_3 project, it is exactly 100 per cent, and for project A_4, it is somewhat less than 100 per cent.

The justification for either form of this ranking device is similar to that for the cut-off period. When imitation by competitors or rapid obsolescence is anticipated, or in circumstances of political uncertainty, one of the overriding considerations is safety. One looks for quick returns and prepares for a hasty exit. A project such as A_1, which pays 115 within a year of 100 being invested, is likely, in such circumstances, to be looked on with greater favour than option A_2, which would not show any profit until the fourth year. The method is easy to understand and gives a decision quickly without much further analysis.

In the complete absence of uncertainty, however, it would be impossible to justify either of the above rules-of-thumb. If interest rates happened to be low, A_2 would be far more profitable than A_1 and more profitable than A_3 for that matter. And like the cut-off period, the method takes no account of the time value of money, and favours short-term investment over long-term ones.

4   *The average rate of return* is the simplest way of taking account of all the figures in the investment stream. Just because all the figures are taken at face value in calculating the average rate of return, there is an implied assumption that all the figures have been corrected for uncertainty.

For all investment options with only an initial outlay of 100, such as A_1 and A_2 in Table 22.1, there is no ambiguity in the method. One simply adds together all the subsequent positive net benefits, divides this sum by the number of years and expresses the resulting figure as a percentage of the initial investment outlay. For option A_1, the sum of positive benefits is 115. This sum divided by the number of years, in this case only one year, gives an average net benefit of 115 per annum. Expressed as a percentage of the outlay of 100, it is 115 per cent. For A_2, the sum of positive net benefits over four years is 270 and, dividing by four, gives an annual average return of 67.5. Expressed again as a percentage of the outlay of 100, it is 67.5 per cent.

For investment options A_3 and A_4, which happen to have outlays also in later years, we add together all the figures, both positive and negative, after the initial outlay of 100 and proceed as before. For A_3, the algebraic sum of net benefits over three years (years 1, 2 and 3) comes to 160. This sum divided by three yields an average of 53.33 per cent per annum. Similarly for option A_4 which yields an average return of 32.5 per cent per annum.

The weakness of this method is apparent at once, for it is by no means evident to anyone thinking of investing 100 that A_1 with an average of return of 115 per cent is superior to A_2. It might be added in passing, however, that the weakness is not particular to this method, but arises also in the more familiar internal-rate-of return method, which will be treated later.

5 *The average rate of return including the initial outlay* is an obvious modification of the preceding criterion. The average rate of return is calculated in the same way *except* that the initial outlay of 100 has to be included as a negative net benefit before dividing by the number of years.

Thus, in option A_1, we subtract the outlay of 100 from 115 to give 15, this being a 15 per cent net benefit on the outlay of 100. In A_2, subtracting the 100 outlay from the 270 of net benefits leaves us with 170 net benefits, and dividing by four yields a net average return of 42.5 per cent per annum on the outlay of 100. Similar calculations yield a net average return of 20 per cent per annum for three years on the 100 outlay for the A_3 option, and an average of 7.5 per cent per annum for the four years for option A_4.

Under conditions of certainty, at least, this criterion, although clearly superior to the others, is unsatisfactory for two reasons. First, the results depend critically upon the number of years counted on this criterion. But determining the length of the investment stream by reference to the number of years for which there is a net benefit, positive or negative, is arbitrary. If, for example, option A_1 were altered so as to yield a slight positive net benefit, say 0.1, in year 2, the annual net benefit, spread over two years, would be little more than 7.5 per cent on the outlay of 100, which makes this slightly altered A_1 option far less attractive.

Second, a less apparent but no less serious defect is that this criterion takes no cognizance of the *profile* of the net benefits over time. Given the algebraic aggregate of all the net benefits following the initial outlay of 100, it makes no difference to the calculation whether the net benefits are bunched together over the first years, spread evenly over the time span, or are bunched together toward the end of the time span. Thus, an investment stream of −100, 5, 20, 25, 250 is valued as highly on this criterion as one of −100, 250, 25, 20, 5; or, for that matter, an investment stream of –100, 1, 1, 1, 297 is valued as highly as an investment stream of –100, 297, 1, 1, 1.

Yet, who would not prefer the latter stream to the former! People do indeed take account of the timing of benefits: they are not indifferent as between receiving 100 now and 100 in ten years' time. Once we take account of the time dimension of the net-benefit stream, we are impelled to move away from these rather primitive investment criteria and move on to those that are more familiar to economists – those in which 100 in any year is valued more than 100 in any subsequent year.

6   Although all investment criteria resort to the common procedure of reducing a stream of net benefits to a single figure at one point in time, usually the present time,[2] the economist invariably uses some rate of interest (or some combination of rates) as a means of weighting the net benefits in successive years.

The more familiar criteria fall into two categories: (i) those that draw on a given rate (or rates) of interest in reducing the investment stream to a present discounted value, and (ii) those that, in contrast, are used to discover just what is the average rate of return on the initial outlay. This latter criterion, known as the internal rate of return, may be defined as that rate of discount which reduces the entire investment stream (including the initial outlay) to zero.

These two popular criteria, the present discounted value and the internal rate of return, will be compared in the following two chapters.

---

2 However, as we shall propose later, the future compounded value, taken at a terminal year, offers certain advantages.

23 The discounted present value criterion

1 If we have an investment -100, 50, 150, and we are given a rate of interest or discount rate of 10 per cent per annum, the DPV of the net benefits alone that are generated by the initial outlay of $100-50$ at the end of the first year, and 150 after the second year is given by the calculation

$$\frac{50}{(1+0.1)} + \frac{150}{(1+0.1)^2} = 169.4$$

In this connection, an initial outlay of 100 has a present value also of 100, being incurred at the end of the zeroth year.

The DPV of the *entire* stream, -100, 50, 150, is equal to the DPV of the net benefits (positive or negative): here, 169.4, *minus* the DPV of the outlays, here 100, and is therefore equal to $169.4-100$, or 69.4.

In more general terms, given a stream of benefits generated by only a single initial outlay K_0, but which for the time being may be designated as B_0, so enabling us to represent the entire stream as $B_0, B_1, B_2, \ldots, B_n$, where the Bs are positive, negative or zero, its net DPV is given by

$$B_0 + \frac{B_1}{(1+r)} + \frac{B_2}{(1+r)^2} + \cdots \frac{B_n}{(1+r)^n}$$

or more briefly by

$$\sum_{t=0}^{t=n} \frac{B_t}{(1+r)^t}$$

where r is the rate of discount.

The necessary instrument in this criterion is the appropriate rate of interest or rate of discount by which the net benefit at any point of time is weighted. It is commonly assumed that the correct rate of interest is that which reflects society's rate of time preference. (If, for example, society is taken to be indifferent between having $100 million today and $106 million next year, the *social* rate of time preference is 6 per cent per annum.) We shall, for the present, go along with this assumption, though later on it will be argued that it is correct only under special conditions. In a Crusoe economy, if 120 bushels of corn next year are deemed by Crusoe to be equivalent in satisfaction to 100 bushels of corn today – by which is meant that he is perfectly indifferent, to having either 100 bushels of corn today or 120 bushels of corn in a year's time – Crusoe's rate of discount is 20 per cent per annum. Until Man Friday arrives and has some say in the decision, Crusoe's individual rate of discount can also be thought of as the social rate of discount.

2   To be more accurate, however, Crusoe's reaction to the choice presented to him gives us no more than the social rate of discount for the one year and, for that matter, is strictly valid only for 100 bushels of corn this year, not for more or for less. If, indeed, the same rate of discount did hold for successive years, then Crusoe would be indifferent as between 100 today, 120 next year, 144 in the year following that, and so on. It is, however, quite possible that his discount rate rises with the passage of time. Instead of being indifferent as between 100 today and 144 in two years' time, he might specify 150 in two years' time. This would mean that for the first year his rate of discount is 20 per cent, but for the second year he uses a discount rate of roughly 25 per cent per annum.

Again, even if we confine ourselves to the one year, it is not true that the same rate of discount holds for *any* amount of corn. If Crusoe agrees, though only just, to postpone consumption of 100 bushels of corn this year in order to have an additional 120 bushels next year, it does not follow that he will be prepared to forgo another 100 bushels of corn this year in exchange for another additional 120 bushels next year. It is more plausible to suppose that he should want more than an additional 120 bushels next year to persuade him to forgo this year the consumption of yet another 100 bushels; say an additional 140 bushels next year. We could say that Crusoe's marginal willingness to sacrifice 100 today for 120 next year reflects a discount rate of 20 per cent per annum, while his marginal willingness to sacrifice 200 today for 260 tomorrow reflects a discount rate of 30 per cent overall. Put otherwise, we could say that for the first 100 bushels the marginal discount rate was 20 per cent, and that the marginal discount rate for another 100 bushels was 40 per cent.

These possibilities are to be noted before passing on. For it is also the case in society at large that, however the social rate of discount is determined, it is invariant neither with respect to the magnitudes of the inter-temporal exchange of goods nor to the length of time involved. If we have information about the variation in the rate of discount with respect to either magnitude or time, however, there is no difficulty, in principle, in adapting our chosen investment criterion accordingly. In the meantime, our task will be simplified by assuming but a single social rate of discount. Moreover, since we are to examine this concept in Chapter 25, we shall also assume that this social rate of discount is known to us. If the reader prefers, he can suppose, provisionally, that it has arisen from the interplay of market forces plus, perhaps, some form of government intervention that has the object of ensuring that the resulting rate of interest in the economy correctly reveals society's preference as between present and future goods. If, for instance, the social rate of discount is 10 per cent per annum, we shall take it that society as a whole is indifferent as between 100 today, 110 in a year's time, 121 in two years' time, and so on. And that, therefore, the *present* value of 110 to be received in one year's time, or 121 in two years' time, is exactly 100.

3   Having made these provisional simplifications, let us go on to consider the following propositions, all of them commonplace in the literature on the subject.

The net present value[1] (or excess of present value over cost) of a particular investment stream depends upon the rate of discount used. If, for instance, the stream of net benefits is −100, 0, 150, the net present value of the stream would be a little less than 48 if the discount rate were 1 per cent, but would be −33$\frac{1}{3}$ if the discount rate were 50 per cent.

It follows that, which one of a number of alternative investment streams yields the largest net DPV must depend, in general, on the rate of discount that is employed. Only if there is one investment stream that is "dominant" over all the others being contemplated, will it have a higher DPV irrespective of the discount rate. Thus, if there are but two investment streams, *A* having the stream −50, 20, 80, and *B* the stream −50, 20, 70, then stream *A*, being dominant, will have a higher present value irrespective of the discount rate. But if, instead, there is an *A* stream of −100, 0, 180, and a *B* stream of −100, 165, 0, a discount rate of 0.01, or 1 per cent, ranks *A*, with a net present value of about 76, above *B*, which has a net present value of about 63. If, however, the appropriate rate of discount is 0.5, or 50 per cent, the net present value of the *A* stream is −20 and is therefore ranked *below* the *B* stream, which has a net present value of 10. From these two examples, it should be manifest that there is a particular social rate of discount between 1 per cent and 50 per cent for which the two streams have exactly the same present value. Let us call this social rate of discount *r**. Then *r** is easily determined by equating the net present value formulae for the two streams, i.e. we set

$$-100 + \frac{180}{(1 + r^*)^2} = -100 + \frac{165}{(1 + r^*)}$$

and solve for *r**, which turns out to be about 9 per cent.

In general, we can determine a net present value of a particular investment stream, say *A*, for each conceivable rate of discount. The resulting relationship can be plotted in Figure 23.1, where the vertical axis measures PV_r, or net present value of the investment stream in question, and the horizontal axis measures *r*, the social rate of discount. The net present value of the *A* stream becomes smaller, the larger the rate of discount *r*; hence the negative slope of the *A* curve. It will be noted that the negative slope crosses the horizontal axis and continues below it into the south-east quadrant. This indicates that, at discount rates above some critical rate of discount, the net present value of the stream becomes negative (for example,

1   The term 'net present value' will be used occasionally as an abbreviation of 'net present discounted value' or 'net discounted present value'.

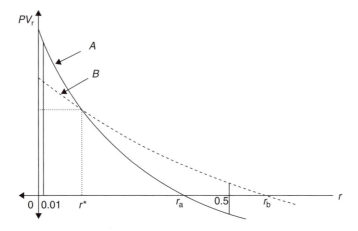

Figure 23.1

at a 50 per cent discount rate, the stream −100, 0, 180, has a net present value of −20). A similar relationship can be plotted for the *B* investment stream.

If one of these two investment streams were dominant, it would lie above the other at all rates of discount. In the absence of dominance, the *A* and *B* curves will intersect, either in the positive quadrant, as in the figure, or else in the negative quadrant (not shown).

For all conceivable (positive) discount rates – save one, r^* – the present values of the two streams differ. At discount rates below r^*, the *A* stream has a higher net present value than the *B* stream, the reverse being true for discount rates above r^*. Only at r^* do both streams have the same net present value. It is obvious that if the rate of discount, from being a little above r^*, fell to a figure below r^*, the net present value of the *A* stream would change from being less than that of the *B* stream to being greater than it.

It may be observed finally, that there is a discount rate corresponding to each investment stream, r_a and r_b respectively, for which the net present values of the *A* and *B* streams are both zero. By definition, therefore, r_a and r_b are, respectively, the internal rates of return of the *A* and *B* investment streams.

4   If now, the annual net benefits that are generated by an initial outlay (eventually) become smaller over time and, also, instead of dividing the relevant time span into years or other unit periods, it is treated as a *continuum*, the resulting net benefit profile over time can be envisaged as a growth path, it being understood that no benefit is reaped at any date earlier than some given point of time, at which point the cumulative benefit may be discounted. Thus, rather than plot a profile of marginal net benefits over time, we can plot a profile over time of the *total* benefit, in effect a growth path as represented in Figure 23.2, where time is measured along the horizontal axis and the *total* net benefit, or total value, reached at any point of

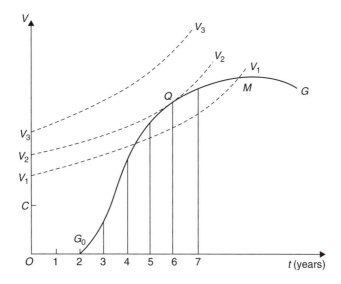

Figure 23.2

time, is measured vertically. The vertical axis *OV*, which cuts the horizontal axis at time zero, can be used to measure the DPV reached at any point of time, given the rate of discount.

Common examples of such growth curves are those of trees or wine. Once a tree is planted, its value increases after a point in time, roughly in proportion to the increase in the volume of its timber (assuming a constant price of timber).

As for a barrel of wine, its value increases over time (up to a point) in consequence of the improvement in its flavour. Let us consider the timber example.

A continuous growth path is represented *by* G_0G in Figure 23.2. At time zero, total costs *OC* (measured above *O* along the vertical axis *OV*) are incurred in purchasing the sapling and in employing the labour to plant the tree. Although the sapling may begin to grow immediately after planting, its wood will be worth nothing until, say, the end of the second year, from which point of time it grows in value – at first more rapidly – to a maximum, after which it declines. Thus, the net value of the timber at any point in time is given by the vertical distance from that point of time.

In order to appreciate better the connection between this growth curve and the preceding Figure 23.1, along with its examples, we could split the time axis into discrete units, say years, and measure vertically the total value, of the timber at the end of each successive year. Instead of a continuous growth path, we should then have a succession of vertical lines increasing in height up to point *M*. The heights of each of these vertical lines could then be regarded as the value of *alternative* investment streams. For instance, the vertical line above 4 on the horizontal axis could measure exactly 100. If OC measured an initial cost of 50, the investment option corresponding to $t = 4$ would be $-50, 0, 0, 0, 100$. The investment option corresponding to $t = 5$ could be $-50, 0, 0, 0, 0, 112$. The investment option corresponding to $t = 6$ could be $-50, 0, 0, 0, 0, 0, 120$, and so on for $t = 7, 8, 9, \ldots, n$.[2] Which of all the investment options would we choose? Bearing in mind the preceding proposition, we need have no hesitation in affirming that, in general, it will depend upon the social rate of discount.

For any given discount rate, we may construct a number of V curves over time, each corresponding to a different present value. For a social discount rate that is equal to 5 per cent, one such discount curve V_1V_1 would measure, say, 80 along the vertical axis at time zero. At a point directly above $t = 1$, the height of the curve would be 80 $(1 + 0.5)$, or 84; at $t = 2$ the height of the curve would be 84 $(1 + 0.5)$, or 88.2, and so on, the height at the end of each successive year being 5 per cent greater than that of the preceding year.

At a social discount rate that is supposed to equal to the social rate of time preference of, say, 5 per cent, society is deemed indifferent to receiving timber worth, say, 100 as measured at some point in time by the height of the V_1V_1 curve, and receiving timber worth 105 a year later. Other 5 per cent discount curves such as V_2V_2, V_3V_3 and so on may be constructed on the same principle. The family of such 5 per cent VV curves is conceived as being 'infinitely dense', and optimization requires we select among them the highest VV curve that just touches the G_0G growth curve. In Figure 23.2 this is V_2V_2, which just touches G_0G at Q. The optimal growth period, or gestation period, is then exactly six years. And the net present value of the timber that is cut down at the end of the sixth year is measured by the height OQ *less* the initial cost OC. It will be correctly surmised that point Q is one of mutual tangency between a VV discount rate curve and the growth curve.

It will be understood that, if the tree were not cut down at the end of the sixth year, it would continue to grow for a number of years. After point Q is reached at the end of the sixth year, however, the increase in its value falls below 5 per cent per annum. There is, therefore, more to be gained by cutting down the tree at the end of the sixth year, selling the timber and investing the proceeds at 5 per cent than the alternative of cutting the trees at a later date.

---

2 For expository convenience, we are ignoring the costs of tending the tree while it is growing. If these were constant at, say, 10 each year, the investment option correction to $t = 4$ would be $-50, -10, -10, -10, 100$.

24 The internal rate of return

1   The internal rate of return (IRR) is a more respectable form of the average rate of return mentioned in Chapter 22 in that, like the DPV method, it takes account of time.

A simple example will illustrate how the IRR is calculated. If we have a stream of net benefits −100, 50, 86.4, we can discount each of these net benefits to the present, $t = 0$, using a discount rate of 20 per cent. The present value of the net benefit of 50 in year 1, when discounted at 20 per cent, is $50/(1 + 0.2)$, or 40, while the present value of 86.4 in year 2, when discounted at 20 per cent, is $86.4/(1 + 0.2)^2$, or 60. The present value of both 50 in year 1 and 86.4 in year 2 is, therefore, $40 + 60$, or 100; which is exactly equal to the initial *negative* net benefit, or net outlay, of 100. This 20 per cent discount, just because it equates the present value of the positive net benefits to the present value of the net outlay, is taken to be the internal rate of return of the above stream of net benefits.

The above example serves to illustrate a common definition of the IRR as being equal to that rate of discount, say λ, which when applied to a stream of net benefits, would make them equal to the initial outlay K; hence, the formula

$$K = \sum_{t=1}^{n} \frac{B_t}{(1 + \lambda)^t} \text{ or, alternatively, } K - \sum_{t=1}^{n} \frac{B_t}{(1 + \lambda)^t} = 0$$

in which we solve for λ.

2   There could, however, be additional outlays in future years. If, for example there were additional outlays, say K_2 and K_5 in years 2 and 5, respectively, these outlays have somehow to be discounted to the present and added to the initial outlay K in year 0. And if discounted, the relevant rate must also be λ which has, it may seem, yet to be determined.

Yet, on reflection, it will be understood that these later outlays can be left in place and, regarding them as negative net benefits to be discounted to the present along with the positive net benefits, so retaining the above formula. For example, given an initial outlay of 100 at time zero, a net benefit of 220 at the end of the first year and an *outlay* of 121 at the end of the second year – thus an investment stream equal to −100, 220, −121 – a discount rate equal to 10 per cent, reduces the present value of that stream to zero. The IRR is, therefore, equal to 10 per cent.

Inasmuch, then, as in conforming to the formula, both outlays and benefits are to be discounted to the present at the IRR, it will sometimes be neater to obviate mention of the initial outlay K and any subsequent outlays, treating them instead as negative net benefits in the year they occur. The formula then becomes

$$\sum_{t=1}^{n} \frac{B_t}{(1+\lambda)^t} = 0, \text{ in which } B_t \text{ can be positive, negative or zero}$$

It will be convenient, henceforth to continue using negative Bs for any *subsequent* outlays. Nonetheless, it should be understood that, although there can also be negative net benefits in future years that are in fact not cash outlays, being instead possible losses arising from environmental damage or compensatory payment, it makes no difference in the calculation of the IRR – or, for that matter, of the DPV, given the discount rate.[1]

3   The sense in which the internal rate of return, so defined, is an average over time is conveyed by the example of a man investing, say, 100 for five years. If the internal rate of return of some given investment stream were 25 per cent per annum, the man would have in mind *an equivalent*, though simpler, investment in which his 100 in the present grows by 25 per cent each year. He sees his 100 in the present becoming 125 by the end of the first year, $156\frac{1}{4}$ by the end of the second year, and so on, to reach $100(1 + 0.25)^5$ by the end of the fifth year. More generally, if the investment stream in question were $-100, B_1, B_2, B_3, B_4, B_5$, where the Bs are any pattern of benefits, and the internal rate of return were known to be 25 per cent, then an *equivalent* investment stream would be $-100, 0, 0, 0, 0, \ 100[(1 + 0.25)^5]$, for this given investment stream, when discounted to its present value at 25 per cent, is, by assumption, equal to zero, and so also is the equivalent stream. Consequently, if a man is told that the internal rate of an investment stream over n years is equal to λ, he is justified in thinking of the investment as equivalent to one in which his initial outlay is compounded forward at the rate of λ per annum for n years.

Thinking of the IRR in this way, the man will want to compare any such investment with the opportunities for putting his money into other securities, either equities or government bonds. If the only alternative open to him, or the only

---

1 Later, when we come to introduce a normalization procedure in which net benefits, positive or negative, are to be compounded forward, the composition of each net benefit must be considered. In that case, a negative net benefit that is a cash outlay will, in general, be treated differently from a negative net benefit that is, say, a collective bad (such as the ambient pollution) that is inflicted on the community.

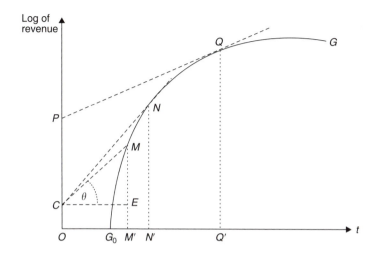

Figure 24.1

alternative he will consider, is long-term government bonds, perpetuities say, yield-ing 6 per cent per annum,[2] an investment yielding a rate of return of more than 6 per cent (always assuming certainty or, at least, equal certainty) will be preferred to the purchase of these 6 per cent government bonds.

4   Let us now return briefly to the growth curve of the preceding chapter, depicted here in Figure 24.1. The reader will recall that using the tangency condition between the growth curve G_0G and the highest 5 per cent discount curve at Q determined the optimal gestation or investment, period. Here however, we have followed the convention of drawing the discount curve as straight lines by measuring the *loga-rithms* of the values along the vertical axis – thus successive x per cent differences appear along it as equal distances.

If the highest discounted present value OP, at the given social rate of discount (which we continue to suppose is 5 per cent) determines the optimal period OQ', do we obtain the same result using, instead, the IRR? We should hardly expect so, since this optimal OQ' period itself will vary with the particular magnitude of the rate of discount adopted, being longer the lower the rate of discount.

But first, how do we represent the IRR on this diagram? The answer is that it can be represented by the slope of a straight line from C to any point of the growth curve, say M. For this slope is determined by $\tan \theta$, which is equal to the *excess*

---

2 In the modern economy there is, of course, a wide diversity of government bonds even if we restrict ourselves to long-term issues. We simplify the treatment, for the time being, by assuming there is only one type of long-term government bond, say 'perpetuities', i.e. interest-bearing bonds with no redemption date, such as British Consols.

benefit *EM* at time *M'* (that is, total benefit *M'M less* the cost *OC* at time zero) divided by time *OM'* in years. This ratio given by tan θ must be the IRR simply because, as required by definition, it is the rate of interest which reduces the *total* future benefit *M'M* to a present value that is equal to the initial cost *OC*.

Now the highest IRR possible is, on this construction, determined by the slope of the straight line from *C* that just touches the growth curve G_0G at point *N*, there being no straight lines from *C* steeper than *CN* that can also just touch this growth curve.

If the optimal investment period is now defined as that yielding the highest IRR, this will be a period equal to *ON'*. This *optimal* IRR period is clearly shorter than *OQ'*, the optimal period on the net present value criterion with a given rate of discount. So which is it to be? Do we let the tree grow for a period *OQ'*, or do we cut it down after *ON'* years? This is not the only sort of problem in which the results obtained using these two investment criteria differ. We shall defer the resolution of this apparent discrepancy,[3] however, until we have illustrated other discrepancies in the results obtained using IRR as compared with using DPV.

---

3 A hint may be allowed the impatient reader, however. If, after time *ON''* the proceeds *NN'* could be reinvested in an identical tree-growing project, there would be a loss by, instead, letting the tree continue to grow to *Q'Q*. What is at issue, then, are the reinvestment possibilities whenever the tree is cut down. This reinvestment aspect of the problem is treated in some detail in later chapters on the 'normalization' procedure.

25 The alleged superiority of the discounted present value criterion compared with the internal rate of return criterion

1 Consider the three alternative investment streams *A*, *B* and *C*, shown in Table 25.1. The *undiscounted* net benefit ratio $(B - K)/K$, in which *B* represents the net benefit in the first and only year in which benefits accrue, with *K* representing the initial capital outlay in year zero, will here serve as the criterion, one that will rank *C* above *B*, and *B* above *A*. Why the *undiscounted* net benefit ratio? For the simple reason that, whatever the rate of discount used, it will affect the net benefit at t_1 of *A*, *B* and *C* in exactly the same proportion. We may therefore infer that, irrespective of the discount rate used, the resulting *discounted* net benefit ratio would give the same *ranking* as the undiscounted net benefit ratio.

This conclusion is valid, however, only for a two-period investment in which the outlay appears in the first period and the benefit in the second. Add but one more period, and the ranking will, in general, depend upon the discount rate. For instance, a stream −100, 10, 100 cannot be ranked in relation to the stream −100, 90, 10 without knowing the discount rate. If this were 1 per cent, the first would clearly yield a larger net benefit ratio than the second. If, however, the discount rate were 50 per cent, the second would yield a larger net benefit ratio than the first.

The original two-period investment stream has another property: the internal rates of return of each of two-period streams *A*, *B* and *C* (as shown in Table 25.1) are equal to their corresponding net benefit ratios (also shown in the table), and therefore produce the same ranking, *C*, *B*, *A*. There is no mystery about this: for the net or excess benefit $(B - K)$ produced over the year, taken as a fraction of the capital cost *K*, is of course equivalent to one year's growth of the initial capital *K*. Thus the capital of 100 invested in *A* will have been perceived to grow by 5 per cent over the year, in *B* by 15 per cent, and in *C* by 25 per cent. A discount rate of 5 per cent for *A*, of 15 per cent for *B* and of 25 per cent for *C* will reduce

Table 25.1

	t_0	t_1	$(B - K)/K$	Internal rate of return
A	−100	105	5/100	5%
B	−100	115	15/100	15%
C	−100	125	25/100	25%

the magnitudes of their respective benefits to their original outlays, 100 in each case – such discount rates being, therefore, by definition, the respective internal rates of return of *A, B* and *C*.

For such two-period investment streams, then, the ranking C, B, A is the same whether we use the IRR or the DPV method. Moreover, whatever the rate of discount that is employed, whether positive, zero or negative, the ranking remains unchanged.

2   This harmony between the net present value criterion and the IRR criterion will, however, as the reader probably suspects, break down if any of the investment streams being compared contains more than two periods. Indeed, this implication accords with the proposition exemplified above: that, for investment streams in excess of two periods, the ranking will vary with the rate of discount used. The IRR ranking does not, however, at all depend on the adopted rate of discount, but is independently determined. If it then so happens that at the ruling discount rate a number of investment streams show the same ranking by the two criteria, an alteration of the discount rate, which changes the net present value ranking of the investment projects, will also produce a discrepancy between this new net present value ranking and the ranking by IRR.

We illustrate this latter statement using two different investment streams, *A* and *B*, as in Table 25.2. Both of these are ranked equally by the IRR criterion, being 10 per cent in each case. Not surprisingly then, if the discount rate employed also happened to be 10 per cent, the discounted net benefit ratio $(B - K)/K$ would be zero for both *A* and *B*, as $(B - K)$ would equal zero using a 10 per cent discount rate. Were the discount rate equal to only 1 per cent, the three-period *B* stream would show a $(B - K)K$ ratio of 19/100 and would rank above the $(B - K)/K$ ratio for *A*, of 9/100, the reverse ranking being produced if the discount rate were doubled to become 20 per cent. In that case, *B*'s discounted net benefit ratio would be equal to $-16/100$, which is therefore ranked below that of $-8/100$ for the *A* stream.

A diagrammatic representation of the variation in the discounted net present value, $PV_r(B - K)$ with respect to the rate of discount for each of these investment streams, *A* and *B*, is displayed in Figure 25.1, where $PV_r(B-K)$ is measured along the vertical axis and the rate of discount *r* along the horizontal axis. It can be seen at a glance that discounted net benefit $PV_r(B - K)$ for each of the two streams of investment – indeed, for any investment stream – varies inversely with the rate of discount *r*.

Table 25.2

	t_0	t_1	t_2	Internal rate of return	$(B - K)/K$ at 1%	$(B - K)/K$ at 10%	$(B - K)/K$ at 20%
A	-100	110	0	10%	9/100	0	$-$ 8/100
B	-100	0	121	10%	19/100	0	$-16/100$

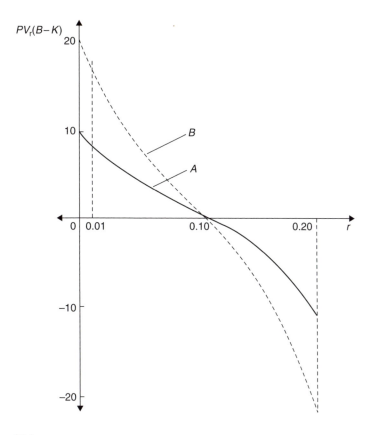

Figure 25.1

It will be noticed that there is some rate of discount, here 10 per cent, at which the two investment streams will have exactly the same discounted net present value. In this particular case, moreover, it so happens that this same discounted net present value is equal to zero; hence, the IRR for each will be 10 per cent. For discount rates below 10 per cent, B's $PV_r(B - K)$ exceeds that of A, the reverse being true for discount rates above 10 per cent.

3   In spite of this discrepancy between the two criteria, the IRR has been rec-ommended in some circumstances, particularly as a method of allocating a given capital budget among a number of potential investment projects. Thus, one might select a number of public investment streams, subject to a budget, provided that the IRR on each investment stream that is chosen exceeds the adopted rate of discount. The scheme is illustrated in Table 25.3, which shows five investment streams in declining order of IRR. The DPV of their net benefit ratios is also given for a discount rate equal to 3 per cent.

Table 25.3

	t_0	t_1	t_2	Internal rate of return	$PV_r(B-K)/K$ (for $r = 0.03$)
A	−100	110	0	10%	7/100
B	−100	0	115	7%	8/100
C	−100	106	0	6%	3/100
D	−50	52	0	4%	1/100
E	−200	2	208	2%	−2/100

If the available budget were 1,000, on the IRR criterion, only 350 of it would be spent. We should admit A, B, C and D, but not E, since the latter has an IRR of only 2 per cent, whereas the discount rate is taken to be 3 per cent. The reader will doubtless observe that the IRR ranking A, B, C, D and E differs from that resulting from the DPV criterion, which is B, A, C, D and E. Yet, this latter ranking holds only for rates of discount close to 3 per cent. As we move further from a 3 per cent discount rate, so the ranking may change, in general, for any set of investment streams.

Were the available budget only 100, the IRR criterion would choose investment option A, in contrast to the selection of the B option if, instead, the DPV criterion were used. But which is the better option?

4 Although the ranking of a number of alternative investment streams will, in general, differ according to whether we use one criterion or the other, we have no reason, so far, for preferring one to the other. We may now introduce at least one consideration that tells against the use of the IRR criterion as usually defined:[1] more than a single IRR may be yielded by a given investment stream. A necessary, though not sufficient condition, for this to occur is that not all outlays (or negative net benefits) take place in the initial period. There have to be negative net benefits in later periods.

A simple example of such an investment stream, call it the H stream, could be −100, 420, −400. This stream is one that yields two IRRs, λ_1 of 46 per cent, and λ_2 of 174 per cent, since using either of these rates as a discount rate would reduce the discounted net present value of the H stream to zero.[2]

---

1 A more accommodating definition is proposed in Chapter 28, following the critique of the DPV criterion.

2 From this definition of the IRR, say λ, we require a λ for which

$$-100 + \frac{420}{(1+\lambda)} - \frac{400}{(1+\lambda)^2} = 0$$

The reader will recognize the expression as a quadratic equation with two solutions, $\lambda = 0.46$ and $\lambda = 1.74$. A negative net benefit in the second period is not a sufficient condition for two IRRs, however. If it were small enough, there would still be a single IRR. An example would be the stream −100, 121, −1, which yields an IRR of a little over 20 per cent.

Figure 25.2 depicts the curve relating the net present value of the *H* stream to the rate of discount *r*. The curve will be seen to cut the horizontal axis, not once (as does each of the investment streams in Figure 25.3), but twice: once at the point where *r* is 0.46 and once where *r* is 1.74. Since either of these two discount rates reduces the present value of the *H* stream to zero, they are identified as the two IRRs λ_1 and λ_2.

Of course, the reader might think that, of these two IRRs, λ_1 (46 per cent) is the more reasonable. If he were obliged to adopt an IRR for such a stream, he would probably choose 46 per cent. But he would find it difficult to justify such a choice, if he were not allowed to draw on intuition. Moreover, even if the reader did feel confident about the 46 per cent IRR for the *H* stream, this example of two IRRs is only a special case. For one can devise investment streams to yield three, four or indeed any number of IRRs.[3] However open-minded the reader may wish to remain, he cannot deny that the case for preferring the present value criterion above the IRR criterion looks very strong.

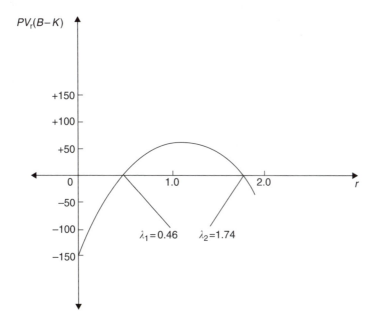

Figure 25.2

3 Determining the values of the IRRs corresponding to any investment stream implies solving for the roots of a polynomial. Any investment stream with *n* periods can be transformed into a polynomial with a maximum of *n* − 1 different roots, each being a possible IRRs. Only those that are positive will matter for investment criteria. Negative IRRs make sense, but are not usually of much importance. Complex roots do not appear to make sense in this context.

5   If, provisionally, we accept the DPV criterion, there remains the question of whether we are to rank (i) by excess benefit over cost $(B' - K')$, (ii) by the ratio of benefit to cost B'/K', or (iii) by the ratio of excess benefit to cost $(B' - K')/K'$. These alternative ranking methods are worked out in Table 25.4 for investment options A and B, where K' is taken to be the DPV of all outlays, initial and subsequent ones, if any, and B' is understood to be the DPV of all net benefits, the discount rate being given.

In the $(B' - K')$ column, A, which has excess benefit over cost of 50, is ranked above C, which has an excess benefit over cost of only 30. In the next, B'/K' column, however, C, with a ratio of benefit to cost of 2.5, is ranked above A, which has a ratio of benefit to cost of only 1.5. In the final column showing $(B' - K')/K'$, the ratio of *excess* benefit to cost continues to show C ranked above A. A glance at the last two columns will assure the reader that B'/K' and $(B' - K)/K'$ will give the same ranking, as the latter ratio is derived from the former simply by subtracting unity from it. We can, then, ignore the B'/K' ratio and compare the $(B' - K')$ with the $(B' - K')/K'$ ranking.

Now, if there is a capital budget of exactly 100, it may seem reasonable to be guided by the $(B' - K')/K'$ ratio ranking, and therefore to choose C rather than A. This is rational enough if it is established that one can have either A alone or, instead, five of the C streams. The outlay for five of the C streams uses up exactly the budget of 100, and produces a DPV of five times 50, or 250 – which is 100 more than can be obtained by choosing to put the whole of the 100 in option A. But if it is not possible to have more than one C investment option, we could be misled by using the ranking method $(B' - K')/K'$, for although this ratio is higher for C than it is for A, the excess net benefit for A, 50, is greater than that for C, which is only 30.

Let us, therefore consider ranking by the $(B' - K')$ method and, to make things more awkward, let us assume also that option A is indivisible. In that case, by choosing option C, we are left with an outlay of 80 from the original budget of 100. The relevant question now is: are there any opportunities for investing this remaining outlay of 80?

Allowing that there are no other public investment options available, we must recognize that there is always the private investment sector. If the average rate of return over time in this private sector happens to be equal to perpetuity of 8 per cent per annum, then a sum equal to 80 invested in the private sector could be said to yield a return of 6.4 in perpetuity.

At a given rate of discount of 5 per cent, this perpetuity of 6.4 has a DPV of 128. Adding this B' of 128 to the B' of 50 (from putting 20 in the C option) gives a

Table 25.4

	K'	B'	$(B' - K')$	B'/K'	$(B' - K')/K'$
A	100	150	50	1.5	0.5
C	20	50	30	2.5	1.5

total B' of 178, which is more than can be obtained by investing the 100, instead, wholly in option A, which yields a B' of only 150, at least if we ignore further reinvesting possibilities.

Thus, if we do adopt the ranking method $(B' - K')/K'$, it is tacitly assumed that each of the investment options being considered may be multiplied in such a way as to ensure that the magnitude of the K' is the same for each of them. Where this cannot be assumed, we should be advised to use the $(B' - K')$ method of ranking and use the stratagem above in order that each option use a K' of the same magnitude. This can always be done, in the last resort if necessary, by investing the 'spare' funds of any option in the private investment sector.

In sum, for a valid ranking of alternative investment options, we must first make sure we have created for each option a K' of the same magnitude. Once this is done, we shall, in fact, obtain the same ranking, whichever of the three methods we use $- (B' - K')$, B'/K' or $(B' - K')/K'$.

6 Finally, a brief word about the treatment of a set of investment streams that have different life spans, some beginning earlier than others, some later.

A correct ranking of such streams requires, ideally, only one particular adjustment: that each of these investment streams be compounded forward to a common terminal year, this common terminal year clearly being that year in which the final net benefit (positive or negative) occurs in that investment stream stretching furthest into the future.

To illustrate, if we measure time in years along a horizontal axis, four investment streams to be compared can be represented as successive horizontal lines of different lengths, as in Figure 25.3.

It will be seen that investment stream A begins in year 0 and ends in year 7. Two successive and complementary streams are generated by project B, the first beginning in year 3 and ending in year 7, the second being from year 8 to year 10.

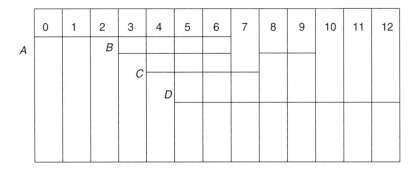

Figure 25.3

The *C* investment stream is from year 4 to year 8, while the *D* stream is from year 5 to year 12.

Year 12 is then to be accepted as the common terminal date for the four investment streams. In Chapter 28, where the normalization procedure is elaborated, we shall find that there is no difficulty in compounding the first three investment streams, *A*, *B* and *C*, to the terminal year 12.

26 Investment criteria in an ideal capital market

1 Investment criteria, whether based on DPV or IRR, are devised so as to enable us to choose between alternative uses of investable funds. If there are two or more alternative investment options, each must be compared with the others.[1] If there is only one investment project under consideration, the alternatives are to use the funds either for private expenditure or for buying government securities. The latter course of action may be thought of as a financial transaction that does not of itself result in any new investment. Initially, it is but a purchase of government bonds on the open market: a transfer of cash from the individual to the government. For society as a whole, however, and certainly for public investment, we must transcend all financial transactions and, in the last resort, consider at least two alternatives: either consumption or else investment in this particular project.

Only in the absence of a progressive income tax would an ideal capital market be possible.[2] And, for the present, we shall also assume only one rate of interest which is to be used as the relevant rate of discount in the DPV criterion and which also reflects society's rate of time preference. A rate of interest of 5 per cent that reflects this society's time preference implies that such a society is wholly indifferent as between having $1 today and $1.05 in exactly a year's time. If, therefore, by reducing the consumption of $1 worth of goods today it becomes possible to gain $1.06 worth of goods next year, society is deemed to gain by the transaction.

---

1 It is just possible that the reader may be wondering why we have continuously ignored mention of depreciation in the treatment of investment criteria. The short answer is that the principles which guide the rate of *amortization* are unrelated to those that arise in *selecting investments*. There is nothing mysterious about this. All investment criteria, whether based on DPV or IRR, implicitly make allowance for the maintenance of capital through the requirement that the outlays on the investment project be (more than) covered by the DPV of its expected future benefits.

2 Given the existence of a progressive income tax, a man who pays 40 per cent tax on his income will receive no more than 3 per cent net return on a market yield of 5 per cent whereas to the man who pays 20 per cent tax on his income, the 5 per cent market yield receives a net income of 4 per cent on his investment, and so on. It will be convenient, above, to assume zero income tax.

If, instead, one returns $1.04 in a year's time, society is deemed to be worse off from having postponed consumption. Consequently, if a particular investment yields more than 5 per cent in a year's time, society is deemed better off from switching resources from the production of consumption goods to this particular investment good, and vice versa.

In circumstances where the only alternatives open to the use of present resources are either investment today or consumption today, an investment will be chosen if its rate of return exceeds the 5 per cent rate of time preference. If it does so, the DPV of its outlays and benefits over time will be positive, and the investment will be undertaken. Thus, given a rate of discount that is equal to the rate of time preference, a positive net present value indicates that the present value of a sum when invested exceeds its net present value if, instead, the sum is used to consume goods today. It follows that society is better off investing the sum today than using it to consume goods today.

2   In an ideal market economy, in which the only existing rate of return on investment is equal to society's rate of time preference, the economy is in equilibrium, at least with respect to the capital market. If, for example, the existing rate of interest is 5 per cent, the marginal product of the existing capital stock is also equal to 5 per cent, as is also the rate of return on current investment or 'marginal efficiency of investment'. In such an ideal capital market, any new investment opportunity that has, with certainty, a net present value above zero (when its outlays and benefits are discounted at 5 per cent) must add to society's welfare and would therefore be undertaken. The consequent incentive to invest may be supposed to continue until equilibrium is restored, the rate of return being, once more, no greater than society's rate of time preference. In this ideal situation, there is apparently no problem about the appropriate rate of discount.[3]

However, once the yield on current investment tends to remain above society's rate of time preference, as it tends to be for a number of reasons, the choice of the appropriate discount rate is far from simple. In fact, the variety of proposals has engendered much controversy about the considerations that should enter into the devising of an appropriate rate of discount.[4] We shall examine the chief differences between these proposals in Chapter 28.

---

3 Even in this seemingly ideal economy, the prevalence of external economies in investment will result in a sub-optimal volume of capital formation which perhaps could be corrected only if the market rate of interest were appropriately reduced. This aspect was originally developed by Marglin (1963b), but it is not directly relevant to investment criteria for reasons given in footnote 4 following.

4 What may also seem to complicate the issue is that any long-run equilibrium rate of interest is, in any event, not uniquely determined by the interaction of individual time preference and investment opportunities. Such long-run rate of interest may be varied through monetary and fiscal policies.

  Such policies, however, are of macroeconomic interest. They are not directly pertinent to cost-benefit analysis. Stated briefly, the required data for the application of an investment criterion is (ought to be) the relevant opportunity yields of investment, on the one hand, and the social rate of time preference, on the other.

27 Calculation of rates of return and of time preference

1   We must now reconsider our supposition of a single rate of time preference for society, say r, and a single yield, say ρ, on private investment.

The latter task is simple in principle. On the assumption that risk-aversion among investors predominates, received doctrine has it that there is a tendency for private investment with a greater expected risk to carry a higher actuarial rate of return – that is, a higher average rate of return over a long-term period.[1]

Provided that classification of private investment according to actuarial rates of return is feasible, it might be thought that the highest actuarial rate of return (corresponding to the riskiest private investment) is the appropriate opportunity rate of return for public projects – on the argument that the outlay K raised to finance the public project could always have been invested in this type of private investment. Even if the argument were accepted, however, there may be relatively little of this riskiest private investment about, and it may therefore take too long to discover its actuarial rate of return. The economist might then choose for the appropriate opportunity rate ρ the rate of return on a less risky private investment, but one that is more common and more likely to be maintained over the future.

2   The reader is reminded, however, that, where the necessary funds for the public project are to be raised entirely by borrowing from the public, the relevant opportunity rate of return, which is to be used as the discount rate, has to be calculated, in general, not by reference simply to the rate paid by the government on the nominal value of the bonds issued. In so far as private investment is displaced – 'crowded out', in the jargon – the higher actuarial rate of return on private investment ρ is the appropriate rate.

Only in the limiting case in which the full amount of the initial outlay K that is borrowed by the government does not in fact displace any private investment – so

---

1   Under a progressive income tax, the total tax paid over, say, a 20-year period is greater for a riskier investment with the same total gross return than for a less risky investment in as much as the gross return on the former is more unevenly spread than the same gross return on the latter. Thus, even in the absence of risk-aversion, the gross rate of return – which is what ρ measures – has to be higher for the riskier private investment simply in order to yield the same *net* return over time as for the safer private investment.

that the aggregate volume of investment that would have taken place during the year is increased by the amount K – does the relevant rate of discount (which has to have reference to the opportunities forgone when the amount K is diverted from the use to which it would otherwise be put) equal society's rate of time preference, inasmuch as those who buy the K value of government bonds are reducing some part of their current consumption for some additional consumption over the future.

In the more general case where the amount borrowed by the government has the effect of displacing some part only of this amount of private investment, say $4 million of an outlay K of $10 million, the opportunity rate of this $4 million is equal to ρ, with society's rate of time preference r on the remaining $6 million. The appropriate discount rate in this general case is, therefore, a weighted average of r and ρ.

3   An estimate of the social rate of time preference is more elusive. We have already discussed an ideal capital market in which everybody's rate of time preference, whether or not he is a borrower or lender, is the same and exactly equal to the rate of interest prevailing on the market, and equal also to the rate of return on existing capital and new investment.

Although we can move a little in the direction of realism by envisaging a large number of loan markets, each differing from the other according to the terms of the loan, it is not possible to suppose that a person can borrow all he wishes at the going rate of interest. For if he could, he would also be able to renew the loan when it expired, so postponing repayment indefinitely. Yet, even if borrowers were all equally honest, unless we want also to suppose them equally wealthy, prudent and shrewd, they would not be equally creditworthy. For example, for an initial $100,000 loan to run for five years, the more creditworthy the borrower the lower, in general, will be the rate of interest charged.

In order to estimate a community's rate of time preference, however, it is not enough to take account of all the different loan markets, and within each such market the different categories of borrowers, for, as a result of rationing the amount of money lent to each borrower, the rate of interest he pays on the marginal dollar borrowed may be well below his rate of time preference. For more reliable estimates of people's time preferences, then, we must go beyond market data. We must use questionnaire surveys.

4   Following the basic maxim, it would seem that, if a person says he will defer consumption of 100 this year for no less than 105 next year, the implied rate of time preference of 5 per cent has to be accepted.[2] And if this 5 per cent holds over

---

2 From the fact that a person is indifferent as between consuming an additional 100 this year and consuming an additional 105 next year, it is not to be inferred that he is 'myopic' or 'impatient'. As demonstrated in Appendix 10, in the complete absence of a loans market, a person may regard a given sum as being of equal worth whether he receives it today or some time in the future. Yet, once a loans market is introduced, this same person may adjust his pattern of consumption so that, indeed, he then becomes indifferent as between, say, 100 today and 105 in a year's time.

the entire time span, he will be indifferent as between consuming 100 this year, year 0, and consuming 100 $(1.05)^t$ in year t.

Can the rate of time preference r be higher than ρ, the average rate of return on private investment? Although virtually impossible for society as a whole, we must recognize the possibility that some individuals who perforce must, via taxation, reduce their consumption have very high rates of time preference. Let us take an extreme example of a man of 90 years of age, Mr A, who has to put a value on the amount of consumption he would require in 10 years' time in order to compensate him for sacrificing the consumption today of an additional 200. His average rate of time preference over the next 10 years may be inordinately high, and not unreasonably so. If he believes that his chances of surviving the next 10 years are very low, he may truly claim to be indifferent as between consuming an additional 100 this year and an additional 20,000 in 10 years' time. This average rate of time preference of about 100 cent per annum is clearly expressive of his impatience to consume while he is still alive: it is the minimum incentive needed to persuade him to forgo present consumption in favour of consumption in the tenth year.

It would seem to follow that the age distribution of the beneficiaries and the losers in the different projects being compared would significantly affect the weighted average rate of time preference and, therefore might be a critical variable in determining their ranking. For example, a public investment whose beneficiaries were largely elderly people would certainly have a higher average rate of time preference and, in so far as it enters the discount rate, would reduce the present value of that project below that of a project whose beneficiaries were mainly young people.

5 It would seem reasonable to calculate society's rate of time preference as the weighted average of the several groups in the community that are affected, making society's rate of time preference R equal to $\Sigma^n w_i r_i$, where there are n different groups, r_i being the rate of time preference of group i, and w_i being the weight of group i, with $\Sigma^n w_i$ equal to unity.

It transpires, however, that the R so calculated is generally slightly smaller than an exact measure of society's rate of time preference as, if a sum x is compounded for a number of years at this rate R, it will compound to a sum that is slightly smaller than the sum compounded for each group separately and then added. Over the years, of course, the absolute difference between R and the true measure will grow. But save in exceptional circumstances the difference will remain relatively slight.[3]

---

3 To illustrate with only two groups (group 1 with a weight of 0.7 and a rate of time preference of 10 per cent, the other group with a weight of 0.3 with a rate of time preference of 0.05): R would then be equal to $(0.7 \times 0.1) + (0.3 \times 0.05)$ equal, therefore, to 8.5 per cent. If x is \$1,000, then compounded at R for two years it becomes \$1000$(1.085)^2$ or \$1,177.25. For five years, it becomes equal to \$1,503.65. If now we compound each group separately, after two years we have \$700$(1.1)^2$ plus \$300$(1.05)^2$, a total of \$1,177.75 – a difference from compounding R of only 50 cents. After five years, the compounded sum of the two separate groups becomes \$700$(1, 1)$ plus \$300$(1.05)^5$, a total of \$1,510 – a difference now of less than \$7.

Where the range of the different rates of time preference for the community affected is not great, at least for the larger groups, the use of this weighted average R as society's rate of time preference is unlikely to make a significant difference to the calculation as compared with the use of the rate of time preference of each of the separate n groups.

28 Critique of the discounted present value criterion (I)

1   All the well-known criteria proposed for evaluating public investment streams embody in one form or another a DPV procedure.[1] A distinction must be made, however, between (a) the older type of criterion, which simply applies what is thought to be an appropriate discount rate to the stream of benefits (positive or negative) in question, and (b) a newer type of criterion, in which provision is made for the allocation of the resulting benefits of a project as between consumption and further investment and within which category there can be differences between behavioural, institutional and political assumptions.

The differences within the (a) category are elucidated in a comparison of equations (28.1)–(28.4) which follow. Those within the (b) category are basically less controversial and may be represented by equation (28.5) alone. The latter differences, as we shall see, arise only from the degree of elaboration thought to be appropriate, and deserve only passing mention.

2   In order to economize on inessential elaboration of the analysis, the practice common in the literature of ignoring (initially at least) uncertainty in order to focus on a critical part of the logic of investment criteria is followed here.

Although, in general, there may be different rates of time preference for the different groups affected by the project and also different yields on private investment according to risk, an analysis conducted in terms of such generality adds only an elegant complexity to the exposition that is more likely than not to obscure the basic outlines of the argument. We shall, therefore, regard the rate of time preference r as a single figure (or weighted average of the rates of time preference of all groups affected by the project) and the yield ρ also as a single figure (or weighted average of the different rates of return on sums invested by the project).

If we write $PV(B)$ as a shorthand for the DPV of the stream of all the (net) benefits, $B_0, B_1, B_2, \ldots, B_T$, some of which may be negative, and K as the

---

1 Mishan's proposed normalization procedure (1967c) is an exception, one that informs this and the following chapter.

initial outlay, then under the older type of criteria (a) we may distinguish four alternatives:

$$PV_r(B) > K \tag{28.1}$$

$$PV_\rho(B) > K \tag{28.2}$$

$$PV_p(B) > K, \text{where } p = \sum_{n+1}^{n} w_i r_i + \sum_{n+1}^{s} w_j \rho_j \text{ and } \sum_{1}^{n} w_i + \sum_{n+1}^{s} w_j = 1 \tag{28.3}$$

$$PV_q(B) > K (\rho > q > r) \tag{28.4}$$

3   Criterion (28.1), the staple of textbook instruction, is superficially plausible enough. If r is rate of time preference, the community is indifferent between receiving the stream of benefits $(B) = B_1, \ldots, B_T$, and receiving its present value $PV_r(B)$. In particular, any project with a benefit stream that meets criterion (28.1) tells us that the present value of that stream of benefits exceeds the value of its initial outlay at time zero and, therefore, introducing the project realizes a potential Pareto improvement.

The rationale for criterion (28.2) is no less plausible. It suggests that, if funds equal to K are to be spent on a public project, the average yield from the project should be no less than the ρ per annum that the sum K could fetch if it were placed in the private investment sector instead. If, over the period, the benefit stream yields on average more than ρ, the $PV_p(B) > K$ criterion would be met, and there would be a net gain from adopting the investment project.

Clearly, criterion (28.3) is a generalization of (28.1) and (28.2) extended to cover all the different rs and ρs in the economy. Since the weights, the ws, are the fractions of K contributed by separable components of the reduced amount of consumption and of the reduced amounts of private investment, the resultant weighted rate of return represents society's actual opportunity yield per dollar of investing a sum K in a public project. In general, then, ρ will vary according to whether K is raised by tax finance, loan finance or as a mixture of both. Although (28.3) was originally proposed by Krutilla and Eckstein (1958), it was advanced again by Harberger (1968) in connection with a rise in interest rates in response to government borrowing,[2] which is supposed to check both private investment

---

2 Not surprisingly, Chicago School economists favour loan finance of public investments. Others favour tax finance, either on the grounds that it tends to reduce the volume of private investment less than does loan finance (see Musgrave, 1969) or else on the grounds that loan finance entails future tax levies in order to service the debt.

and consumption.[3] With such a weighted discount rate, Harberger (1968: 308) claimed (erroneously, as we shall see) that the 'so-called reinvestment problem disappears'.[4]

This criterion is also open to a more serious reservation. In essence, it is pre-Keynesian, ignoring as it does the stabilizing effect of 'liquidity preference' – the shape of the demand curve to hold the total stock of securities in the economy – on rates of interest. If, therefore, government borrowing for the public project has no effect or a negligible effect on interest rates, there may be no 'crowding out' of private investment and no reduction in current savings.

In so far as the economy is close to full employment, any government expenditure on a public project that is financed by borrowing – by an issue of bonds – must add to aggregate demand in the economy, and is therefore inflationary.[5]

If, in contrast, there is ample slack in the economy, the addition to aggregate demand arising from spending a sum K as initial outlay on a public project has no inflationary effect. In such circumstances, the cost of the public project could be negative, as argued in Chapter 13.

We turn finally to the well-known Arrow–Lind paper of 1970, which produced criterion (28.4) as a modification of the popular criterion (28.2), $PV_\rho(B) > K$. We shall accept without criticism their argument that the risks associated with public projects, when divided among a large population of taxpayers, are felt by each taxpayer to be negligible compared with the sense of risk apprehended by investors in private enterprise. A person can then be supposed to be indifferent between a rate of return ρ on private investment and the greater certainty of a somewhat lower rate of return q on his money when it is invested instead in a public project – a risk premium equal to $(\rho - q)$ being attributable to the greater risk entailed by investing in the private-investment sector. A potential Pareto improvement may then be realized if funds are removed from private investment, so forgoing yield ρ, and placed instead in a public investment at a yield greater than q. For

---

3 However, Dreze (1974: 60) asks whether if government borrowing does affect the rate of interest and, if so, whether a higher rate of interest increases current saving. His answer is simply that 'there undoubtly exist cases where government borrowing does not affect the rate of interest, but is simply offset by rationing of private investment'. Dreze compares his view with that of Arrow (1966), who argues that the divergence between 'the rate of interest implicit in consumption decisions and any market rate is so great that it must be accepted that savings are largely independent of the latter' and then goes on to say that the issue is 'to decide whether some consumers do react, at least, for some forms of consumption'.

4 Indeed, all formulae that assume a voluntary increase in savings in response to a rise in interest rates are suspect, for, in the absence of a well-functioning capital market – one in which interest rates move freely so as to bring the current flow of savings into equilibrium with the current flow of investment – an additional $1 million saved (although, by definition, entailing a reduction of current consumption by $1 million) may have no effect whatever on the current demand for investment.

5 Equilibrium mechanisms that are invoked by the inflation can act eventually to reduce aggregate consumption and/or investment. But there is no simple theory from which we may deduce reductions in the rate of inflation.

then, everyone who invests in the public project will be made better off by a yield of a little more than q than by the higher yield ρ from private investment. Hence, the proposed criterion (28.4), $PV_q(B) > K$, for investments in the public sector.

This proposed criterion (28.4) is, however, no less vulnerable than the other three. Even though we assume that the government is not permitted to undertake any investments comparable with those undertaken in the private sector, adherence to this criterion might deprive the economy of worthwhile investments. If the sum K is raised wholly by taxation, it *may* involve a reduction in consumption only. The opportunity rate that is to be forgone on the sum K raised by taxation is then no more than society's rate of time preference r. It follows that a Pareto criterion would be met if the public project were to yield more than r, as in criterion (28.1).

In sum, although this (28.4) criterion is an interesting, though controversial variation of the (a) type of criteria, it is – apart from the above criticism – subject to a more fundamental critique along with the other three.

4   We turn briefly to the newer type (b) criterion, which recognizes that more care has to be taken of the reinvestment aspect of the returns on an investment project. Such criteria can be formulated as

$$PV_r(B) > AK \tag{28.5}$$

where A is the ratio of the social opportunity costs both of the public project itself and of the actual alternative use of the outlay K. Let us consider these two social opportunity costs.

Marglin's (1963a) treatment, in his classic article, assumes that the required sum K is raised from tax revenue and that, of every dollar so raised, a fraction θ_1 comes from an *initial* reduction in private investment with yield ρ, the remaining fraction $(1 - \theta_1)$ coming from a reduction in current consumption.[6] In addition, θ_2 is the fraction of each dollar of any return that is placed in the private investment sector. Under these conditions, an amount K left in the private sector of the economy would generate a stream of consumption over the future which, when discounted at r, would converge to aK, a being greater than unity.[7] This aK is the 'social opportunity cost' of a project requiring a nominal outlay of K.

However, the employment now of criterion $PV_r(B) > aK$ can be justified only if the stream of benefits are entirely consumed as they occur. If, instead, the fraction $(1 - \theta_2)$ of each of the benefits is consumed as it occurs, the remainder being invested in the private sector at ρ, and the returns to these investment components

6 In fact, Marglin produces three models in this paper. His third model introduces alternative and less plausible behaviour assumptions, while his first model is little more than a stepping stone to the second model, which is treated above as *the* Marglin model.

7 In order for the infinite stream of consumption thus generated to converge, when discounted at r, to a finite sum, Marglin assumes that $\theta_2 p > r$.

treated in the same way, the consumption stream so generated can be discounted at r to a present value of $\alpha PV_r(B)$, with $\propto$ greater than unity. The corrected criterion $\alpha PV_r(B) > aK$ can then be written as[8]

$$PV_r(B) > AK \left(A = \frac{a}{\alpha} \right)$$

Later contributions that explicitly recognized the reinvestment problem produced models which, though interesting in themselves, reproduced the same essential features of the Marglin model. Feldstein's three papers (1964a,b, 1972), for instance, extend the formulation to cover other behavioural and institutional parameters. Bradford's (1975) paper is of the same family and, though he begins somewhat differently, his results conform to the same basic formula as Marglin's.[9] As there is no fundamental novelty of conception in the later papers adopting this approach, remarks on the Marglin model are applicable also to their analyses.

Without doubt, the introduction of the type (b) criteria, which face up to the reinvestment problem, is an important step forward in the art of project evaluation and goes far to remedy the defect inherent in the older DPV formulae. Yet, the insight that inspired the innovation was channelled into the conventional mould.

It is possible, however, to break out of this conventional DPV mould by adopting, instead, a normalization procedure with the singular feature that each of a stream of benefits is compounded forward to a terminal date rather than being discounted backward to the present, a procedure that is illustrated in the following chapter.

---

8 In a limiting case, where $\theta_1 = \theta_2 = 0$, a will equal α, and $PV_r(B) > AK$ becomes equal to $PV_r > K$. (In Bradford's 1975 model, θ_1 and θ_2 are denoted, respectively, as α_t and α_{t+1} and, when these are equal, his criterion also reduces to $PV_r(B) > K$.)

9 Bradford's (1975) paper, in some ways a development of his earlier paper of 1970, constructs a model which closely resembles that of Marglin. This resemblance is easier to appreciate by comparing Marglin's equation (8), condensed and cast in discrete form, with Bradford's equation (15), using a common notation. Marglin's criterion then appears as

$$\sum_{t=0}^{\infty} \alpha \beta_t \delta_t - aK_0 > 0$$

while Bradford's takes the form

$$\sum_{t=0}^{T} \alpha_t B_t \delta_t - \sum a_t K_t \delta_t > 0$$

where B_t is the tth benefit from the public project, K_t is the tth net outlay, and a_t is the shadow price of a dollar of the tth net outlay. The discount factor to be applied to B_t, and K_t is δ_t. Bradford's public investment benefit stream is finite (and not infinite as is Marglin's), and his shadow prices a_t and α_t vary with t. For the special case $\alpha_t = a_t$, both reduce to the general form $PV_r(B - K) > 0$, which form includes the possibility also of a stream of net outlays.

29 Critique of the discounted present value criterion (II)

1 Since, for the purpose in hand, any one of the five criteria discussed in the preceding chapter will serve, we shall use criterion (28.2), $PV_\rho(B) > K$, for demonstration.

Given, therefore, the initial outlay K in year zero, and the subsequent stream of (net) benefits, $B_1, B_2, \ldots, B_T$, we can re-write criterion (28.2) as

$$\sum_{t=1}^{T} \frac{B_t}{(1+\rho)^t} > K \tag{29.1}$$

By multiplying through by a scalar $(1+\rho)^T$, we obtain the equivalent inequality

$$\sum_{t=1}^{T} B_t(1+\rho)^{T-t} > K(1+\rho)^T \tag{29.2}$$

which may be summarized as $TV_\rho(B) > TV_\rho(K)$, where $TV_\rho(B)$ stands for the terminal value of the stream of benefits when each is compounded forward to terminal date T at rate ρ, and $TV_\rho(K)$ stands for the terminal value of the outlay K when it also is compounded forward to terminal date T at rate ρ.

If and only if $PV_\rho(B) > K$ does $TV_\rho(B) > TV_\rho(K)$; one form of the criterion, that is, entails the other. But the latter form is far more revealing: it makes clear that, for the criterion to be met, the aggregate of the benefits, B_1, B_2, B_T, when each benefit is wholly and continually reinvested to time T at this same weighted rate of return ρ, must exceed the sum which K amounts to when it also is wholly invested and reinvested to the terminal year T. Such a criterion would, of course, be applicable in the rare case when, in fact, both the benefits and the initial outlay of the project were to be used in exactly this way. It could be justified only if all benefits were encashed and wholly invested and reinvested at ρ, the return to private investment, until the terminal date, and similarly for the amount K.

Inasmuch as this implicit requirement is seldom complied with, the use of a criterion that is valid only if such a requirement is, in fact, assured can be seriously misleading. Certainly, any of these four criteria is misleading when it is applied to a public project without information in the particular case about the disposal of the returns to the project and without information also about the sort of stream that would have been generated by the sum K had it not been taken from the economy.[1]

To illustrate, suppose that the outlay K required by a particular public investment is to be drawn entirely from the private investment sector, where it would otherwise have been reinvested continually at ρ to reach a terminal value at T of $TV_\rho(K)$. Suppose also that the project's benefits, in contrast, are expected to be wholly consumed as they occur over time. The value of such benefits therefore grows in value at the rate of time preference r to reach a terminal value at T of $TV_r(B)$. Now if $TV_r(B)$, as is likely, happens to be smaller than $TV_\rho(K)$, the terminal value of the sum K, the project has to be rejected on a Pareto criterion: society would be better off leaving the amount K in the private investment sector (there to be continually reinvested at ρ) rather than using it to finance a project whose benefits are consumed as they occur.

It should be evident that the use of criterion (28.1), $PV_r(B)K$, would fail to reveal this possibility. Employing it could then sanction projects that would be rejected on a Pareto criterion. By reversing these suppositions in the above example, so that the outlay K is raised entirely through a reduction in present consumption so that it is to be compounded to the terminal year T at society's rate of time preference while, in contrast, all the returns over time to the project are to be wholly invested and reinvested at ρ to the terminal year, the employment of the $PV_r(B) > K$ criterion could reject projects that do, in fact, meet the Pareto criterion.

2   Thus transforming the criterion $PV_r(B) > K$ into its compounded terminal form $TV_r(B) > TV_r(K)$ enables us immediately to appreciate that, for its valid employment, all the returns from the project should be *wholly consumed* as they occur and that the sum K should be raised entirely from current consumption. Similarly, transforming the other limiting case $PV_\rho(B) > K$, into the form $TV_\rho(B) > TV_\rho(K)$ enables us also to appreciate at once that its Pareto validity is assured if, in fact, it is applied to a case in which the benefits, as they occur, are wholly invested and reinvested in the private investment sector at prevailing yield ρ, until the terminal date T, and if the sum K raised from the private sector is also wholly invested and reinvested at yield ρ until T.

In other words, the *correct* terminal value of a project's benefit stream and the *correct* terminal value of the opportunity cost of its outlay are both functions, in the simplest possible case, of three variables, r, ρ and c, where c is the fraction of any income or of any return on investment[2] that is consumed, the remainder $(1 - c)$ being invested (unless otherwise determined) in the private sector at ρ.

---

1 This critique, incidentally, applies as well to the usual DPV methods employed by private corporations for evaluating alternative investment streams – though in so far as the returns over time are likely to be treated more uniformly, the error may be less important.

2 For there may be public projects for which all or part of any of the expected returns over the future are required to be invested in designated public enterprises. Again, the amount K may be raised wholly or in part using the sums that are available simply in consequence of the non-renewal of existing public investments.

In contrast, criterion (28.2), $PV_\rho(B) > K$, is valid only if both the initial outlay K and the stream of returns that it generates are all wholly invested and re-invested to the terminal year at ρ. And this condition is transparent once this criterion (28.2) is transformed into the more explicit form $TV_\rho(B) > TV_\rho(K)$.

By subtracting $TV(K)$ from $TV(B)$, we obtain the *net* terminal value of the project in question. Once this net terminal value is correctly calculated for a number of projects, all with an initial outlay K, the resultant ranking can be maintained whatever rate of discount is then used to discount them to the present.

3   In order to complete the critique, we need to re-examine the standard IRR criterion. Although, on the face of it, there should be an advantage in being able to calculate the IRR without reference to the prevailing interest rates or investment yields in the economy, it has fallen into disfavour among economists since, as we have seen, we can derive more than one IRR for a given investment stream.[3]

The more important reason, however, is that, even in the more usual case in which all net benefits are positive, the standard IRR calculated for an investment stream does not accord with the true average rate of return of the net benefit stream. It transpires that, as conventionally defined, the IRR suffers from the same defect as common DPV criteria; namely, that the implied reinvestment rate of the net benefits has no necessary relation to the actual rates.

Given the standard definition of the IRR as that λ for which

$$\sum_{t=1}^{T} \frac{B_t}{(1+\lambda)^t} = K$$

If we multiply through by the scalar $(1+\lambda)^t$ we obtain

$$\sum_{t=1}^{T} B_t(1+\lambda)^{T-t} = K(1+\lambda)^T$$

So explicated, the standard IRR is shown to be defined as that rate λ which, when it is used to compound each of the benefits B_t to the terminal year T, produces a terminal outlay that itself is equal to K compounded forward to year T also at λ. But this resulting λ has no necessary relation to the average rate at which the benefits B_t are being actually compounded forward to T.

Since in any given project it cannot be assumed that each of the benefits B_t is wholly invested at λ when it occurs, the standard definition is misleading. In fact, the disposal of each B_t as it occurs depends upon behavioural and institutional factors, in general on the values r, ρ and c. In order, then, to calculate the IRR as a uniquely determined average rate of growth of the initial outlay K over period T,

---

3 The reader is reminded that a necessary though not a sufficient condition for the standard IRR to have more than one value is that one or more of the net benefits be negative, a contingency not often encountered.

we must first calculate the *actual* terminal value of each of the benefits that are generated by the outlay K.

A correct calculation of the IRR, consistent with the normalized procedure being proposed, must therefore be defined as that rate of discount λ which would reduce the actual terminal value of the sum of each of the benefits, so compounded, to equality with the initial outlay K. This can be formulated as that λ for which

$$\frac{TV(B)}{(1+\lambda)^T} = K$$

It follows that if, with a given outlay K, the terminal value of the benefit stream of project X exceeds that of project Y, which in turn exceeds that of project Z – which we can write as $X > Y > Z$ – then, by our definition above, their respective IRRs λ_x, λ_y and λ_z are those for which

$$\frac{X}{(1+\lambda_x)^T} = \frac{Y}{(1+\lambda_y)^T} = \frac{Z}{(1+\lambda_z)^T} = K$$

from which it follows that $\lambda_x > \lambda_y > \lambda_z$.

However, for ranking purposes, at least, it would be pointless to calculate these normalized IRRs, as they will follow that of the terminal value of their respective benefit streams.

30   The normalized compounded terminal value criterion (I)

1   The normalized CTV procedure is designed to transform the stream of net benefits $B_1, B_2, \ldots, B_T$, arising from an initial outlay K into an equivalent stream, $0, 0, \ldots, TV(B)$, this being shorthand for the terminal value of the stream of net benefits generated by the initial outlay K. From this $TV(B)$ we are to subtract $TV(K)$, or the terminal value of the outlay K, conceived as the terminal value of the opportunity cost of investing the sum K.

What we call normalization is the requirement that, in ranking two or more projects, not only must they have the same terminal date T, but also a common initial outlay K. This requirement is in no way restrictive.

If, for example, of two mutually exclusive projects, the initial outlay required for project Y is, say 80, this 80 being less than the outlay of the 100 that is required for project X, the outlay that is to be common to both projects must be the larger, being 100 in this example. If the project Y is to be undertaken then an additional 20 of outlay must be spent. It may be possible to spend this 20 on an additional project that is a quarter the size of Y and yields benefits that are also a quarter the size of project Y. If, however, the project is not one that is divisible, the 20 to be spent can, at least, be returned to the private investment sector where, if returns are continually reinvested, will produce a terminal value of $20(1 + \rho)^T$, which must be added to the terminal value of project Y that requires an outlay of only 80. If, however, this 20 is returned to the government, it will generate a terminal value that will depend upon how the government disposes of it.

Similarly, if the life-span of project X is 20 years, and that of the alternative investment is only 16 years, the common terminal period is 20 years. The original terminal value of the benefits of the project that is reached in the sixteenth year must then be compounded forward to the twentieth year. This compounding for the additional four years must, however, follow the relevant pattern of behaviour.

To illustrate, consider first the simple case in which all the benefits, $B_1, B_2, \ldots, B_{16}$, are wholly consumed. If their terminal value in the sixteenth year amounts to, say, 250, this being the equivalent worth in the sixteenth year when all the preceding Bs are compounded to this sixteenth year at society's rate of time deference r, then the terminal value of the Bs in the twentieth year will be $250(1 + r)^4$.

The other simple case is that in which all the annual returns are directed by the political decision maker to be invested and reinvested in the private sector at rate ρ until the sixteenth year. If the resulting terminal value in the sixteenth year comes to, say, 350 – this 350 being conceived as an increase in the capital stock – the terminal value in the twentieth year is equal to $350(1 + \rho)^4$.

In a more general case in which, of the *full* returns annually paid to subscribers, fraction c is consumed, the remaining $(1 - c)$ invested at ρ, the terminal value of the benefits in the sixteenth year may be divided into two parts: [1] (a) the equivalent terminal worth in the sixteenth year of all the amounts consumed, say 220, and (b) the increase in the capital stock in the sixteenth year that arises from the amounts each year that are invested in the private sector at the average yield ρ. We suppose this increase in the capital stock to be equal to 60.

Part (a) of the terminal value in the sixteenth year, equal to 220 will become equal to $220(1 + r)^4$ in the twentieth year. As for part (b), equal to 60, of the return to this additional capital in each of the additional years, the fraction c is consumed and the remaining fraction $(1-c)$ invested. Therefore, at the end of four more years, we must add, first, the value of consumption (equal to the amounts consumed over the four years compounded forward at rate r), say this is equal to 20. Then, we must also add the further increase in the capital stock for four more years that results from the amounts invested in each of those years. We suppose this to equal 8.

Thus, using the figures we have adopted, the terminal value in the sixteenth year, equal to $220 + 60$, or 280, is extended to a terminal value in the twentieth year that is equal to $220(1 + r)^4 + 60 + 20 + 8$.

Needless to remark, similar principles must be used in extending for an additional four years the terminal value in the sixteenth year of the initial outlay K.

Finally, it should be noted, that this method of extending projects to a common terminal year where necessary is applicable also where the alternative to one or more projects is that of two (or several) successive projects that, usually, have relatively shorter lifespans: applicable also where one or more of the projects can be undertaken at a later date than the others.

2 The principle to be followed in compounding forward requires attention to the disposal of each of the benefits right through to the terminal year T. In the general case, the fraction c of the benefit in each year is consumed, the remaining fraction $(1 - c)$ being invested at ρ (unless otherwise directed). The terminal value of the amount consumed in year t being cB_t, it is compounded forward to become $cB_t(1+r)^{T-t}$ in the terminal year T. The remaining part $(1 - c)B_t$ that is invested

---

1 There can also be a general case with yet another behaviour pattern: namely, that in which each year only a part of the returns that year, say two-thirds, is paid out to subscribers, the remaining one-third being invested in the private sector at yield ρ (or else invested in some other designated public project). Of the amounts, received each year by the subscribers, fraction c is, again, consumed, the remainder being invested at yield ρ. Although the calculation required to extend the terminal value in the sixteenth year to that in the twentieth year is a bit more elaborate, no new principle is involved.

in year t is to be conceived as an addition to the capital stock. As such, it yields an annual return that is equal to $(1 - c)B_t(1 + \rho)$ in the following year and in *each* subsequent year to year T, of which annual returns, the fraction c is consumed and the remainder invested, and so on.

We may as well consider, first, the two simple cases mentioned earlier, (28.1) $PV_r(B) > K$ and (28.2) $PV_\rho(B) > K$, when each of these is transformed correctly into the CTV criterion. The first case, that in which c is equal to unity, requires that each of the benefits, being wholly consumed, is compounded to the terminal year at society's rate of time preference r. Their terminal value is therefore equal to $B_1(1 + r)^{T-1} + B_2(1 + r)^{T-2} + \ldots B_T$, while the terminal value of the initial outlay is equal to $K(1 + r)^T$.

The second simple case is that in which c is equal to zero, as a result of which each of the benefits is invested and reinvested at rate ρ. The stream of benefits given by the project will then have a terminal value equal to $B_1(1 + \rho)^{T-1} + B_2(1 + \rho)^{T-2} + \ldots B_T$, this terminal value being conceived as the increase in the capital stock that is contributed by the project in question. As for the initial outlay K, its terminal value is equal to $K(1 + \rho)^T$.

In the more general case in, which c is a positive fraction greater than zero but less than unity, we must treat the part of the benefit that is consumed differently from the part that is invested. The amount of the benefit B_t that is consumed has a terminal value of $B_t(1 + r)^{T-t}$. The terminal value of the remaining part $(1 - c)B_t$ that is invested is not so easy to calculate. Although this much is to be added to the terminal capital stock, this addition to the capital stock in year t also produces, in each of the following years until year T, an annual return equal to $(1 - c)B_t(1 + \rho)$ of which, again, fraction c is consumed each year and the remainder invested at rate, ρ. And so on.

3   The exact method of calculation will be easier to understand if we suppose that the project to be considered is one that generates a stream of benefits, $B_1, B_2, \ldots, B_T$, each annual benefit being equal to 10 million. In addition, we shall let $c = 0.8$, $r = 0.05$ and $\rho = 0.1$ and take T to equal 10.

(i) Of the B_1 of 10 million, therefore, 8 million will be consumed, the remaining 2 million being invested in the private sector at interest rate $r = 0.05$. The 8 million consumed has a terminal value, when compounded at the rate of time preference r, equal to 8 million $(1.05)^{T-t}$. As for the 2 million that is invested that year, it is far more prolific, as we shall see, for it adds that much to the private capital stock which is then a part of the terminal value.

(ii) This 2 million of additional capital yields an annual return of 200,000 beginning in the *second* year and ending in the terminal year, or tenth year. Of *each* of these nine annual returns of 200,000, 160,000 is consumed, its terminal value therefore requiring that it be compounded to the tenth year at a rate equal to 0.05. Altogether, they contribute to the terminal value a total of $160,000(1.05)^8 + 160,000(1.05)^7 + \ldots + 160,000$.

The remaining 40,000 that is invested each year, from the *second* to the tenth year, must also be added to the capital stock.

(iii) Now each one of the successive annual investments of 40,000, beginning in the second year, will itself generate an annual return of 4,000, starting the year after the investment took place, and continuing until the tenth year. (Thus, the 40,000 invested in the second year will generate a return of 4,000 in year 3, 4,000 in year 4, and so on until year 10. The 40,000 invested in the third year will also generate a return of 4,000 in the fourth year, 4,000 in the fifth year, and so on until year 10, and similarly for each of the 40,000 in subsequent years).

(iv) Of each of these annual returns of 4,000, the amount 3,200 will be consumed, the remaining 800 invested, each 800 invested giving rise in the following year to an annual return until the tenth year of 80, and so we can continue.

Thus, we may reckon up the total number of additional returns so far that have been generated by the 2 million invested from the first benefit of 10 million, as follows: (ii) 9 of 200,000 plus (iii) 8 of 4,000 plus (iv) 7 of 80, and so on to the terminal year.

Having completed all these calculations, we now recognize that the amount we have added to the capital stock and the terminal value of all amounts consumed are those that flow only from B_1 – from the 10 million generated by the project in year 1. Clearly the same calculations must be undertaken for each of the subsequent benefits. $B_2, B_3, \ldots, B_T$ that we have conveniently assumed to be also equal to 10 million. Clearly, the calculations required for each of the successive year's benefits will, as we approach closer to the terminal year, be smaller than the calculations required for the preceding year.

4 Turning to the calculation of the terminal value of the initial outlay K, the procedure is no different from that above. Thus, only in two simple cases mentioned in which the two criteria, $PV_r(B) > K$ and $PV_\rho(B) > K$ are correctly transformed into their corresponding CTV criteria, will the terminal values of K be, respectively, $K(1 + r)$ and $K(1 + \rho)^T$.

In all cases, the terminal value of K, so calculated, is conceived as the terminal value of the opportunity cost of any one of the public projects under consideration; that is the terminal value of K is calculated as what it would amount to if it were left in its current use or in some specifically designated alternative use.

5 The preliminary calculations above have been undertaken to show how the correct terminal value of the given ten-year stream of net benefits is to be determined on the simple but common assumption that, in ordinary circumstances, people generally save a proportion of their annual incomes. And since it follows that their incomes grow over time, so also does the amount being saved annually.

Wherever the actual behaviour pattern differs from this common assumption, the terminal value of any given stream of net benefits will, of course, also be different. In particular, it may be necessary to modify the simple assumption that people save a given proportion of each annual net benefit in two ways: (i) where only a proportion of the annual net benefits, say w, is paid out as income to subscribers to the project; and (ii) where, in addition, such income is subject to income tax.

In either case – often in both cases – the calculation of the terminal value will be yet more exacting. In case (ii), where each year a proportion of income received by the subscribers to the project is taxed, it is necessary to follow to the terminal year the disposal by the government of the additional revenues it receives in that year – at least if the government's annual disposal of the additional revenues takes a pattern that is different from that which would be taken if, instead, such revenues were left to be disposed of in the usual way by the subscribers to the project (since, if the patterns were the same, the terminal value would remain the same whether the annual income received by the subscribers were taxed or not).

6   Finally, a brief word about the possibility that some or all of the sum needed for the project is to be borrowed from abroad.

Clearly, the eventual repayment of the sum borrowed, say M, takes place in some future year or years. If the whole of M is repaid in the terminal year T, it will feature as a negative benefit in year T. In addition, each of the annual interest payments to the foreign country will appear as negative benefits. Consequently, there may be negative net benefits in some years.

There can, of course, be different arrangements for the payment of interest on the sum borrowed and also for the eventual repayment. But the above guidelines will suffice to determine their treatment.

31 The normalized compounded terminal value criterion (II)

1 We should not be surprised if the student seeking to master the techniques of CBA demurs at the prospect of having to subject himself to so taxing and tedious a calculation, which is apparently unavoidable if a correct investment criterion is to be employed. For it must be admitted that, allowing for the magnitudes of the annual benefits and disbenefits to be reliable, the calculation of the project's exact terminal value of its stream of net benefits $TV(B)$ and of the exact terminal value of its outlay $TV(K)$ would be a daunting task: one that requires more time and concentration than even the most sophisticated DPV criteria discussed in Chapter 28. It must, nonetheless, be recognized that familiarity with the application or the principles necessary to calculate these normalized terminal values – which, alone, can determine whether or not implementation of the project meets a potential Pareto criterion – may be said at least to serve as a template by which the conscientious economist may judge the adequacy of the DPV criterion or of proposed proxies in the various textbooks.

Familiarity with the principles needed to calculate these normalized terminal values, however, is not to be regarded simply as a means by which to judge the adequacy of the more commonly used DPV criteria, for, on reflection surely the student will realize that modern sophisticated computers are quite capable of managing such calculations: one has only to 'feed in' the relatively simple instructions for compounding forward to the terminal year the annual net benefits or disbenefits at the appropriate rates r and ρ and, where necessary, the fractions w and c.

2 What is more, the possibility of contriving some preliminary approximations to the exact terminal values deserves consideration, in so far as in some cases they may eliminate the necessity of exact calculation.

In this connection, it should be evident that – in the absence of political constraints that would require returns over future years to be directed into public projects that have, on average, a yield greater than ρ, which we take to be the actuarial annual return on private investment – the correct terminal values of the project's net benefit stream and of its initial outlay $CV(B)$ and $CV(K)$, respectively, must lie between $CV_r(B)$ and $CV_r(K)$, on the one hand, and $CV_\rho(B)$ and $CV_\rho(K)$, on the other; in other words, between the two terminal values when compounded forward to year T at rate r and their terminal values when compounded forward to year T at rate ρ.

The former, the lower limits, $CV_r(B)$ and $CV_r(K)$, are correctly used when c equals unity. The latter, the higher limits, $CV_\rho(B)$ and $CV_\rho(K)$, are correctly used when c is zero. In the unlikely case that r and ρ are not very different, then irrespective of the values of c, the terminal values $CV_r(B)$ and $CV_\rho(B)$ will not differ by much, at least for projects that have a short time span: similarly for $CV_r(K)$ and $CV_\rho(K)$. In the usual case, however, in which ρ is significantly greater than r (say, at least one percentage point greater), the difference between compounding at r and compounding at ρ will (save for very short time spans) mean that neither alone will serve as an approximation for the terminal values of a project.

3   Useful approximations, for the general case, to the correct terminal values $CV(B)$ and $CV(K)$ may be contrived from three suppositions: (i) that the investment of a sum in any year remains entirely invested until the terminal year T at the yield ρ; (ii) either that income tax is negligible or that we may ignore the government's disposal of the revenues received from taxation in the belief that it is comparable with the ways in which beneficiaries of the project would themselves have disposed of them if not taxed; and (iii) that w is close to unity. Given these somewhat heroic suppositions, and provided that parameters r and ρ and also the overall propensity to consume c are maintained over the time span of the project, the *approximation*, App. $TV(B)$, to the correct terminal value of the net benefits $TV(B)$ becomes equal to

$$\sum_{t=1}^{T} cB_t(1+r)^{T-1} + \sum_{t=1}^{T} (1-c)B_t(1+\rho)^{T-1}, \quad \text{where} 1 \geq c \geq 0$$

In view of our supposition (i), the longer the time span of the project, the less reliable the approximation; that is, the greater *proportionally* will App. $TV(B)$ be above $TV(B)$.

Turning to the *approximation*, App. $TV(K)$, to the correct terminal value of the outlay $TV(K)$, let us first formulate the more general case, one in which fraction G of outlay K ($1 \geq G \geq 0$) is raised by taxation, the remainder $(1-G)$ being raised by borrowing from the public. The App. $TV(K)$ becomes equal to

$$G[cK(1+r)^T + (1-c)K(1+\rho)^T] + [(1-G)K(1+\rho)^T]$$

Clearly, if the initial outlay K is raised entirely by taxation ($G = 1$) the App. $TV(K)$ reduces to

$$cK(1+r)^T + (1-c)K(1+\rho)^T$$

If, however, K is raised entirely by borrowing ($G = 0$), the App. $TV(K)$ is reduced to

$$K(1 + \rho)^T$$

It transpires that, although these approximations to $TV(B)$ and to $TV(K)$ are sure to exceed those of their correct terminal values irrespective of how K is raised, the *proportion* by which App. $TV(K)$ in all cases exceeds $TV(K)$ will exceed the *proportion* by which App. $TV(B)$ exceeds $TV(B)$. What this implies is that, whenever App. $TV(B)$ exceeds App. $TV(K)$, the Pareto criterion is met, indeed a fortiori met. On the other hand, where App. $TV(B)$ is less than App. $TV(K)$, one cannot be sure that the Pareto criterion is not met: it is still possible, that is, when calculating the exact terminal values, $TV(B)$ will exceed $TV(K)$.[1]

To be sure, if we chose to abide by these approximations, we may occasionally reject a project that, using exact terminal values, would indeed meet a Pareto criterion. Yet, it may be argued that this sort of error is tolerable because, if App. $TV(B)$ does exceed App. $TV(K)$, we can be sure the exact measure of the excess of $TV(B)$ over $TV(K)$ is significant, if not substantial.

4   Once we turn our attention to special cases, however, even the exact calculations of the terminal values can be much easier. Among the more popular public projects are those that are undertaken to produce a collective good only: often environmental improvements such as a reduction of pollution or effluent. The collective benefits so generated over time are therefore to be deemed wholly consumed in each successive year. Moreover, inasmuch as such benefits are in kind – no part being paid out in cash – no tax is levied on the beneficiaries. The exact terminal value of a stream of such benefits is therefore simply equal to $\Sigma_1^T B_t (1 + r)^{T-1}$. It would be too much, however to expect the terminal value of the outlay K also to be simply equal to $K(1 + r)^T$ – which it would be only if K were raised solely by reducing consumption by this amount at time zero.

Another special case in which the calculation of the terminal value is much simplified is worth mentioning, even though it is less common. This is one in which all the benefits are cash returns – all goods being produced by the project being sold on the market – which cash returns each year are then wholly invested and reinvested until the terminal year T in the private investment sector at yield ρ. Were this to be the case, the exact terminal value would be equal to $\Sigma_1^T B_t (1 + \rho)^{T-1}$. Again, corresponding to this simple calculation of the terminal value of the benefits, there can be an equally simple calculation of the terminal value of the outlay K. Were the sum K raised entirely by a loan and were the investors who subscribed to it to consume no part of the annual returns but continually reinvest returns until

---

1 Moreover, for all cases in which App. $TV(B)$ exceeds App. (K) and, which therefore do meet the Pareto criterion, the *ranking* of the projects accords with that of their respective *difference* – the difference, that is, between App. $TV(B)$ and the corresponding App. $TV(K)$.

the terminal year T, the terminal value of the outlay K would then be equal to $K(1 + \rho)^T$.

Before ending this chapter, we must acknowledge the possibility that students who become familiar with the calculation of terminal values may wish to face the problem of selecting from a number of technically feasible projects that meet one or more given requirements, but subject to a stated budget. A procedure for the efficient selection of projects that meet the budget constraint is presented in Appendix 12.

32 The Pareto criterion and generational time

1 The Pareto criterion on which a CBA is raised has regard also to the economist's basic maxim that the value to be attributed to a good or bad at any point in time is that value which is placed on it by the persons themselves at that point in time. Its application requires, in particular, that, if a person values a sum, say $400, expected to be received with equal certainty ten years from now as exactly equivalent in welfare to $60 received this year, the economist accepts this trade-off as part of his 'objective' data.

If, however, gainers or losers in the projects being ranked are expected not to be alive at the common terminal date of the projects or at the common commencement date, it is easily shown that a positive figure calculated by reducing all gains and losses to a single date – for instance, to a terminal value as proposed or the currently more popular present value – does *not* in fact meet the Pareto criterion.

Although not necessary for its demonstration, it will simplify the exposition if, for the time being, we conceive of a public project for which the finance is raised wholly by reducing current consumption. Further simplification is gained by assuming also the existence of institutions so accommodating as to produce a single rate of discount that is the rate of time preference common to all people affected by the project, this rate being exactly equal to the current yield on all investment.

With these highly convenient assumptions, it would follow in the usual way – that is, with the implicit proviso *that all persons affected are expected to remain alive over the investment period* – that the benefit–cost *ratio* would remain constant no matter what point of time was adopted in discounting and/or compounding gains and losses. Inasmuch as a benefit–cost ratio greater than unity entails an excess of benefits over costs, it also meets a Pareto criterion.

Thus, the problem addressed in this chapter is that which arises when the italicized proviso above is *not* met; that is, when gainers and losers come into being at some point of time later than the commencement of the project or else expire before its terminal date. To illustrate, suppose a benefit of $1,000 is to be received by person X in year 100. The common rate of discount r, which also corresponds to X's rate of time preference, is such, we shall suppose, as to discount this $1,000 to the sum $2 in year zero. But even though this r remains constant over his own lifetime, if person X is born in year 60, he cannot properly be said to be indifferent as between receiving $1,000 in year 100 and receiving $2 in year zero when he is in fact not alive in year zero, this being 60 years before he was born.

2   This difficulty has been circumvented up to now by assuming (implicitly) that each person affected by the project remains alive during the entire investment period, which assumption is incidentally too strict, as we shall see later. A popular alternative that simplifies matters wonderfully is to adopt a particular 'social' rate of discount, one the economist is to accept as a political datum and one to be used to cover any number of years, whether or not more than one generation is involved. Yet, as indicated earlier, the implications of introducing politically determined valuations or parameters into what are putatively economic calculations are unacceptable. Such a device entails a rejection of the economist's basic maxim (that only the person himself is to determine the valuation of the effect on him of the good or bad) and therefore also of an economic or Pareto criterion. And in so far as the political authority in question is requiring the economist to come up with a strictly economic calculation, the economist's surrender to such a requirement not only prevents the economist from discharging his responsibility, but involves him in deception.

3   Let us first highlight the inter-generational problem by a simple three-person model, one that may also be interpreted as a three-generation model.

In Figure 32.1, chronological time is measured as t along the horizontal axis, and the logarithm of the net benefit for persons X and Y, and of the net loss for person Z, is measured as B along the vertical axis. The three sloping lines are to be conceived as 'time-indifference' curves for the three persons who alone are affected by a particular project, it being assumed that each person is indifferent between any two points. Although not essential to the analysis, it simplifies further to assume a common rate of time preference for the three persons r, say one that

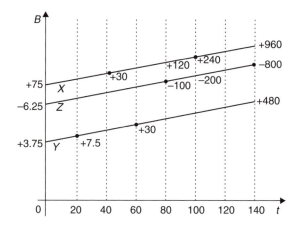

Figure 32.1

indicates indifference between having $1 at any time t and having $2 twenty years later. All three indifference lines therefore slope upward from left to right at the same angle.

Consider first case (i), in which person Z, who lives from year 80 to year 140, is shown to be indifferent between losing consumption equal to $100 in year 80 and losing consumption equal to $200 in year 100. Person X, who lives from year 40 to year 100, is indifferent between consuming $120 in year 80 and consuming $240 in year 100. As there is an overlap of 20 years between the lifetimes of Z and X, extending from year 80 to year 100, a Pareto comparison can be made without violating the basic maxim. Whether year 80 is chosen or year 100 or any year between 80 and 100, the ratio of X's gain to Z's loss – 6/5 – remains valid. If, for instance, the year chosen is year 80, Z actually loses $100 of consumption in that year, whereas X, who actually gained $30 of consumption in year 40, would agree to accept, instead, $120 in year 80. Thus, whether or not X actually postpones consumption, his gain of $30 in year 40 is equivalent to a gain of 120 in year 80. Consequently, a potential Pareto improvement is realized in year 80, since X's gain of 120 in that year exceeds the loss of $100 by Z.[1]

The same exercise may be carried out for persons Y and X inasmuch as, between years 40 and 60, their lifetimes overlap. Y is indifferent between consumption of 7.5 in year 20 and 15 in year 40, whereas X actually receives 30 in year 40. In this case, both persons gain. But if, for argument's sake, we change Y's gain of 7.5 in year 20 into a loss of 7.5, equivalent to a loss of 15 in year 40, since it is then exceeded by X's actual gain of 30 in year 40, a potential Pareto improvement again exists.

Now consider case (ii) in which persons Y and Z alone comprise the community affected by the project. Since there is no point of time common to the two of them, a direct comparison between their actual or equivalent gains or losses is not possible. Y's gain of 7.5 in year 20 can be compounded forward as far as year 60 when he is still alive, but Z's loss of 100 is suffered in year 80, at the start of his life. Were it possible meaningfully to compound Y's gain forward beyond year 60 or to discount Z's loss backward from year 80, we should be able to talk of the project producing a potential Pareto loss for the $Y–Z$ community – or, if the signs were reversed, a potential Pareto gain. But it is not possible, and therefore a valid comparison of gains and losses cannot be made for any single year.

For example, Y cannot be indifferent as between receiving 7.5 in year 20 and receiving 60 in year 80, as he will not be alive in year 80. Nor can a valid comparison be made for year 60, as Z cannot be indifferent between losing 100 in year 80 and losing 50 in year 60, 20 years before he is born. Inasmuch as the basic maxim cannot be met in a case where no common point of time is shared by Y and Z, a Pareto comparison of their gains and losses is not possible.

---

1 Clearly, discounting these two sums in year 80 to present values, or else compounding them to terminal values, simply multiplies each sum by the same scalar, leaving the benefit–loss ratio unchanged at 6/5.

It should be evident that we can multiply the number of persons and also reduce the time overlap between successive persons indefinitely. But once a time gap between any two persons exists, their comparison via compounding or discounting through time must be ruled out as an invalid procedure.

We conclude then that, in the absence of some dependable mechanism enabling us to transform the project's original net benefit stream into some new pattern over generational time, it is not possible to compare gains and losses on the Pareto criterion. In particular, where a time gap exists between two or more persons affected by the project in question, a potential Pareto improvement cannot be said to be met by a cost–benefit calculation that results in a positive discounted present (or compounded terminal) net benefit.

4   Among other facile but inoperative proposals to somehow circumvent the problem, in addition to the adoption of a politically determined social rate of discount, is that of recourse to the oft-touted economist's Nirvana, 'a well-defined social welfare function'. However we imagine this abstraction to be created, it is even more far-fetched than the idea of a social rate of discount.[2]

It has also been proposed that projects that show modest benefits in the first years to be succeeded by heavy losses falling on future generations could be made acceptable if a state agency were established charged with appropriating a portion of the gains accruing in the early years, investing it at market rates of return. By the time the heavy losses occurred, the amount invested would have compounded to a sum that would fully compensate for the losses.[3] But until such an agency is indeed established, the economist cannot interpret the results of his CBA as if in fact it exists.

5   The question then naturally arises: when, over a period that covers two or more generations, the terminal years show an excess of benefits over costs which, as argued, cannot be said to result in a Pareto improvement, just what criterion can it be said to meet?

In fact, the answer is quite simple. Indeed, the answer is deducible from the proposal considered above, that a state agency be established to act in such ways as

2 This "well-defined social welfare function" may be visualized perhaps as emerging from a sort of conclave representatives of present and future generations who, between them, will debate and eventually reach agreement about what is an equitable inter-generational distribution of real income and, possibly, other momentous issues. Yet, whatever that distribution of income agreed upon, even if it could somehow be brought about, it does not ensure that a positive DPV or CTV can be interpreted as realizing a potential Pareto improvement.

3 The reverse of a hypothetical investment stream – one that imposes costs on current generations from which future generations will reap great benefits – would seem to be more difficult for our state agency to handle. But although one cannot appropriate a portion of the gains of future generations so as to compensate losers in the present, as much may be achieved by compensating present generation for their losses by 'eating' into the existing stock of capital. In practice, this would translate into the state's taking action to increase current consumption through a reduction in income tax, the fall in revenue being met by a fall in public investment (or else by an issue of bonds that would 'crowd out' current commercial investment).

to ensure that, in implementing projects that show a positive net terminal benefit, no generation suffers a net loss. With such an investment project, it would be possible to make sure that each generation then enjoyed a potential Pareto improvement.

Since such an agency does not, in fact, exist, and a potential Pareto improvement in any period over the entire lifespan of the project could be assured only if such an agency did exist, the required potential Pareto improvement is hypothetical only – contingent, that is, on the actual establishment of the agency. In other words, the standard potential Pareto improvement, which rationalizes the economist's acceptance of projects that show an excess of net benefits, must itself be regarded as potential only, so long as such an agency itself remains a potential, and not an actual, institution.

It must be concluded, therefore, that the excess net benefit criterion, when realized for a long-lived project does not in fact meet the standard economist's test of a potential Pareto improvement: the criterion confers no more than a *potential* Pareto improvement.

On reflection, moreover, it will transpire that a time span long enough to cover two or more generations is not necessary for interpreting a positive excess net benefit as no more than a *potential* Pareto improvement, for even for projects with short lifespans, say of five years or less, it will almost be impossible to avoid some generational overlap. In fact, it is enough for a person who contributes to the cost of the project to expire before receiving the later benefits to warrant regarding the net excess benefit criterion as fulfilling only a *potential* improvement.

6   It cannot be denied that a *potential* Pareto improvement is less compelling a sanction in warranting the economist's excess net benefit criterion than is the more generally accepted potential Pareto improvement. Certainly, for those who are apt to regard CBA, or allocative economics in general, as a normative study, at least in the sense that the economist's criterion would command a consensus or near-consensus, would be disconcerted to discover that the criterion involved no more than a *potential* improvement.

For those economists like ourselves, however, who regard CBA as an exercise in positive economics, there need be no heart searching. For the decision to sanction a proposed project is not the economist's responsibility. It is the responsibility of the political decision maker – in a liberal democracy, that of the community's representatives. Yet, in order for decisions to be taken in full awareness of the economic implications of cost–benefit calculations, the economist has a duty to explain its limitations. He is to emphasize in particular that the values he attributes to the goods and bads produced by the project are all derived, ultimately, from the subjective valuations of the persons affected by the project: also that the excess of net benefits over costs that is calculated must be interpreted not so much as a material improvement for the community as a whole, nor even as a potential improvement over the given time span, but as a *potential* improvement – with no account being taken of the distribution of gains or losses over time, whether progressive or regressive on balance.

Part VI
Notes on particular goods

33 The value of time saved

1 Transport projects are designed chiefly either to accommodate an increasing number of travellers or to reduce journey time. Less frequently, they are designed to increase comfort or convenience of travel.

It is hardly necessary to remark that, if a project does save journey time, the required compensating variation is equal to the largest sum a person is willing to pay in order to save that amount of time. And, indeed, there have been a few interesting but unsophisticated attempts to estimate this willingness-to-pay figure for travel time saved for different income groups. Although further refinements would take account of the element of comfort and reliability, it will be argued in this chapter that, notwithstanding frequent recourse in CBA to arbitrary calculations based on hourly earnings, the value of time saved (or spent) necessarily varies with the context in which time is saved (or spent).

2 It is possible also to put a value on the time saved from improvements in industrial technology. If, for example, the introduction of a new method of producing good x turns out to increase productivity by 50 per cent, which enables a given output to be produced in one-third less than the previous time, the valuation of the time that is saved will depend on the output of the good x that is subsequently produced.

Following the above, if, to take one extreme, the workforce employed in producing x is constrained to work the same number of hours for the same pay, output will rise by 50 per cent, and the supply curve of x will fall by one-third. In a competitive economy, the resulting increase in consumer surplus – which will then be the chief measure of social gain – is likely to be less than it would be if the output of x that was produced were such that price is equal to marginal cost.

At the other extreme, the whole of the gain from increased productivity is appropriated by the workers employed in producing x by a rise of 50 per cent in their wages. In consequence, the supply curve of x remains unchanged and (ignoring any additional demand for x resulting from the increased income of the x workers, which is apt to be negligible) also the demand curve for x.

Although, more generally, the outcome will be somewhere between these two extremes, we need not trouble to elaborate further because, in CBA, the need to value time saved, when it arises, is almost invariably in connection with improvements in transport or travel, whether by land, sea or air.

3   In the attempts to measure the value of time saved, at least under the assumption that there are no changes in comfort, etc., a once-common method was to value an hour saved by a given person as equal to the social value of his (marginal) product.[1] Thus, if an improvement in public transport had no other effect than that of enabling a man to save exactly one hour from his journey to work each day, this method of valuing time saved would be valid only if (i) our man would accept an offer, if it were made, of working an additional hour at the existing rate of pay, and (ii) the social marginal product of the additional hour worked were a valid measure of the additional social benefit.

While (i) is far from certain, (ii) is certainly not true. For one thing, a part (generally the greater part) of the measured value of the additional hour's output will be some minimal compensation to our man for the additional work undertaken – which, by definition, does not increase his welfare. This method of valuing time saved cannot therefore be accepted as a proxy for the true value of time saved, namely, the amount a man is willing to pay for the time saved, ignoring any externalities.

4   Although it is indeed correct to value the amount of time saved by the most a person is willing to pay for it, which will therefore vary widely between one person and another, we are not to suppose that the saving of time is always a good thing. The tacit assumption that travelling is but an unavoidable disutility, simply a means to reach a destination, is not generally valid.

There can be situations when reducing time is far from being a good thing. Indeed, when a person is willing to pay for additional time, whether in travelling or in some other activity – a prime example being that of the plea of the lover in the once-popular song, 'Give me five minutes more, only five minutes more . . . in your arms'. Apart from the joys of a prolonged embrace, however, there can be many familiar instances when the saving of time is a negative benefit or, put more positively, the availability of *more* time is a positive benefit.

If a person is on a train bound for a seaside holiday, some delay at a small railway station that allows him to detrain, to stretch his legs and enjoy the views, might be much welcomed. A summer holiday along the coast of the Costa del Sol that is unexpectedly prolonged for a couple of days is a delay that is more likely to be thought of as a bit of good luck than otherwise. Again, a representative of a firm who is on a business trip may not mind a delay in congenial surroundings, as it is in the firm's time anyway. He may well enjoy travelling much more than

---

1 For a good review of the literature on the value of travel time savings in project evaluation, see Abelson (2003).

spending time in the office and will always prefer say, crossing the Atlantic by ship rather than by plane. So far as he is concerned, any shortening of his travel time is regarded as a loss.[2]

5   Turning to those cases which the cost–benefit economist more frequently addresses, those in which any time saved is unambiguously a good, the valuation of time saved will obviously vary according to the circumstances. A young man desperate to be on time for his first date would be willing to pay a large sum to avoid delay if his car were stuck in a traffic jam.

In more ordinary circumstances, a reduction by, say, a half hour of his daily commuting time would be valued by a person according to the anticipated use to which he would put the spare half hour. He might use some of the extra time available at the gym or jogging. He might stay longer at home in the mornings, extending his breakfast time, reading the newspaper or watching television. The satisfaction he obtains from the way he chooses to spend the additional half hour will, of course, determine the most he is willing to pay for it. (It is not impossible, however, that he preferred the original journey if he travelled by train, there being just about enough time to relax, read the newspaper and perhaps finish the crossword puzzle).[3]

A more interesting case would be that in which there are enough people, each willing to pay an additional $3,000 several times a year to fly the Atlantic in no more than an hour if the opportunity arose. If this were known, it might prove worthwhile to construct and operate such an aero-engineering phenomenon. Were it to be so, were such flights to take place, we should be able to make a rough calculation of the worth (on average) of the saving of five hours of flying time to those who choose regularly to fly on the new supersupersonic plane.

6   Finally, in considering any reduction in an existing delay, the extent of the delay is important. There is obviously some *minimum sensible* level below which any delay has no perceptible value for society. An investment that would save about ten seconds' time on a daily journey is not worth having, even if many millions of people 'benefit' from it. No one would really care much. Indeed, in a journey that

---

2 To the corporation who employs him, however, the saving in time might be a gain, but only if the time saved were large enough to enable his presence in the office to add something to profits. Obviously, a few hours' saving would be useless in this connection, and it is uncertain whether even a few days would make a difference. Furthermore, even though a saving of the executive's time can be counted on to increase the corporation's profit somewhat, the economist engaged in *social* CBA does not necessarily equate the increased profit with increased social benefit. The increase in profit may well be at the expense of the profits of competitors. Only if the saving in the executive's time resulted in some additional value of output to the economy as a whole (*net* of external effects) would it rate as a social benefit. In contrast, the owner of a small business, say a retail shop, who can travel only by closing his shop, or by suffering a reduction in sales, would benefit by the saving of a few daylight hours of travelling.

3 One of our colleagues enjoys reading journal papers by deliberately choosing public transportation over private cars!

currently takes, say, six hours, a ten-minute saving of time is hardly likely to have a perceptible effect on people's welfare, and there would be a case for ignoring it, irrespective of the number of people involved. In general, it is the proportion of time saved that counts as much as the absolute amount of time saved.[4]

4 As stated earlier, there are other fairly obvious factors such as comfort to be considered also. Many people will prefer a journey during which they can sit and read quietly to a shorter journey during which they can do neither, or to a shorter journey during which they have to make one or more changes. They may also prefer a means of transport *A* which arrives punctually to a means of transport *B* which, although it *averages less on* the journey, sometimes takes longer than the *A* transport. Greater frequency of public transport or a more convenient timetable may be rated more highly than some perceptible saving in existing journey time. Although it appeared some time ago, an excellent article by Tipping (1968) discusses such factors in more detail. For a study that relates the value of automobile travel time with implications, and for congestion and public policy, see Small *et al.* (2003). Here, the authors use a variant of stated preference models to estimate the value that commuters are willing to pay to save travel time.

34 Measuring the benefits of recreational areas (I)

1 Increases in population, in income per capita, in leisure opportunities, in health consciousness and improvement in transport infrastructure have, to a large extent, accounted for much of the growth of recreational activities. This, in turn, has led to the increasing importance given to issues of public planning and managing of land and water resources.

2 In most discussions on the value of facilities for recreation, there is some mention of 'non-economic' considerations. Recreational activity may be seen, for instance, as promoting creativity or individual freedom, or as encouraging democratic participation or inculcating a healthy outlook. Whether such values or attitudes can, or should, be brought into the calculus is an open question. There is certainly a repugnance at the idea of attempting to bring humane and perhaps transcendental considerations 'into relation with the measuring rod of money', and though we are in sympathy with it, we are uncertain just where the line should be drawn. For that reason, we shall steer away from this controversy, at least until the close of the following chapter, and confine ourselves to the concepts of the direct benefits that the economist should certainly attempt to measure.

3 Let us restrict the analysis to parks, particularly large national parks, as an interesting exercise in the application of cost–benefit principles. Clearly the economic justification for introducing a park of any size whatever is that its total social benefits, will exceed its total opportunity costs. As for the *optimal* size of the park under consideration, it is required in addition that the marginal social benefit be equal to the marginal cost.

4 Now consider in more detail the long-run determination of the *size* of a park within some given location. The information we should need from each potential visitor to the park is as follows: for any x acres of a park in a given location, what is the incremental value he places on the number of separate trips per annum? To illustrate, for a specific kind of park of one acre, the value the ith person places on each of a number of successive trips per annum can be plotted in Figure 34.1 As he is not constrained to take more trips to the park each year than he chooses, we

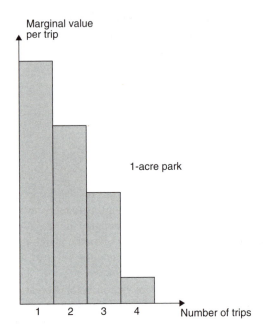

Figure 34.1

shall count only trips with positive values. The figure reveals that he will choose to make four separate trips each year, the fifth trip having a zero or negative value for her. The total area of these four rectangles represents the maximum sum he is willing to pay per annum for this specific kind of park of one acre.

For a park in the same location of two acres, his marginal valuation of successive trips will be somewhat larger. In consequence, he would choose to make more trips as depicted in Figure 34.2; in our example, six trips per annum.

We could then repeat the exercise for parks of three, four, five acres and so on to some maximum acreage possible.

For the *i*th individual visitor, we now plot the *differences* in, or increments to, his *total* valuation for successively larger parks as in Figure 34.3. The total valuation of a park with only one acre is given by the area of that first rectangle in Figure 34.3 which area is, of course, equal to the total area of the four trips he would choose to make each year to a one-acre park, as already shown in Figure 34.1. The size of the second rectangle in Figure 34.3 is equal to the difference between the total area of Figure 34.2 and that of Figure 34.1, this difference being the additional amount of money he would pay for a park that is of two acres – one acre larger than the original park. Clearly, the size of the third rectangle in our Figure 34.3 must be equal to the additional money the individual is willing to pay for a park of three acres, and so on until the increment he is willing to pay

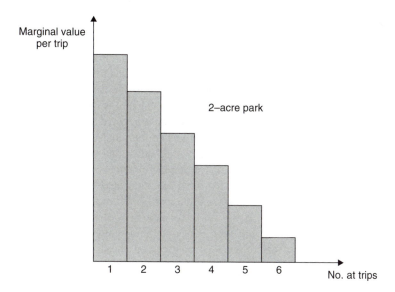

Figure 34.2

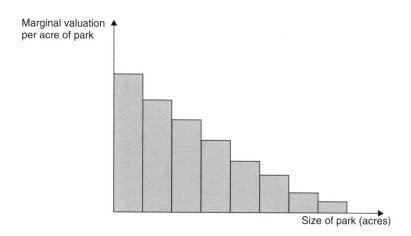

Figure 34.3

for the park of an additional acre is shown to be just a little above zero when the eight-acre park is contemplated.

It should be evident that these successive increments of value for successive one-acre increments of parkland (assumed to be declining) would become more like a smoothly declining marginal valuation curve as the increments became smaller.

If, for convenience, we assume continuity in the construction of this individual marginal valuation curve, and also for marginal valuation curves of all prospective visitors, they must now be added together to construct a marginal valuation curve for all the prospective visitors taken together. As a park is a collective good inasmuch as, in the absence of congestion costs, the costs of creating and maintaining the park are not attributable to any one person (the benefits being simultaneously enjoyed by all the visitors) their marginal valuation curves are to be aggregated vertically, whereby, we end up with a *collective* marginal valuation curve with respect to the size of the park, each increment of valuation being equal to the sum of the valuations of all the individuals for that increment.

The intersection of this collective marginal valuation curve with that of the long-run marginal cost of extending the size of the park determines the optimal size of the park to be built.

Formally speaking, then, the necessary (marginal) conditions to be met for determining the optimal size of the park are given by

$$\sum_i^n V_i \geq k$$

where V_i is the ith person's marginal valuation with respect to park size, and k is the long-run marginal cost. (Since the park is an optional collective good, all the V_i are positive.[1])

The necessary total condition that has to be met is that $\sum_i^n V_i \geq K$, where V_i is the total valuation of the chosen park by the ith person, and K is equal to the total long-period opportunity cost of the park.[2]

5   Two issues must now be faced: the implications of the *ceteris paribus* clause relevant to the problem, and the treatment of costs and benefits over time.

The calculation of the benefits by the above method is designed for the introduction of an additional park and for the determination of its size, given the existing spread of population, the existing resource endowments and the

1 For a park of x acres, $V_i = \delta V_i / \delta x$ and $k = \delta K / \delta x$, where K is the total cost.
2 The reader might think that, if such information were readily available, he could perhaps use linear programming methods to determine the number, size, location and other specific features of parks serving the community. But inasmuch as the parks are substitutes, the value people attach to any one of them depends, *inter alia*, on the existing number of parks, their size, location, etc. The objective function to be maximized cannot therefore be calculated. In order to devise some optimal system of parks, we should have to use a sequential procedure; finding, say, the highest discounted benefit–cost ratio for the location of some minimal size park, followed by the next highest benefit–cost ratio for some minimal additional park area, either attached to the first or located elsewhere – and so on down to a point where the budget is exhausted, or where the benefit–cost ratio of the marginal park acreage is no higher than that of investment projects generally.

existing product and factor prices, in particular the existing number of parks and recreational facilities provided either free or at some set of prices. Clearly, if there are already a number of such parks available in the community, the *apparent* aggregate benefit of all these parks, if obtained simply by aggregating the areas under the marginal benefit curves of the community obtained on the above principle, will overstate the *true* social benefit – the difference between the apparent and the true benefit being larger the closer can the parks be regarded as substitutes for one another. A correct method of calculating the aggregate social benefit of a number of parks is that outlined in Chapter 5. In principle, the method would require that the parks be introduced in hypothetical sequence: to the total benefit of introducing only a single park in the community, there is then added the total benefit of introducing a second park on the assumption that the first park is, indeed, already in existence, and so on. A correct calculation of the total social benefit is, of course, important whenever the economist is concerned with the total contribution to society's welfare of an existing number or a proposed number of parks.

6   If the calculations of the economist do indeed reveal that using the land in question to create a national park confers excess benefits over cost – valued either in the present or the terminal year – he may yet have to reckon with a political requirement; one that the magnitude of this excess benefit be greater than, or as great as, that which would be conferred by any one of several alternative specified uses of the land. In the calculation of the excess benefit figure, however, and whether the land in question is to be used for the creation of a national park or for any other politically sanctioned purpose, the initial outlay has to be equal to or include the value of the land in its current use which, in a competitive economy, has a market priced equal to the capitalized value of the expected future returns. Thus, the initial outlay includes this opportunity cost of using the land.

Subsequent outlays – chiefly the variable costs over time of maintaining the park and its facilities so as to cope with the expected number of visitors – are, as indicated earlier, effectively the opportunity costs of the factors that are employed for this purpose.[3]

Turning, to the calculation of the terminal (or present) value of the net benefit stream, since the annual benefits enjoyed by the visitors are, so to speak, in kind – conceived as being consumed as they occur – they may be compounded forward to the terminal year (or discounted to the present) using society's rate of time preference r.

7   Finally, we remind the reader that an excess of benefits over cost – whether calculated as a terminal value or a present value – may be interpreted as conferring

3 Should the number of visitors prove to be greater than the number anticipated, and congestion costs are incurred, we conclude that we have underestimated the number of visitors and, therefore, also the excess benefit.

on the community a potential Pareto improvement only if all who are affected by the project remain alive over the period. If, as is likely, generations overlap during the life of the project, the inter-generational difficulty broached earlier has to be faced. The excess benefit over cost that is calculated must then be understood as conferring only a *potential* potential Pareto improvement.

35 Measuring the benefits of recreational areas (II)

1 Although we are primarily concerned in this volume with the validity of the concepts and techniques used in CBA, and with particular attention to what exactly it is that we should be seeking to measure, we cannot in this instance resist some brief discussion and comments on the ingenious attempt made as far back as 1959 by Marion Clawson to derive a demand curve for recreational activity, in particular for national parks, under a number of simplifying assumptions.[1]

The Clawson concept is that of an already existing park of given acreage and facilities, so the question of determining the optimal size of the park does not arise in his paper. In principle, and considering only direct benefits for the present, one could discover for each person the maximum sum he would be willing to pay (over and above the costs of the journey) for the privilege of one trip a year to this particular park, for two trips a year and so on, until he would pay nothing for an additional annual trip. The aggregate over all persons of such maximum sums constitutes a measure of the total direct social benefit per annum.

The first relationship estimated by Clawson could be looked at as a sort of gravity model, inasmuch as the traffic from any particular area to the park is inversely related to the distance and directly to the population of the area. From areas of varying distance to Yosemite National Park (the park example he used), Clawson estimated the total dollar cost per one-day visit in the year 1953 on the basis of time and mileage, using a number of assumptions of varying degrees of plausibility, such as four persons per car travelling 400 miles a day and, more restrictive, that the main purpose of the journey was to visit Yosemite and there being then no entrance charge to the park.

2 The elements of his method can be brought quickly into focus by inventing figures for only three hypothetical areas A, B and C, situated at varying distances from Yosemite, rather than by introducing his more elaborate estimates. The hypothetical data required are given in Table 35.1.

1 Also see the seminal work on recreational valuation and parks by Clawson and Knetsch (1966). More recent work on comparing benefits and costs in recreation economic decision can be found in Walsh (1986) and Loomis and Walsh (1997).

Table 35.1

Area	Population	Distance from Yosemite	Number of visits to Yosemite as a percent of population[a]	Journey cost per visit[b]
A	10,000	100 miles	50%	$20
B	20,000	300 miles	15%	$40
C	30,000	800 miles	5%	$100

Note

a There is, of course, nothing to prevent the number of visits per annum exceeding 100% of that area's population, though in fact, this was not the case caused by Clawson.

b If it can be assumed that expenditure on food etc., once in the park is little different from what it is at home, we could add together for the visitors coming from any one area, say the sea area, two-day, three-day, and n-day stays in the park along with the one-day stay stays there. Since the journey costs are the same for the marginal n-day visitors, the total benefit enjoyed by this n-day visitor can also be taken to be just equal to the total travelling costs. If these assumptions are implausible, it would be necessary to separate the demand curves for one-day, two-day, and up to n-day visitors.

The corresponding figures of the last two columns enable us to plot three points, *A*, *B* and *C*, in Figure 35.1.

If we now make the strong assumption that the population of each of these areas is a perfect sample with respect to all relevant variables of the population of all three areas taken together, a curve fitted through points *A*, *B* and *C*, can be interpreted as a relation between the proportion of the total population visiting Yosemite and the cost per visit. Thus, if, as stated, 50 per cent of the population of area *A* is willing to make the trip when the cost is $20, we may infer that this sum is the *least* any person from area *A* is willing to pay for the trip – the marginal trip, that is, is worth just $20, and the intramarginal trips are worth more. This means

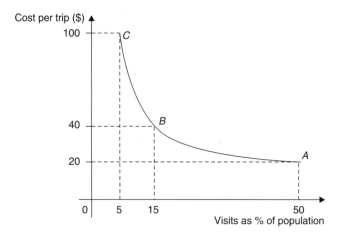

Figure 35.1

that a sort of marginal valuation curve passes through point A and – inasmuch as the population samples of areas B and C are identical with that of A – it also passes through points B and C.[2]

3   Having made the assumption that the inhabitants of A, B and C may be regarded as identical with respect to the value they place on Yosemite National Park, the percentages along the horizontal axis of Figure 35.1 can be translated into actual numbers of visits from a total population of 60,000, this being the combined populations of areas A, B and C. Corresponding to the cost per visit of \$20, \$40 and \$100 along the vertical axis of the figure, the annual numbers of visits are 30,000, 9,000 and 3,000, respectively.[3]

This resulting curve, referred to by Clawson as a demand curve, can properly be interpreted as a willingness-to-pay or marginal valuation curve. Thus, if we imagined that all the 60,000 inhabitants lived so close to Yosemite that the cost of the trip itself is virtually zero, the dollar cost per trip measured along the vertical axis of the figure can be translated into the price charged for entry into the park; the lower the price, the greater the number of annual visits to the park.

On the one hand, a monopolist contemplating this demand curve would, of course, set a price or entrance fee that would maximize his net revenue, as a result of which the number of visits would be fewer than the optimal number. On the other hand, although a perfectly discriminating monopolist would vary the entrance fee so as to attract the optimal number of visits, he would, by definition, appropriate to himself the whole of the consumer surplus that would otherwise be enjoyed by the visitors.

The effect of congestion or crowding at recreational sites may have a significant negative impact on the demand for park recreation. Congestion can be estimated directly by eliciting users' willingness to pay for its reduction.

4   In predicting demand over the future, information about population growth, per capita 'real' income growth and income distribution over time would be required for all types of investment yielding a stream of future benefits. What is perhaps of particular relevance to the demand for recreation, and is brought out in some of the charts drawn by Clawson and Knetsch (1966), is the relation between the reduction in the working week, and the improvement in roads and travel conditions generally, on the one hand, and the demand for recreation facilities, on the other.

2 If it were assumed, instead, that some benefit arises from the journey itself, the curve passing through points A, B and C in Figure 35.1 would be closer to the horizontal axis, for the 'true' cost of the journey requires that any incidental benefits are to be subtracted from the calculated time and resource costs of the journey.

3 It may be remarked that the curve in Figure 35.1 bears resemblance to a rectangular hyperbole. This just happens to be the curve that emerges from our postulated data, however, and is unlikely to be the case in any empirically constructed demand curve for recreational areas.

Other factors that bear emphasis are the external diseconomies or adverse spillover effects resulting from a rising population and its agglomeration about urban centres and, consequently, the increase in congestion, noise, air pollution and the resulting stress and frustration that are likely, over time, to increase the demand for national parks or wilderness areas. Even if there are as yet no dependable estimates of such trends, one may be disposed to make generous allowance for them. Thus, unless there is a radical reversal of current trends in population, traffic and industrialization, the world inhabited by our grandchildren will be more crowded and built-up than the world today. The average person at some time in the future is then sure to be willing to pay more for recreation facilities, for natural beauty and wilderness areas, than is the average person today with the same 'real' income. In other words, if the trends associated with sustained economic growth persist into the future, the terms of trade between manufactured goods and natural goods will tend to move increasingly in favour of the latter.

5   Two other factors should be entered into the benefits of such reserved areas of natural beauty which, though they appear related, are in fact quite distinct. First, there is the 'option demand' arising from a willingness to pay by all those people who do not anticipate making specific use in the foreseeable future of the particular area, notwithstanding which they are aware of the possibility that their customary sources of recreation might be reduced or withdrawn. They therefore have an interest in supporting the preservation of the area. For instance, they may, at some future date, have to move to another area of the country and, as a form of insurance, they would be willing to make some contribution to a number of reserved areas that they cannot use today but may be able make use of later.[4]

Second, there is a 'non-participant' (or 'disinterested') demand (sometimes called "existence" demand) arising from the willingness to pay by all those people who are concerned simply that such goods be available to the nation or to humanity at large. They may not be concerned in the least with insuring themselves against future contingencies, and they may well believe that they will never have occasion to enjoy the good in question, but it gives them satisfaction to know it exists. There are, for instance, a large number of people who do indeed care that wilderness areas be left on Earth, that Venice should not sink beneath the waters, that whales and other species should be preserved, and yet will readily admit that they will never visit a wilderness area or travel through Venice or behold a whale. Their welfare would be reduced if they were to know that such things had disappeared from the Earth.

Such non-participant demand might indeed be thought of as translating into money values, at least, some of those 'non-economic' considerations referred to at the beginning of the preceding chapter. If people's feelings about what is 'right

---

4 A more common example of an optional demand for some facility is that of the willingness of a veteran motorist to pay something toward the upkeep of a bus or rail service that he would not normally make use of but to which he may have recourse if his car should break down.

and proper' are sufficiently strong to induce them to contribute something in order to have their aspirations realized, there is no good reason for excluding them in principle from a cost–benefit calculation – always provided that the ends sought are not such as to be precluded by an ethical consensus.

6 Finally, we should remind ourselves that willingness-to-pay used as a measure of the valuation of a benefit is the appropriate CV^{12} measure for the introduction of a good. If, however, the situation is one where some public good is already in existence and the issue is to decide whether it should be demolished in order, say, to erect an industrial estate, the CV^{12} measure of the loss endured is the minimum sum necessary to compensate people for the loss of the park. And this loss will have to include that suffered by those people who, although they do not use the park or even expect to use it, yet derive satisfaction from the knowledge that it exists.

As indicated earlier, the use of the CV^{12} measure in cases of environmental destruction – which measure, in effect, confers property rights, or rather amenity rights, on the beneficiaries of recreational areas – will favour preservation of the environment.

36 The value of life

1   The question to be faced by economists interested in CBA is how to calculate the loss or gain that arises from changes in the incidence of death or disablement during the construction or operation of a project.

Since the analysis of saving life is symmetrical with that of losing it, we may concentrate initially on the loss of life, bearing in mind also that the analysis applies equally to loss of limb or health, to disablement or disease.

Consistency with the basic axiom of mainstream economics, that the only acceptable valuation of a good or bad is that placed on it by the individual affected, requires that the loss of a person's life has also to be determined by reference only to his own valuation,[1] more precisely by his compensating variation. Choosing the CV^{12} measure, the value of life to person A is the minimal sum he is prepared to accept for its surrender.[2] In ordinary circumstance, his value would be infinite: no sum would be large enough to persuade a person to part with his life. So valued, it might seem that no project, no matter how worthy, could be undertaken on the Pareto criterion if, during its construction and operation over time, one person at least can be expected to meet with a fatal accident.

This would be true, however, if a specific person A were known in advance as the person destined to expire, which is never the case in fact. All that can be known in this connection is that a number of persons engaged in a project can be expected to be killed or disabled over a given period. Each person engaged in working for that project is faced with a known risk. And if the risk is known to him, it will be costed as the minimum sum acceptable to him for taking the risk, given the wage available for the same work in a riskless enterprise or project.

---

1   Earlier attempts by economists to calculate the value of human life depart from that axiom, They include (a) those based on the expected lifetime earnings and or consumption of the individual, (b) those held to be implicit in the policy decisions of society, and (c) those deriving from insurance premiums. They are examined and revealed as inadequate in Mishan's (1971a) article. Also see Viscusi and Aldy (2003).
2   The alternative measure, CV^{21}, which would be finite, is the most a person is willing and able to pay to avoid being put to death. Where the prevailing ethos is one that believes that each person has a right to life, the CV^{12} measure is the appropriate one to use.

Assuming risk-aversion in such cases, the relevant sum to be subtracted from the estimated benefits of a project is simply the aggregate of these minimal payments required annually by the workers to compensate them for the risk they undertake in working for that enterprise or project. Thus, if there are n workers employed in the risky project, the additional labour cost for the risk of death and disablement will be measured as $\sum_{i=1}^{n} CV_i^{12}$.

2 In general, of course, every activity will incur some degree of risk (even staying at home in bed bears some risk of mishap: the bed might collapse; the wind might blow the roof off; a marauder might enter). A change from one environment to another, from one style of living to another, may alter the balance of risk, imperceptibly or substantially. Only the dead opt out of all risk. However, the actual risk attaching to some activity may be so small that only the hypersensitive would take account of it. In common with all changes in economic arrangements, there is some *sensible minimum* beyond which some slight change in risk will not register or matter.

Again, since it is a change in risk – a reduction or increase in risk – that is often at issue, what is important is the person's response to the change that matters. It will be useful, therefore, to use the standard indifference diagram in Figure 36.1 to bring out the characteristic response of the individual to changes in risk.

Thus, the sum of money is measured along the vertical axis of the figure – here as a capital sum, although it could also be measured as a period payment – and the degree of risk of death is measured along the horizontal axis increasing by equal increments from right to left (from left to right, therefore, one can measure the increasing probability of survival). Point r_0 is virtually riskless, while point r^* is the critical or highest risk along the horizontal axis – that beyond which no sum of money will compensate the individual.

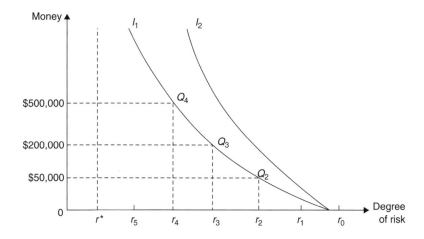

Figure 36.1

The indifference curves are ordered in the usual way, I_2 having a higher welfare level than I_1, the locus of each indifference curve being a continuum of alternative combinations of money and risk, between which our individual is indifferent. The assumption of risk-aversion over the operative range requires the curves to slope downward from left to right, while the concavity of the curves indicates that successively larger sums are needed to compensate the individual for assuming successive increments of risk. For instance, movement along the I_1 curve from Q_2 to Q_3 shows that the individual would require \$150,000 to increase his risk from r_2 to r_3. For a further equal increment of risk, however, that from r_3 to r_4, the movement along the curve from Q_3 to Q_4 reveals that the minimal compensation required is now \$300,000.

It will be noticed that, although the indifference curves are asymptotic to the vertical dotted line passing through point r^*, they will all touch the horizontal axis at r_0, where the risk is zero, or may also be drawn to touch the horizontal axis for a short distance to the left of r_0, so indicating that although there is some discernable risk, it is too slight to warrant attention by the individual.

3   It may be thought that a cost–benefit calculation must take account not only of the cost of risks incurred in the production process but also in the consumption process: the costs, that is, of risks run by those who use the goods produced by the projects.

Although the larger the risk associated with the use of a good, the smaller is the amount the buyer is willing to pay for it, no adjustment is necessary to the economist's calculation of willingness to pay, since the consumer himself may be supposed to have made the adjustment. When a new car is bought, the buyer who is to drive the car is assumed to know the risks over time to which he will be exposed in driving the car. The most he is willing to pay for it is adjusted accordingly. Allowing that he is risk-averse, the higher the risk, the larger the deduction from his willingness to pay.[3]

4   In order to formulate a more general expression of the social cost of a given risk, that is of society's valuation of the loss suffered by having to bear with a given risk, a little taxonomy will be useful.

For the introduction of a known risk of death r, affecting equally each of m persons in a community, the cost of only the direct physical danger to all of them can be written as $\sum_{j=1}^{m} c_j$, where the letter c_j is shorthand for the CV[12] measure of the jth person.

---

3 The same may be said of the consumption of tobacco products where the damages of smoking are widely advertised, but there is evidence to support the belief that awareness of the dangers of smoking attract young people to take it up; at least to be seen by their peers to be smoking, in which case the risks add to the sum they are willing to pay.

To this direct cost of the risk must be added the indirect cost arising from the possible impact on the welfare of any of the other remaining $(n - m)$ members of the community who are not themselves exposed to the risk in question. Thus, it may be that a person A who is not exposed to the risk, being fond of person B who is so exposed, or expecting to lose financially from B's demise, suffers a reduction in his welfare, the measure of his loss being a negative CV^{12} (the minimum sum acceptable to A for having to bear with the risk imposed on B). *Per contra*, if person A hates person B, or if he stands to gain from B's demise, his increase in welfare can be measured by his positive CV^{12} (the most A is willing to pay to maintain the risk of B's death).

Although it is unlikely that any one of the $(n - m)$ members of the community will be affected, emotionally or financially, by this risk of death of more than a few of the m persons, the aggregate sum of these reactions can be formulated as equal to the sum $\sum\limits_{i=m+1}^{n} \sum\limits_{j=1}^{m} c_{ij}$, where c_{ij} is the CV^{12} of the ith person who reacts to the risk sustained by the jth person in the m group. Needless to remark, most of these C_{ij} will be zero for the reasons given above.[4]

Clearly, if this aggregate sum is negative, the dollar figure measures a loss to the $(n - m)$ members of the community of the risk borne by the m members. If it is positive, the impact on the $(n - m)$ members of the community is, on balance, favourable, the net benefit being equal to the magnitude of the sum.

It is worth mentioning in passing that the summation expression above remains unaltered if the risk in question is that arising from an infectious disease which may be caught by any of the remaining $(n - m)$ members. The relevant CV^{12} measures of the consequent decline in welfare will all be negative, the resulting aggregate being a net loss.

5 Two developments arising from the proposed measurement of risk in CBA deserve comment: (i) a proposed extension of this measure of risk to the value of life, and (ii) a recognition of the seeming irrationality of those people placing a value on risk or chance.

(i) The proposed extension of a calculated risk premium to the value of a person's life can be illustrated by a simple example, one in which the individual at risk is concerned only with his own safety – not, that is, the effect of him having an accident on the welfare of anyone else.

Suppose that for a large group of men engaged in the same sort of work, the compensatory sum required for a risk of a fatal accident of 1 in 1,000 is, on average, equal to $800 then, for every 1,000 workmen, one workman may be expected to be killed each year. Since the aggregate sum that has to be paid to 1,000 such men

---

4 If we wish to allow that some of the m group who are directly at risk are themselves affected by some of those in that m group, we should re-write the above expression as $\sum\limits_{i=1}^{n} \sum\limits_{j=1}^{m} c_{ij}$ (where, again, a number of the c_{ij} are equal to zero).

each year comes to $800,000, this sum may be regarded as an agreed payment for the life lost.

Put generally, if the risk of a fatality, or an increase in the risk of a fatality, is equal to $1/n$, and the appropriate compensatory sum is, on average, equal to C, the value of a life is calculated to be equal to Cn.

But some caveats are necessary here. Although, in the simple example below, it may be convenient for the employer, who can expect such fatalities to occur over the years, to reckon the cost of each life lost as equal to $800,000, it does not follow that he or anyone else actually believes that the life of any particular person who dies in an accident is worth $800,000. Certainly, the person who died would not have agreed to surrender his life for $800,000.

It may be prudent to call this $800,000 the value of a *statistical* life. Even so, we should have to recognize that any such derived statistical life is pertinent only for that particular occupation in a particular region at a particular time: it is also applicable only for the existing degree of risk from which the increment of risk is to be calculated. By reference to Figure 36.1, if the existing degree of risk was taken to be equal to r_0, or about equal to zero risk, a small increment of risk may warrant an average compensatory sum of no more than $5 per annum, yielding a statistical life equal to $5,000. If, however, the existing risk of a fatality were r_1, an equal increment of risk would require a much larger average compensatory sum, say, $50, yielding the value of $50,000 for a statistical life. And if, instead, the existing risk of a fatality in that work were already as great as r_3, the same increment of risk would not be borne for less than an average sum of, say, $2,000, the resulting value of a statistical life being then equal to $2 million.

Obviously, any calculated statistical life has no claim to generality and no relation whatever to the value a person places on their own life – which, as indicated earlier, is likely to be infinite. It may, of course, continue to be regarded as an alternative to the calculation of the compensatory sum for a specific risk or increment of risk. But it is an alternative that is unnecessary and misleading.

6   Turning to (ii), although the method proposed in this chapter for measuring the valuation of any specific risk by reference to the compensating variation cannot be faulted, it transpires that, when it comes to the individual valuations of risks, they are far from being consistent. This apparent inconsistency may be attributed to the difficulty people have in apprehending the import of significant differences in very large numbers and very small fractions. For instance the risk of, loss of, say, 1 in 100,000 – or, alternatively, the chance of a gain of 1 in 100,000 – is not apprehended as being much smaller than a risk or chance of 1 in 10,000, or much smaller even than 1 in 1,000.[5]

This would be the case in an experiment in which a person is willing to pay as much as $50 for the reduction of an existing risk by $1/1,000$, yet willing to pay the

---

5 Mishan's (1971a) paper suggested, *inter alia*, that this interesting fact of life also explains why people both gamble and insure without invoking the ingenious hypothesis about the shape of the utility curve advanced by Friedman and Savage (1948). Also see Mishan (1971b).

same sum also for a reduction in that risk by 1/10,000 and, indeed, willing to pay this same $50 for a reduction of the risk of 1/100,000.

Yet, something like this sort of reaction has been shown to exist in papers written some time ago, for when we take this same compensatory sum of $50 for a reduction in risk of 10^{-3}, 10^{-4}, and 10^{-5}, in that order, the resulting statistical value of life itself works out to be equal to $50,000, $500,000 and $5 million, respectively.

These figures are, in fact, not that different from the findings of Mulligan (1977). For corresponding to these alternative reductions in risk of 10^{-3}, 10^{-4} and 10^{-5}, he comes up with a statistical value of life equal to $62,000, $428,000 and $3,756,000, respectively.[6] Clearly, this difficulty in apprehending the numerical significance of differences in very small fractions must be taken seriously – as it presumably is by insurers and lottery promoters.

Although this fact of life is admittedly disquieting, the economist engaged in cost–benefit calculations may not allow himself to become overwrought for, in most cases, the increase or reduction in risk he has to evaluate is likely to be much larger than, say, 10^{-3}. He may therefore be justified in expecting a reasonable degree of consistency.

Therefore, although it is a matter of conscience to enter the above caveat before concluding, it is also as well to recognize that, for the usual order of change in risk that he meets within cost–benefit studies, the expressed compensating variations may be accepted as valid estimates for calculating the loss of incurring a risk or the benefit of reducing risk.

7   A word on the deficiencies in the information available to each person concerning the degree of risk involved. These deficiencies of information necessarily contribute to the discrepancies experienced by people between anticipated and realized satisfactions. For all that, in determining whether a potential Pareto improvement has been met, economists are generally agreed – as a canon of faith, as a political tenet, or as an act of expediency – to accept the dictum that each person knows his own interest best. If, therefore, the economist is told that a person A is indifferent between not assuming a particular risk and assuming it along with a sum of money V, then, on the Pareto principle, the sum V has to be accepted as the relevant cost of him being exposed to that risk. It may well be the case that, owing to either deficient information or congenital optimism, person A consistently overestimates his chances of survival. But once the dictum is accepted, as indeed it is in economists' appraisals of allocative efficiency, CBA must accept V as the only relevant magnitude – this being the sum chosen by A in awareness of his relative ignorance.[7] Certainly, all the rest of the economic data used in a CBA,

---

6 If the relevant segment of the indifference curve is linear, these empirical findings by Mulligan can be expressed as equal to a compensatory sum of $62 for a reduction of risk by 10^{-3}, of about $43 for a reduction of risk of 10^{-4} and about $37 for a reduction of risk of 10^{-5}.

7 Person A, for example, may find himself disabled for life and rue his decision to take the risk. But this example is only a more painful one of the fact that people come to regret a great many of the choices they make, notwithstanding which they would resent any interference with their future choices.

or any other allocative study, whether derived from market prices and quantities or by other methods of enquiry, is based on this principle of accepting as final only the individual's estimate of what a thing is worth to him at the time the decision is to be made. The thing in question may, of course, also have a direct worth, positive or negative, for persons other than the buyer or seller of it, a possibility which requires a consideration of external effects. Yet, again, on the above dictum, it is the values placed on this thing by these other persons that are to count. Thus, while it is scarcely necessary to urge that more economical ways of refining and disseminating information be explored, the economist engaged in allocative studies traditionally follows the practice of evaluating all social gains and losses solely on the basis of individuals' own evaluations of the relevant effects on their welfare, given the information they have at the time the decision is taken.

8   To sum up and conclude, given the common set of relevant economic characteristics of any group, the benefit of a given reduction in the existing risk (or the cost of an increment in that risk) as calculated from the valuations of people who are directly or indirectly affected by the change will vary (i) according to the existing degree of risk and to the magnitude of the change in risk, (ii) according to the kind of casualty associated with the change of risk, and (iii) according to the way that the risk translates itself into casualties. A quick word about each of these.

(i)   A project that is expected to save each year no more than about one life in 10 million is likely to yield (in the absence of any other benefit) a zero contribution *by direct reference to individual valuations*. However, the installation of a plant that is expected to increase the death rate by 10 per cent within a certain area may inflict an average loss per person of several thousand dollars. Needless to say, it would be as absurd to derive a social value for human life from the former instance as from the latter – and quite arbitrary to use any other instance for the purpose.

(ii)   The particular kind of death envisaged also plays a part. For exactly the same increase in the risk of death, say 5 per cent, beginning from exactly the same existing risk, the individual valuation of loss may be much higher if the kind of death being risked is that by nuclear radiation than if it is that by drowning or by influenza.

(iii) Again, even the same risk of the same kind of death may be valued differently according to whether (a) expected deaths take the form of a probability distribution, so that the number tends to vary from one year to the next: the smaller the variance, the less bearable is the given risk; (b) the expected number of deaths – irrespective of the variance of the probability distribution – occurs within a particular community located *within* a larger population, rather than the same number of deaths being dispersed throughout the larger population.

9   There can therefore be no question of the economist engaged in a cost–benefit calculation having recourse to some all-purpose value of human life, however ingeniously calculated. In a CBA, the economist is to attend directly only to the observable data that lends itself to valuation: thus he is to value an increased or reduced risk of death, or of other misfortunes, as simply one among the several goods or bads associated with the construction or operation of a specific project. And, as argued in the chapter, the valuation of the given change of risk is correctly measured only by the compensating variations of those who are directly or indirectly affected by it.

To be sure, the general economic literature offers occasional examples of economic models putatively designed to produce formulae for calculating the monetary value of a human life, models that again, though with greater sophistication, draw on the expectations of a person's economic activities over the duration of his life, and their effect on himself and others.

Whatever one's reaction to such models, there is no way of testing their validity. As indicated earlier, in ordinary circumstances, the value of a person's life to himself is unlikely to be finite; no sum of money, no matter how large, will induce him to surrender his life. As for checking the monetary value produced by such models by reference to some chosen statistical value of life, the exercise would be pointless for, even were the model's calculated value of life 'confirmed' by the statistical value of life, the model's calculated valuation would be worse than superfluous; it would be a case of 'love's labour lost', as it would be far simpler to derive the statistical value of life directly from the relevant compensatory sum for the risk in question.

At all events, since such models, however regarded, have nothing to contribute to CBA, what brief comments we have on their character are relegated to Appendix 12.

Part VII

Uncertainty

37 Risk and certainty equivalence

1 The treatment in this section of the methods for dealing with uncertainty in project evaluation is, inevitably perhaps, the least satisfactory feature of this introductory volume. In the evaluation of any project, there is sure to be some guesswork about the magnitudes of future costs and benefits, arising mainly from technological innovations and shifts in demand which may affect the prices of the inputs and outputs. In this consequence, economists making use of the methods discussed in this section cannot be sure of arriving at a common figure or set of figures for a specific project. The problem of how to make decisions in any situation where the past affords little, if any, guidance is not one that can be satisfactorily resolved by either logic or empiricism, and what rules have been formulated are either of limited application or of no practical value. We shall, however, consider briefly and in a simple-minded way the various methods that have been proposed to deal with this problem of uncertainty, beginning with the device of reducing an uncertain prospect to an equivalent certainty.

2 Suppose that I am uncertain of the price my house will fetch on the market when I come to sell it in five years' time. Though uncertain of the exact price, I will surely entertain some ideas of what the price is likely to be. With luck, I think it could be $60,000, possibly even more. Allowing for this, that, and the other, it is, however, more likely to be $50,000. Yet, it could well be as low as $40,000, and one cannot altogether exclude the possibility of it fetching a sum lower even than this.

I should be glad to be free of the anxiety caused by this uncertainty about the sale price of my house for a guaranteed price of $50,000 five years hence. Indeed, I could be induced to agree to a smaller sum than $50,000. The question naturally arises: what is the lowest guaranteed sum I would be prepared to accept in five years' time to be rid of the uncertainty? If it were $45,000, then $45,000 is said to represent the certainty equivalent that corresponds to the range of my uncertain prospects.

If, conversely, I contemplated buying a particular house in five years' time for a sum which can be as low as $72,000 but might be as high as $100,000, I might be induced to agree to pay, in five years' time as much as (but no more than) $86,000.

If so, $86,000 becomes the certainty equivalent corresponding to the uncertain purchase price.[1]

In general, it is asserted that to any *uncertain* future sum of money – to be paid or to be received – there corresponds a *guaranteed* sum between which and the uncertain sum in question the individual is indifferent.

On the more common assumption of risk-aversion for transactions of some importance, a person is prepared to pay some premium for safety. If, therefore, the expected figure for the sale of his house appears to be $50,000, by accepting a guaranteed price of $45,000 he can be said to be paying a risk premium of $5,000. If, conversely, he is concerned with the problem of buying a particular house in five years' time, and the most likely price is $80,000, by accepting a guaranteed future price of $86,000, he can be said to be paying a risk premium of $6,000. It goes without saying that the higher the degree of uncertainty about the future price,[2] the greater the risk premium a person will be willing to pay.

3   This notion of certainty equivalence is, perhaps, a useful ploy in working through abstract economic constructs where the troublesome fact of uncertainty can be formally accommodated, without any amendment to the theory, simply by attributing a certainty equivalent to every uncertain magnitude. But it provides little guidance to the economist engaged in evaluating a project. If he cannot be sure of a figure at any time in the future, he will have to guess at it and, if he is at all sensible, he will choose to err on the conservative side. There is no way of insuring himself. The knowledge that some rational being, when faced with the problem of placing a value on some future magnitude, might well choose a value very different from that chosen by another equally rational individual may be of some consolation to him in his perplexity. But it cannot provide him with a clear decision rule.

4   Further theoretical elaboration is of interest but of small practical value. For example, by measuring expected value (or arithmetic mean) along the horizontal axis and variance on the vertical axis, a 'gambler's indifference map' can be constructed. The indifference curves will slope upward from left to right indicating that increasing uncertainty (as measured by variance) must be compensated by an increase in expected value. If we now have a number of alternative future benefits to choose from, all incurring the same cost, and each identified by a particular expected value and variance, that touching the highest indifference curve is chosen.

---

1 If there were only two possible outcomes, $100,000, expected with a probability of $\frac{1}{4}$ and $72,000 expected with a probability of $\frac{3}{4}$, the certainty equivalent might be thought equal to ($\frac{1}{4}$ × $100,000) + ($\frac{3}{4}$ × $72,000), or $79,000. In 'normal' cases, it would be less than $79,000, as explained in Chapter 41. In the present chapter, we do not, however, assume that probabilities can be attached to each of a range of possible outcomes.

2 The higher degree of uncertainty might be measured by a higher degree of variance if it were possible to talk of likelihood in a probabilistic sense, one arising from repeated experiment in an unchanged universe – which is not, however, the case for uncertainty.

Such a construction enables us formally to rank a number of alternative uncertain benefits without first reducing each to a certainty equivalent. But though, formally speaking, the method is more direct, exception can be taken to the idea of being able to measure mean and variance in situations of genuine uncertainty. For uncertainty, strictly interpreted, implies ignorance of the probability distribution. Moreover, in the absence of a *community* indifference map and in the absence of agreement on the characteristics of the data, the method provides no more guidance in the face of uncertainty than does the method of uncertainty equivalents; which is to say it provides practically no guidance at all.

5   Finally, a word on the notion of risk. Although there is no universal agreement on the definition of 'risk', the common usage of the term is often associated with the notion of a possibility of loss, injury or other adverse consequences of an event. The driver of a car bears the risk of injury or loss of life to himself or to others when an accident happens. What is uncertain is whether he will be involved in a car crash within the year. A risky event has a number of possible outcomes, but the actual outcome is not known in advance. For instance, storing waste materials in landfills is a risky event, as the groundwater under the landfill may be contaminated by accidental leakage.

Risk can be distinguished between objective and subjective risk. The former refers to the situation when the probability of occurrence of a chance event is objectively known, for example, death from stroke. Such deaths do occur frequently, so that the probability of this event can be determined objectively from the available statistics. If the probability of a random event is not objectively determined, it becomes a subjective probability or an uncertainty. This usually arises when the event happens very infrequently, such as an explosion from a nuclear power plant. Assessing subjective probabilities can be difficult and is much affected by the individual's perception or attitude towards the event.

Nonetheless, the dichotomy between objective and subjective risk is becoming less clear, especially when more data and experiences become available.

It is often the case in practice that the objective and subjective risk estimates of the same event are different. A classic example pertains to nuclear power plants. The subjective risk estimate of nuclear power by the general public is usually greater than the objective risk estimate by the experts. The difference is partly due to the differences in the availability of information to both parties. Nonetheless, such conflicting risk assessments between the experts and lay opinions have been a source of frustration as well as challenge to public policy makers in making the appropriate decisions with respect to such facilities.

38 Game theory and decision rules (I)

1 As game theory can be used as a technique for dealing with cases of complete ignorance of the initial probabilities of possible outcomes, the reader might be inclined to pitch his hopes for useful guidance a little higher. Again, I think he will be disappointed. But before pronouncing judgment, we shall illustrate with one or two simple examples the relevant techniques known as the 'two-person zero-sum game', so called for the rather obvious reasons: (i) that the game is played between two persons or groups, one of which may be 'nature', and (ii) that there are no mutual gains to be made, the gains to one party being exactly equal to the losses suffered by the other party.

2 Consider first a reservoir which is full at the beginning of the season and can be used both for irrigation and for flood control. Without any prior knowledge of whether or not a flood will occur, a decision is required on the amount of water to be released. If a little water is released now, it will be good for the harvest, but it will be ineffectual as a contribution to preventing future flood damage. If, instead, a lot of water is released now, it will make flood damage virtually impossible, but it will damage the harvest to some extent.

Now, the amount of water that can be released from the reservoir can range, in general, from nothing at all to the whole lot. As for the flood, if it occurs, it can be either negligible or highly destructive. In order to illustrate the principle, however, we can restrict ourselves to two possible outcomes: full flood (b_1) and no flood (b_2). The options open to the decision maker are also to be restricted for simplicity of exposition: they will release one-third of the water in the reservoir (a_1), release two-thirds of the water in the reservoir (a_2) and release all the water in the reservoir (a_3).[1] In addition to the possible states of nature, b_1 and b_2 and the options open to the decision maker, a_1, a_2 and a_3, we are also assumed to have a clear idea of the quantitative result corresponding to the particular outcome and the option adopted. If, for example, a decision is taken to release two-thirds of the reservoir, which is option a_2, and a full flood, b_1, happens to occur, the net benefit – that is the value of the harvest *less* the value of the damage done by the

---

1 This example is taken from Dorfman (1962: 130 ff).

flood – is assumed to be known. In this example, we shall assume it is equal to $140,000. Again, if instead we choose the a_3 option, that of releasing all the water, the net benefit that arises if the full flood b_1 occurs is assumed equal to $80,000. Since there are three options or strategies and two possible occurrences or states of nature, there will be six possible outcomes altogether, each identified by a net benefit figure. The scheme is depicted in Table 38.1.

A glance at Table 38.1 will convince the reader that, provided the six figures are all accepted as correct estimates of net benefits, option a_3 – requiring the release of all the water in the reservoir – will never be adopted. Whether b_1 or b_2 occurs, the net benefits of adopting the a_3 option will be lower than those of either a_1 or a_2. In the jargon, option a_3 *is dominated by* the other options, a fact that is revealed by the figures in the a_1 row (130,000 and 400,000) and those in the a_2 row (140,000 and 260,000), both sets of figures being larger than the a_3 row figures (80,000 and 90,000). We could then save some unnecessary calculation by eliminating the dominated option a_3, since there are no circumstances in which it would pay to adopt it. Nevertheless, we shall retain it in this simplified example, as the additional exercise will be useful, while the additional calculation will be slight.

Given no information other than in Table 38.1, we could employ either of two standard methods to produce a decision: a *maximin* procedure and a *minimax* procedure. We shall illustrate the former in the remainder of the present chapter, and the latter in the following chapter.

3 *The maximin procedure*: If he looks along the first row of Table 38.1 showing the net revenues, $130,000 and $400,000, corresponding to each of the two possible alternative states of nature, b_1 and b_2, when the decision maker chooses option a_1, it will be realized that the worst that can happen is the occurrence of b_1, yielding a revenue of only $130,000. Assuming that the decision maker is a conservative person, he will want to compare this worst result, or minimal net revenue, that he can obtain from choosing a_1, with those minima he might obtain if instead he adopts the a_2 or a_3 option. Now the choice of a_2 can realize a net yield of either 140,000 or 260,000 according as b_1 or b_2 occurs, respectively. He can then be sure of at least 140,000. Similarly, if he chooses option a_3 he can be sure of obtaining at least 80,000. These three row minima, 130,000 for a_1, 140,000 for a_2 and 80,000 for a_3, are all shown in the third column of Table 38.2 (which is the same as Table 38.1 except for the addition of two columns).

Table 38.1

	b_1 *Flood* ($)	b_2 *No flood* ($)
a_1	130,000	400,000
a_2	140,000	260,000
a_3	80,000	90,000

Table 38.2

	b_1 ($)	b_2 ($)	Row minima ($)	Maximim (maximum of row minima) ($)
a_1	130,000	400,000	130,000	
a_2	140,000	260,000	140,000	140,000
a_3	80,000	90,000	80,000	

Down this third column he reads off the worst possible outcome corresponding to each option. If he chooses a_1, he can be sure of not getting less than 130,000. If he chooses a_2, he can be sure of not getting less than 140,000. If he chooses a_3, he can be sure of not getting less than 80,000. It will then occur to him that, if he chooses any option *other than* a_2, he might get less than 140,000; for example, if having chosen a_1, b_1 occurs, he will receive only 130,000, whereas, if she chooses a_3, he will receive only 80,000 or 90,000 according to whether event b_1 or event b_2 occurs. The largest net revenue he can be *sure* of obtaining is, then, $140,000. The maximin principle therefore requires that he choose option a_2 (releasing two-thirds of the reservoir) and assure himself of no less than 140,000.

The guiding idea has been to pick out the maximum figure from column three, which column contains the minimum possible net revenues corresponding to each option. Hence the figure chosen – 140,000 in column four of Table 38.2 – is spoken of as the *maximin*.

4   One feature of the above example is that capital costs are taken to be constant for each of the alternative options. This enables us to compare directly the net revenues – annual revenues *less* annual loss – in each of the first two columns. If we assume instead that revenues are fixed and that costs alone vary according to the decision made and the event that takes place, we can go through the same sort of exercise.

An example would be the installation of a boiler in a works.[2] Again, we can suppose three options: a_1, installing a coal-fired boiler, a_2, installing an oil-fired boiler or a_3, installing a dual boiler, one that could be switched from using coal to using oil, and vice versa, at negligible cost. Three possible occurrences are to be considered: b_1, coal prices rise relative to oil prices over the next 20 years by an average of 25 per cent; b_2, the reverse of this; and b_3, the relative prices of the two fuels remain, on average, unchanged.

The outcomes of the relevant calculations are summarized in Table 38.3, the figures being the DPV (in thousands of dollars) of the streams of future costs associated with each option for each of the three possible outcomes.

By convention, costs are to be regarded as *negative* revenues, so the figures in Table 38.3 are all negative. Looking along row a_1, the worst outcome is –13.0. If

2 This example has been adapted from that given in Moore (1968).

Table 38.3

	b_1	b_2	b_3	Row minima	Maximim (maximum of row minima)
a_1	−13.0	−12.0	−12.0	−13.0	
a_2	−11.3	−12.5	−11.3	−12.5	−12.5
a_3	−12.8	−12.8	−12.8	−12.8	

a_1 is chosen and b_1 should occur, the cost would be 13. (13 is the highest absolute figure in the row but, seen as a negative revenue and considered algebraically, −13 is less than −12; thus −13 is the lowest figure in the row.) The largest costs, or the smallest gains, corresponding to options a_2 and a_3 are, respectively, −12.5 and −12.8, which figures are entered in the fourth column. Of these row minima, the maximum (or least cost) is −12.5, corresponding to option a_2 which, on the maximum principle, would be the one to be chosen. Having chosen a_2, we can be sure that the cost to which the firm can be subjected cannot exceed 12.5; this cost would be incurred if event b_2 took place. If, however, event b_1 or b_3 occurred the cost would be only 11.3.

39 Game theory and decision rules (II)

1 There is one implication of this maximin principle that is obviously unsatisfactory. It seeks security above all and is therefore highly conservative. In Table 38.2, for instance, we are led by it to choose a_2 rather than a_1, simply because, in choosing a_2, can be sure of obtaining at least $140,000 whereas, if we choose a_1, we can be sure of obtaining at least $130,000. If we feel pretty certain of getting the least in all cases, we should indeed be wise to choose that least which is largest. And the least for a_2 is $10,000 larger than that for a_1. But if it so happens that the event b_2 does take place, our choice of a_2 yields us only $260,000 whereas, had we instead chosen option a_1, event b_2 would yield as much as $400,000. In other words, if b_2 takes place after all, we shall forgo an extra gain of $140,000 ($400,000 minus $260,000). The cost of playing safe – of ensuring $10,000 more if the worst should happen – is that of losing the opportunity of gaining $140,000 more if the best should happen.

2 We can 'cook up' another set of figures for this example, those in Table 39.1, in order to bring out this defect even more sharply.

The row minima for options a_1 and a_2 are shown in the third column to be 13 and 14, respectively. On the maximin principle, the a_2 option is to be chosen as that which guarantees a net receipt of no less than 14 – but it is clear that the most that can be gained from choosing option a_2 is only 15. By comparing this choice with the rejected option a_1 we cannot but realize that we are sacrificing the chance of gaining 5,000 in order to increase our guaranteed minimum receipts from 13 to 14. With outcomes such as those in the columns of Table 39.1 it is hard to think of anyone employing the maximin method and choosing a_2, for he will be aware that, if event b_2 turns up, he will receive 15 only whereas, if he had instead chosen a_1, he would receive 5,000: he becomes aware, then, that by choosing a_2 (so as

Table 39.1

	b_1	b_2	Row minimum	Maximin
a_1	13	5000	13	14
a_2	14	15	14	

to ensure that if the worst happens he will receive one more than if, instead, he chooses a_1) he lays himself open to a potential loss of 4,985 (5,000 *minus* 15) should the event, b_2, occur.

A less conservative person would not want to guide his choice by the maximin principle even if the figures were less enticing than those in Table 39.1. Indeed, if he were at all enterprising, and had an eye open for the larger gains that are possible, he would adopt something like the reverse of the maximin principle. What he would want to avoid is the possibility of an outcome that will make him regret his choice. Since his regret will increase with the size of the loss of possible gain – 4,985, in the above example, if he chooses a_2 – he will adopt the principle of minimizing his regret. Hence, the alternative *minimax regret* procedure suggested by economists.

3 *The minimax procedure*: We can illustrate this procedure by constructing Table 39.2 using the primary data given in Table 38.1. Suppose a flood occurs, which is to say that the b_1 event takes place, the initial choice of option a_2 would have secured for the b_1, event the largest net revenue of 140,000. If, on the other hand, a_1 had been chosen, the net revenue would have been 130,000, or 10,000 less than could have been obtained had we chosen a_2. We therefore put 10,000 in the cell opposite a_1 and below b_1 in Table 39.2. This 10,000 entry is to be interpreted as follows: if b_1 occurs, the prior choice of option a_2 yields the largest receipt, 140,000. By choosing some other option, say a_1, we receive only 130,000, a *potential loss of 10,000*. Below b_1 and opposite a_3, however, we place the figure 60,000 because, if b_1 occurs, our prior choice of a_3 would yield 80,000 – a potential loss of 60,000 (140,000 *minus* 80,000) compared with the largest yield of 140,000 that would come from having chosen a_2. Opposite a_2 itself, we obviously put a zero, as there is no potential loss from having chosen a_2 if event b_1 occurs.

We now fill the cells down the second column. The highest net revenue if event b_2 occurs is 400,000, corresponding to the choice of option a_1: hence, a zero opposite a_1 and below b_2. If a_2 is chosen instead, only 260,000 can be collected – a potential loss of 140,000 (400,000 *minus* 260,000) is involved. Below b_2 and opposite a_2, therefore, we place the figure 140,000. If, finally, a_3 is chosen, only 90,000 can be collected, involving a potential loss of 310,000 (400,000 *minus* 90,000). Below b_2 and opposite a_3 we therefore place the figure 310,000.

Since the derived figures in the first two columns are now to be regarded as potential losses, row a_3 is again dominated by the other rows. Its potential losses

Table 39.2

	b_1	b_2	Row maxima (of potential losses)	Minimax (minimum of row maxima)
a_1	10,000	0	10,000	10,000
a_2	0	140,000	140,000	
a_3	60,000	310,000	310,000	

for either event b_1 or b_2 are larger than those of any other row. The standard computational procedure would be to eliminate a_3 before calculating the figures for the Row maxima column. But, again, in so simple an example, it adds to the interest while causing no difficulty.

As it is regret-at-potential-losses we now seek to minimize, we glance along the rows and pick out the largest potential loss that could arise from each option in turn. The largest figure along row a_1 is 10,000. It is therefore placed opposite a_1 under the third column containing the row maxima. For row a_2, the largest potential loss figure is 140,000, and it is entered accordingly opposite a_2 and in the third column. For row a_3, the largest potential loss figure is 310,000, and this is shown opposite a_3 in the third column.

Of these largest potential losses from choosing a_1, a_2 or a_3, the decision maker chooses the smallest, which is 10,000, corresponding to option a_1. Accordingly, the figure of 10,000 is entered in the fourth column of Table 39.2. By choosing option a_1, he can be sure of one thing: that whichever event occurs, his potential loss – that is, the additional gain he might, in that event, have obtained had he instead selected one of the other options – can be no greater than 10,000. For clearly, if instead he chooses a_2, the potential loss he may suffer is 140,000. While if he chooses a_3, the potential loss he may suffer is 310,000.[1]

As a further illustration of the minimax-regret method, Table 39.3 is constructed from the primary data given in Table 38.3. For the first column, below b_1 the best choice is a_2, as it would entail the least cost 11.3. If option a_1 were chosen instead,

Table 39.3

	b_1	b_2	b_3	Row maxima	Minimax
a_1	1.7	0	0.7	1.7	
a_2	0	0.5	0	0.5	0.5
a_3	1.5	0.8	1.5	1.5	

1   This 'minimax-regret' or 'minimax-risk' (of loss) principle, as it is sometimes called, is really a misnomer. The figures for losses in Table 39.2 are given without sign. But if we follow the convention of treating losses as negative signs, we should write all the figures in Table 39.2 with a minus sign. For instance, if a_3 is chosen and b_1 occurs, the potential gain is 80,000 minus 140,000 or –60,000.

The largest potential loss in each row of Table 39.2 should then really be expressed as a *negative* figure: –10,000 for a_1, –140,000 for a_2, and –310,000 for a_3. These negative figures can then be regarded as the lowest or minimal row gains. Of these (algebraic) row minima, we choose the (algebraic) maximum, namely, 10,000, corresponding to option a_1.

The formal procedure is in fact no different from that used in connection with Table 38.3, where the negative items happen to refer to costs.

In effect, then, the same maximin procedure as before is employed, with the important difference that the row minima figures we are now maximizing refer to (negative) *potential* gains (compared with other options) instead of *actual* gains.

However, we shall here follow the convention of using positive figures to refer to potential losses, and of describing the procedure as 'minimaxing-regret'.

the cost would be 13, and therefore the loss of potential savings would be 1.7 (13 *minus* 11.3). Similarly, if a_3 were chosen, the cost would be 12.8, and the loss of potential savings would be 1.5 (12.8 *minus* 11.3). The figures in the next two columns are obtained in the same way. In the fourth column, we put the row maxima. From these, the smallest potential loss, 0.5 corresponding to option a_2, is chosen and entered in the fifth column.

4 Not surprisingly, perhaps, the more obvious shortcoming of this minimax method is the opposite of that found in the maximin. The conservatism of the maximin, it will be recalled, is such that cases can arise in which large potential gains are sacrificed for very little extra security. In order to skirt this contingency, the so-called minimax-regret method courts the opposite danger, for cases can arise in which the application of this more enterprising minimax method will effectively jettison the chance of a good gain for the hope of getting a bit more.

The net revenue figures in Table 39.4 are chosen to illustrate this shortcoming of the minimax regret procedure.

Application of the maxim, in principle would select option a_1, so ensuring a receipt of 300. Table 39.5, however, uses the data in Table 39.4 to derive corresponding figures in each cell for potential losses

In the concern (should event b_2 occur) not to regret the loss of 200, the person employing the minimax-regret principle incurs instead the risk of the somewhat smaller potential loss of 180 should any of the other three events, b_1, b_3, b_4, occur. Put more directly, his choice of a_2 ensures that, if event b_2 occurs, he will obtain 500 rather than the 300 he would obtain by choosing a_1. (If, however, b_1, b_2 or b_4 occurs, he will collect only 120 rather than the 300 he would obtain by choosing a_1.)

5 A minor characteristic, sometimes regarded as a defect, arising from the use of the minimax method is that, if one of the rejected options is withdrawn, that option which had been chosen before its withdrawal might not be the option chosen by this method in the new circumstances. This possibility is illustrated using the

Table 39.4

	b_1	b_2	b_3	b_4
a_1	300	300	300	300
a_2	120	500	120	120

Table 39.5

	b_1	b_2	b_3	b_4	Row maxima	Minimax
a_1	0	200	0	0	200	
a_2	180	0	180	180	180	180

figures in Table 39.6, which happen to be the same as those used in Table 38.1 except for the last line.

On the maximin method, a_3 would be chosen. Using the minimax procedure, however, we first derive from Table 39.6 the potential loss figures which appear in Table 39.7, and, from the row maxima column, we choose the lowest figure, namely 160,000, corresponding to option a_2.

Now if option a_1 in Table 39.6 were withdrawn, the resulting potential loss figures for the remaining options, a_2 and a_3, would be those given in Table 39.8. The row maxima are now 160,000 and 60,000 for a_2 and a_3, respectively. Therefore, on the minimax procedure, a_3 becomes the chosen option.

If, on the other hand, option a_3 were to be withdrawn from Table 39.6, the potential loss figures for the remaining options, a_1 and a_2, would be those given in Table 39.9. The row maxima corresponding to a_1 and a_2 are now 10,000 and 140,000, so that, on this principle, a_1 is chosen

There is, however, nothing paradoxical about such results. From the standpoint of the minimax-regret principle, the initially rejected options that are removed are indeed relevant to the decision. Thus, in withdrawing option a_1 the yield of

Table 39.6

	b_1	b_2
a_1	130,000	400,000
a_2	140,000	260,000
a_3	300,000	200,000

Table 39.7

	b_1	b_2	Row maxima	Minimax
a_1	170,000	0	170,000	
a_2	160,000	140,000	160,000	160,000
a_3	0	200,000	200,000	

Table 39.8

	b_1	b_2	Row maxima	Minimax
a_2	160,000	0	160,000	
a_3	0	60,000	60,000	60,000

Table 39.9

	b_1	b_2	Row maxima	Minimax
a_1	10,000	0	10,000	10,000
a_2	0	140,000	140,000	

400,000 if event b_2 occurs (in Table 39.6) is no longer available to us. Thus, when a_1 is no longer available, the potential loss from choosing a_3 falls from 200,000 (when a_1 was available) to only 60,000, as shown in Table 39.8.

Similarly, if option a_3 alone is withdrawn, leaving us with a_1 and a_2, the 300,000 outcome if b_1 occurs is no longer available to us. The potential loss from choosing option a_1 if b_1 occurs falls, therefore, from 170,000 (when a_3 was available) to only 10,000 (when a_3 is no longer available) as a result of which, the a_1 option is then chosen, as indicated in Table 39.9.

We need not therefore regard this feature of the minimax procedure as a defect of the method. Rather, we should confine our criticism to that already indicated in the preceding section as illustrated by Tables 39.4 and 39.5, in which the chance of some minimum gain is put at risk in the hope of securing a bit more

6   In sum, it would appear that the choice of maximin or minimax regret would not be adopted in advance and independently of the primary data by any person unless he was cautious to a fault (in which case he would always apply the maximin principle) or being recklessly opportunistic or, more precisely, fearful of losing potential gains (in which case he would always apply the minimax-regret principle).

One must conclude that, even where conditions are such that these methods can be applied, the fact alone that the choice of whether to use maximin or minimax-regret will depend upon the person and upon the data makes the application of game theory techniques somewhat unsatisfactory. Since subjective judgement enters into the choice of whether to use maximin or minimax-regret, competent economists inspecting the same data can come up with different decisions.

40 How practical are game theory decision techniques?

1 The final stage of a typical cost–benefit study requires that we evaluate a stream of net benefits

$$(B_1 - K_1), (B_2 - K_2), \ldots, (B_n - K_n)$$

in which the Bs or benefits and the Ks or costs are uncertain and, indeed, increase in uncertainty the further they are from the present.

The difficulties we encounter in the attempt to apply game theory principles may be illustrated by recourse to a simple example in which the net benefits of a project are spread over four years as follows: –100, 30, 80 and 50. The –100 figure indicates a net capital outlay of 100 in the first year, and the remaining figures are net benefits in successive years. The penumbra of uncertainty surrounding each of these figures might suggest, for example, that for the –100 figure we substitute a *range* –95 to –105: for the figure of 30, a range 25 to 35, and so on. For practical purposes, however, we would not use a continuous range, only discrete figures. The range –95 to –105 could, for instance, be split into three possible outcomes –95, –100 and –105. The range 25 to 35 could also be split into three outcomes or perhaps five, say, 25, 28, 30, 32 and 35. Similarly for the other two figures. If we take these arbitrarily chosen figures from the range of net benefits in any period to be independent of the arbitrarily chosen figures from the range of any other period's net benefits, a combination that included one of the possible net-benefit outcomes from each of the four periods – say –95 from the first period, 32 from the second, 75 from the third, and 50 from the fourth – would add up to the outcome of a single event. There are obviously as many events as there are combinations of such possible outcomes for the four-year period.[1]

2 The uncertainty about the net-benefit figures in each period can, however, be attributed instead to the uncertainty about future *price* movements of both the inputs and outputs associated with the project. It is true that the price movements themselves depend upon a number of future possible events, such as technical

---

1 It is hardly necessary to say that, in adding these four figures, those for the second, third and fourth periods must be compounded or discounted at the relevant rates.

innovations, changes in domestic and foreign policies, and alterations in the conditions of demand and supply. But for each combination of such possible events, there will be a corresponding range of possible prices for both the inputs and outputs in question. We may therefore express the uncertainty about all future events in each period by reference to some price range of each of the inputs and outputs.

Suppose that in the A_1 investment project, giving rise to a four-year stream of net benefits (including the initial year's capital outlay), there are the prices of only four items to be anticipated: that of homogeneous labour; that of homogeneous material; that of homogeneous machinery; and that of homogeneous output. Since prices do become more uncertain as we move into the future, the range of possible prices becomes wider and, as it becomes wider, it may be split into a larger number of possible prices. In token of this consideration, we shall divide the price range of each item into three alternative prices for the first period, but into five alternative prices for the second, third and fourth periods. In each of the four periods, there will be a larger number of possible net benefits, each possible net benefit corresponding to a different combination of the prices of each of the above-mentioned four items. Thus, for the first period, the three alternative prices for each of these four items will generate 3^4, or 81, possible outcomes, each of such outcomes being an alternative net benefit in the first period. For the second period, the five different prices for each of the four items will generate 5^4, or 625, possible outcomes, each being an alternative net benefit. Similarly, there will be 625 possible net benefits for each of the two remaining periods.

Matching any one of the 81 alternative net benefits in the first period with any one of the 625 possible benefits from each of the other three periods so as to produce a particular permutation of four successive benefits, provides us with (in the terminology of game theory) a single event, b_1. Since there are 81 different net-benefit outcomes in the first period and 625 different net-benefit outcomes in each of the three remaining periods, the total number of different events that are possible is given by 81×625^3, or close to 20 billion different events.

3   If we now introduce another investment option A_2, which also yields a stream of possible net benefits over four years *and uses the same inputs and outputs*, we must calculate figures for roughly another 20 billion events. If, however, the A_2 stream covers more periods than the A_1 stream, or if there are additional inputs or outputs to contend with, we shall have to increase the number of events. Each of these additional events will carry a net-benefit figure for A_2, positive, zero or negative. Corresponding to these additional events for A_2, there will be zeros for A_1. There may, however, be inputs or outputs in the A_2 investment option that replace those in the A_1 option; for example, steel may be the only material used in the A_1 investment option, and aluminium the only material used in the A_2 option. In that case, there will be a number of events that are strictly relevant only to A_1 and a number that are strictly relevant only to A_2. Corresponding to those events that are strictly relevant to A_1, there will be net revenues (positive, zero or negative) for the A_1 option, and zeros for the A_2 option, and vice versa.

One has but to reflect (a) that the price-range of any important item can be split into more than three or five possible prices, (b) that the number of important items to be bought or sold over the lifetime of a project can easily exceed four, (c) that the number of periods of any of the investment streams under comparison can exceed four and, indeed, is often likely to exceed ten, and (d) that there are frequently more than two investment options to compare, to realize that the number of possible events, or outcomes, can run into billions of billions. Attempts to deal with the uncertainty aspects of cost–benefit studies in this game-theory fashion is, therefore, hardly a practical proposition even with the most advanced computers.

When it is further recalled that, as distinct from simple game-theory techniques, not only is the number of distinct events *not* given to us exogenously (as indicated above, it is generated from alternative prices chosen arbitrarily from guesses about the likely range), but also that not all events are equally likely, inasmuch as not all the alternative prices are equally likely, it is not surprising that, in any practical evaluation of investment projects no recourse is had to the formal apparatus of game theory.

41 Simple probability in decision making

1   The techniques illustrated in game theory are based on the assumption that there is no knowledge at all available that could throw any light on the likelihood of each of the alternative events, b_1, b_2, b_3, occurring over the period in question. In the complete absence of such knowledge, we can no more suppose that b_1 is as likely to occur as b_2 than we can suppose that b_1 is more (or less) likely to occur. We can say no more of the events in question than that each is possible. Once a suspicion about the greater likelihood of one or more of the possible events occurring begins to form, the simple game-theory method may require modification. In general, the more information about likelihoods we can obtain, the more agreement about the best decision we can hope to secure. If, from years of keeping records about floods, we could attach probabilities to each of two possible outcomes b_1 and b_2 in Table 38.1, our procedure would be to include those probabilities as weights in working out a solution.

2   Suppose that event b_1 (flood) can be expected with a probability of p_1, say 3/5, and event b_2 (no flood) therefore with a probability p_2 of $(1 - p_1)$, or 2/5, we make our calculations in a way illustrated by Table 41.1.

If option a_1 is chosen, each of the outcomes, 130,000 and 400,000, corresponding to the possible events, b_1 and b_2 respectively, is multiplied by the probability of the occurrence of the event, 3/5 and 2/5. The weighted average, or mathematical expectation, of the gains from choosing a_1 is entered in the third column, as also is the weighted average of gains from choosing a_2 and a_3. The largest weighted average is obviously 238,000, arising from the choice of option a_1, which can be regarded in the circumstances as the proper decision.

Table 41.1

	$b_1 (p_1 = 3/5)$	$b_2 (p_2 = 2/5)$	*Weighted average*	*Largest weighted average*
a_1	130,000 × 3/5	400,000× 2/5	238,000	238,000
a_2	140,000× 3/5	260,000 × 2/5	188,000	
a_3	80,000 × 3/5	90,000 × 2/5	84,000	

Now if this figure of 238,000 could be regarded as the anticipated value of net revenue from choosing a_1, in the sense that there is a stronger likelihood of a net revenue of 238,000 occurring when a_1 is chosen than of any other single value, we might have less hesitation in opting for a_1 rather than a_2 or a_3. But this figure of 238,000 for a_1 can be regarded as the expected value only in the conventional statistical sense; that is to say, if it were possible to repeat this experiment year after year for, say, the next 100 years or so, then – provided that the relevant climatic conditions remain unaltered – the *average* net revenue from choosing a_1, taken over the 100 years, would be close to 238,000. For roughly 3/5 of the century, or for roughly 60 out of the 100 years, event b_1 would occur, and for the remaining years event b_2 would occur.

It is clear, then, that if we are thinking in terms of many years ahead, on the one hand, we can (if relevant conditions are not expected to change very much) expect to come close to the (undiscounted) average of 238,000 by repeatedly opting for a_1. If, on the other hand, we are interested in the outcome next year alone, we obviously cannot expect a net revenue of 238,000 from choosing a_1. For in one year, only one event will occur. If b_1 occurs, the net revenue will be 130,000. If, instead, b_2 occurs, the net revenue will be 400,000. All we can say is that, on the basis of past evidence, there is more chance of b_1 occurring than b_2. And the higher the probability of b_1's occurring, the more we are disposed to expect it and to have our decision governed by the thought of its occurrence.

If, to take more extreme probabilities, we discovered from the records that floods occur, on the average, in nine years out of ten, we should be justified in expecting a flood next year, and in being surprised if it did not occur. The net revenue we can most reasonably expect if we choose a_1 is therefore 130,000. By the same logic, the net revenue we should be inclined to expect by choosing option a_2 is 140,000. This being so, we might conclude that the rational thing is to choose a_2. But once we have probabilities attached to the various events it would not be very sensible to focus our expectations on the event with the highest probability and ignore the possibility of the other events occurring. Thus, whether the probability of event b_1 occurring is 3/5 or 9/10, the decision maker is not completely indifferent to the outcome arising from event b_2 – unless that outcome is the same, say, 200,000, whatever option is chosen. The greater the gain in choosing a_1 (given that b_2 occurs) compared with that in choosing a_2, the more weight he will give to the a_1 option. To illustrate with extreme figures, if choice of a_1 would entail an outcome of 1,000,000 if event b_2 occurred whereas the choice of a_2 entailed an outcome of zero for the same event, the nine chances out of ten that b_1 would occur – conferring an additional 10,000 if a_2 were chosen rather than a_1 – would hardly be likely to prevail against the thought that if, despite its slim chance, b_2 did occur a net gain of 1,000,000 would be collected.

3   We may conclude tentatively that dependable probabilities will be taken into account by the decision maker in such cases; moreover, that the use of these probabilities as weights in the method indicated above (by reference to Table 41.1), would be acceptable to many as a rough general rule. By choosing an option on the basis of a weighted average of events, rather than on the basis of a single most likely event, we are in effect refusing to neglect the possible impact of the less likely event(s) on our decision, and doing so in a systematic and conventional manner.

42 Mixed strategies in decision making

1 Records covering many years can provide information *additional* to the probability of each of a number of alternative events occurring, such as b_1 and b_2. For instance, in addition to discovering that over, say, 100 years event b_1 (flood) occurred in 60 out of 100 years, that is, with a frequency of 3/5, and event b_2 (no flood) therefore with a frequency of 2/5, the records may reveal the following information: (i) prior to event b_1, a period of several weeks of cloudy weather – a condition we refer to as z_1 – was observed in half the number of b_1 events; (ii) prior to event b_1, a period of several weeks of mixed weather – referred to as z_2 – was observed in one-third of the number of b_1 events; (iii) prior to event b_1, a period of several weeks of clear weather – say z_3 – was observed in one-sixth of the number of b_1 events.

The same sort of information will be available for event b_2 which, it is assumed, is completely independent of b_1. Let us suppose, therefore, that z_1 (several weeks of cloudy weather) was observed prior to one-sixth of the number of b_2 (no flood) events; that z_2 (several weeks of mixed weather) was observed prior to one-third of the number of b_2 events; and that z_3 (several weeks of clear weather) was observed prior to one-half of the number of b_2 events. If we can assume that basic climatic and other relevant conditions will remain much the same, we can treat these frequencies as probabilities. And if so, we can get better results than those reached by adopting what are called 'pure' strategies; that is, by adopting *one of* options a_1 or a_2 or a_3. These better results are attained by recourse to 'mixed' strategies, which are no more than a combination of pure options – adopting a_1, a fraction of the time, a_2 another fraction of the time and a_3 the remainder of the time.

2 Thus, instead of the choice between the three simple options, a_1, a_2 and a_3, let the reader think of a larger number of quite arbitrary mixed strategies; call them $s_1, s_2, s_3, \ldots, s_n$. For example, strategy s_1 might require that, if z_1 is observed, a_1 is to be chosen; if z_2 occurs, a_2 is to be chosen; if z_3 occurs, a_3 is to be chosen. Strategy s_2 might be as follows: if z_1 occurs, choose a_1; if z_2 occurs, choose a_2, while if z_3 occurs, choose a_2 again. Strategy s_3 might be, if z_1 or z_2 or z_3 occurs, choose a_2, and so on.

Now suppose event b_1 were to take place, we should, as indicated above, expect to observe weather condition z_1 with a probability of 1/2, z_2 with a probability of 1/3 and z_3 with a probability of 1/6. The expected or average outcome over a period of time from adopting, say, strategy s_1 (in the event that b_1 occurs) is obtained by weighting each of the net revenues attaching to the options designated by strategy s_1 by the probabilities of the zs. Thus, strategy s_1 prescribes that we select option a_1 (with outcome 130 in case of event b_1) should z_1 occur, which it does with a probability of 1/2. The first component of strategy s_1, in that event, is $1/2 \times 130$. The second component of strategy s_1 requires that we select a_2 (with outcome 140 for event b_1) should z_2 occur, which it does with a probability of 1/3. Consequently, the second component of strategy s_1 is equal to $1/3 \times 140$. Similarly, the third component of strategy s_1 prescribes option a_3 (with outcome of 80 for b_1) should z_3 occur, which it does with a probability of 1/6. Hence, it is equal to $1/6 \times 80$.

Given event b_1 then, the expected value of revenue from employing strategy s_1 is equal to

$$(1/2 \times 130) + (1/3 \times 140) + (1/6 \times 80) = 125$$

Given the same b_1 event, we could work out the expected value of the revenue from employing strategy s_2. The same steps in the calculation give it as

$$(1/2 \times 130) + (1/3 \times 140) + (1/6 \times 140) = 136$$

Given the same b_1 event again, the employment of strategy s_3 will realize an expected value equal to

$$(1/2 \times 140) + (1/3 \times 140) + (1/6 \times 140) = 140$$

And so we could go on calculating expected revenues, in the event b_1 takes place, for all the other strategies.

If, instead, event b_2 occurred, the relevant probabilities of z_1, z_2 and z_3 would be 1/6, 1/3 and 1/2, respectively, and employing the original s_1 strategy would, therefore, yield an expected value of revenue equal to

$$(1/6 \times 400) + (1/3 \times 200) + (1/2 \times 90) = 199$$

Employing strategy s_2, however, would yield an expected value of net revenue equal to

$$(1/6 \times 400) + (1/3 \times 260) + (1/2 \times 260) = 284$$

while recourse to strategy s would yield an expected value of revenue equal to

$$(1/6 \times 260) + (1/3 \times 260) + (1/2 \times 260) = 260$$

These results can be displayed in Table 42.1 for all n possible strategies, though in fact only the first three strategies and the last strategy are represented there. Some strategies are likely to be dominated by others and would not stay in the table. After eliminating all the dominated strategies, we are left with a choice of mixed strategies which we could re-number $S_1, S_3, \ldots, S_m$.

3   What is the advantage of all this? On the surface it would appear to offer a larger range of choices.[1] Granted that the use of these strategies offers us more choice, how do we go about selecting the best strategy?

In fact, we are 'back to square one' – *except* that there are apparently many more choices of strategy than the initial three options. With the data given in Table 42.1, that is, we could employ the maximin method, or the minimax-regret method, or some other method in order to select one of these new strategies. Indeed, where we can attach probabilities also to events b_1 and b_2, we can employ the method outlined in the preceding chapter: we can, that is, calculate the weighted average net revenue for each of the listed strategies and choose that yielding the highest revenue.

Again, however, if we are concerned with the outcome over the next one or two years only, the method outlined is of much less use than if, instead, we can adopt the strategy for a largish number of years. Consider, for instance, the calculated net revenue of 125 that arises from employing strategy s_1 in the event that b_1 takes place. True, if b_1 is to occur, we shall observe z_1 with a probability of $1/2$, z_2 with a probability of $1/3$ and z_3 with a probability of $1/6$. But in responding to the zs according to the adopted strategy, here s_1, we cannot hope to realize in this same year a revenue of 125. For in the one year one of z_1 or z_2 or z_3 is observed and, therefore, according to the strategy chosen, one of a_1 or a_2 or a_3 is adopted. The net revenue in that event is one of 130 or 140 or 80 – not 125, however, which

Table 42.1 (in thousand dollars per annum)

	b_1	b_2
s_1	125	199
s_2	136	284
s_3	140	260
"	"	"
"	"	"
s_n	140	160

1   We can, of course, include the pure strategies (the choice of option a_1 alone, a_2 alone or a_3 alone) among these mixed strategies. The choice of a_1 alone might be numbered strategy S_8, with a_1 being chosen irrespective of the occurrence of z_1, z_2 and z_3, so yielding 130 for b_1 and 400 for b_2 as in Table 41.1. The choice of a_2 alone would enter, say, as strategy S_9, with a_2 being chosen regardless of the occurrence of z_1, z_2 and z_3, so yielding 140 for b_1 and 260 for b_2 as in Table 41.1, assuming as before that all the figures are in thousands of dollars.

is but an average figure to which the revenues will converge only if, whenever b_1 occurs (which is about 3/5 of the total number of years), we continue to use strategy s_1. Similar remarks apply to the figure of 199. It follows that if, say, over the next 100 years event b_1 could be expected to occur 3/5 of the time and event b_2 the remaining 2/5 of the time, the repeated use of strategy s_1 could be expected to give a series of (undiscounted) revenues that would average about (3/5 $\times$ 125) + (2/5 $\times$ 199), or 155. If, over the same period, s_2 instead were repeatedly employed, the average (undiscounted) revenue to expect would be (3/5 $\times$ 136) + (2/5 $\times$ 284), or 196. We could work out the (undiscounted) average revenues for all the mixed strategies listed, and expect, in general, that at least one such strategy would produce a weighted average above the highest (238), for the pure strategy makes no use of the zs.[2]

4   We may conclude that the information about such indicators as the zs can be of use in improving the decision process through mixed strategies only when events over a large number of years, or over a large number of similar projects, are anticipated. If, for example, a reservoir is to be used under the same environmental conditions for many years to come, or if a large number of similar reservoirs are to be constructed, there can be advantages in using information provided by the zs in order to produce a variety of mixed strategies. Having chosen the maximum-yielding strategy, it must be employed repeatedly over the future in the first case, or applied to each of the many reservoirs in the second case. If, however, what matters is the revenue for only one or two years and/or for only one or two reservoirs – or if, alternatively, environmental conditions cannot be expected to remain unchanged – (so that one cannot reasonably attach probabilities to events b_1, b_2 or to the indicators z_1, z_2, z_3), the method of contingent probabilities outlined above is of little practical use.

2 Given an appropriate rate of discount, we could, of course, calculate the DPV of any future net revenue and produce a strategy that would yield a highest weighted average *discounted* net revenue.

43 Four additional stratagems for coping with uncertainty

1 If game theory, as a useful method for dealing with future uncertainty, is something of a forlorn hope, the certainty equivalence perhaps too crude, and the more sophisticated conditional probability approach (of the earlier chapter on Mixed Strategies) rather cumbersome, there yet remain a number of proposals that may be employed. In this penultimate chapter, we outline four of these proposals:

   (i) tampering with the discount rate of interest
 (ii) the setting of upper and lower limits to the calculated annual net benefit figures
(iii) the construction of a normal distribution of possible net benefit figures when allowance is made for future price movements
(iv) recourse to yields on commercial investment.

2 The commonly used device (i) consists simply of adding one or two percentage points to the Pareto-determined rate of interest – that used in conditions of certainty and discussed at length in Part V – which, for brevity, we can refer to as the pure rate of discount (or compounding). Bearing in mind the possibility of future losses, it may be thought advisable to add, say, two percentage points to the pure rate of 6 per cent, so that 8 per cent would be used in calculating the net benefit figure of the project before presenting the result to the political decision makers.

There are, of course, some obvious objections to this common device. First, the choice of percentage points to be added to the pure rate is quite arbitrary. Second, the proportional reduction in the initial annual net benefit figures (those calculated with the pure rate) not only increases with the number of years, but does so at an exponential rate, so adding to the arbitrariness of the procedure.

Moreover, the device implicitly assumes that, although the magnitude of the future net benefits are uncertain, they must certainly decline, a built-in pessimism about the movement of prices or valuation over the future that is generally unwarranted.

3 When device (ii) is used, it is implicitly acknowledged that it is no less possible for the annual net benefits to rise over the future as to fall. Thus, if we restricted ourselves to tampering with the discount rate, we should present to the policy makers both a pessimistic net benefit figure for the project from adding some percentage points to the pure rate and also an optimistic net benefit figure from subtracting some percentage points. Although more even handed, such a proposal would still be subject to the objection that the successive resulting magnitudes of the annual net benefit figures increase or decrease at an exponential rate.

It may, therefore, be better to eschew any tampering with the discount rate and, instead, attempt to make allowance for the future uncertainty by setting an upper and lower limit to the net benefit figure for each successive year, such limits becoming wider as we move further from the present. For example, in a first period comprising, say, two or three years, the upper and lower limits could be set, respectively, at 1.5 per cent above and 1.5 per cent below the initial net benefit figure for those years (as calculated with the pure rate of interest). For the second such period, the respective limits could be widened to 2.5 percentage points: the third period to 4 percentage points, and so on.

Although this ruse would obviate the exponential feature entailed in a resort to tampering with the discount rate, the determination of an upper and lower limit to the successive annual net benefit figures is unavoidably arbitrary. Yet it is, on balance, preferable to tampering with the discount rate; not only does it avoid the unwarranted exponential feature, economists with some experience in the application of cost–benefit methods will have some judgement about the extent of upper and lower limits for future annual net benefits.

4 Allowing that we cannot be sure whether future net benefits will rise or fall below those initially calculated, we may resort to (iii), constructing something like a normal distribution of possible net benefit figures for the investment project (whether DPV or CTV), each net benefit figure depending on forecasts of the more relevant input and output prices. One begins with the estimates, or rather 'guesstimates', by one or several experts (if they can be found) of the movement in the prices of these relevant materials over future years. And it is from an average of these informed guesstimates of price movements over the future that the required probability distribution of possible net benefit figures for the project is to be constructed.

The method can be illustrated by supposing, say, four chief inputs, K_1, K_2, K_3 and K_4 – or K_i inputs (where $i = 1, 2, 3, 4$) – the 'guesstimated' prices for each successive period t, where $t = 1, 2, \ldots, 10$, to be set respectively at p_1^t, p_2^t, p_3^t, and p_4^t for each of the four inputs, and allowing a 20-year project to be divided into ten periods of two years each.

Each of our experts is required to offer three alternative prices for each of the inputs in any one period: a most likely figure along with its likelihood of occurring (in percentage terms); and both an upper-limit figure and a lower-limit figure, along with their respective likelihoods. So as not to encumber the exposition we shall suppose that the annual benefits produced by the project are wholly in kind and are enjoyed by a fixed population, as a result of which it may be further assumed that the real value of each of the annual *benefits* remains unchanged over the time span of the project.

For our first two-year period, that is for $t = 1$, our experts are to choose three alternative prices for input K_1, say coke; that is, three alternative prices for p_1 along with their respective probabilities.[1] We then use the average of each of these three prices, along with an average of their corresponding probabilities. We treat the remaining three inputs in the same way for this first period so that, for this one period, there are altogether 12 possible future prices to consider. These 12 possible future prices must then be guesstimated for each of the subsequent nine periods.

5   We now illustrate the procedure, beginning with the three guesstimated p_1^1 prices of the first input, coke, in the *first period*. Let us suppose that the actual price of coke in the immediate present (p_1^0 at time zero) is $20, the most likely price in the first period *averaging* $22 with probability 60 per cent, the upper-limit price averaging $25 with probability 30 per cent, and the lower limit price averaging $18 with a 10 per cent probability.

Given this most likely price of p_1^1 is $22, which is $2 more than the actual p_1^0 price of $20, and the probability attributed to its occurring is 60 per cent, its *weighted* P_1^1 price is calculated as equal to p_1^0 plus 60 percent of $2, or $21.20. Or, put formally, $P_1^1 = p_1^0 + \Delta p_1^0 \ (pr.)$, where Δp_1^0 is the difference above the original price of coke of $20 at time zero, and *pr.* is the probability of its occurrence.

The weighted *upper-limit* price P_1^1 is, in this formula, equal to $20 + $5(0.3), or $21.50, and the weighted *lower-limit* price P_1^1 equal to $20 - $2(0.1), or $19.80. The three weighted prices for the K_2 input in this first period are calculated in the same way, as are also the three weighted prices for the remaining two inputs, K_3 and K_4.

Again, if in the *second period*, the most likely price of the K_1 input, coke, comes to $24 with a 50 per cent probability, the weighted most likely price of P_1^2 is equal to $20 + $4(0.5) or $22. Similarly, a $27 *upper* limit for p_1^2 with a 30 per cent probability, and a p_1^2 *lower* limit of $17 with a 10 per cent probability, will result in a P_1^2 of $22.10 and a P_1^2 of $19.70, respectively. Needless to say, the most likely weighted prices for each of the other inputs, K_2, K_3 and K_4, are calculated in the same way.

Performing the same operation for the three alternative weighted guesstimate prices of each of the four inputs for the remaining eight periods, we end up with a total of, say, *m*, permutations of 40 such prices for each of the ten periods. In consequence, we can calculate *m* distinct net benefit figures for the project in question (although all of these *m* net benefit figures need not be different).

It transpires, however, that the number *m* in our simple example, is very large indeed.

---

1 We could, of course, distinguish these three alternative prices by adding to p_1^1 a suffix, say M, L and U, to indicate the *most* likely price, and the *lower* and *upper* prices, respectively, of the input coke in this first, second and subsequent periods. But we have avoided cluttering up the notation unnecessarily.

If, for ease of exposition, we refer to these weighted guesstimated future input prices simply as future prices, this total number of permutations m can be calculated as follows: For the first period, any one of the three future prices of input K_1 can be combined with any one of the three future prices of input K_2, which two chosen prices can then be combined with one of the three future prices of input K_3, which resulting three prices can then be combined with any one of the three future prices of input K_4. Hence the number of permutations of the four chosen input prices in the first period come to 3^4, or 89, permutations of a set of four input prices.

Each one of these 89 permutations of four prices in the first period, however, can be combined with any one of the 89 permutations of four input prices in the second period. For these first two periods, then, the total number of permutations of a set of eight input prices amount to 89^2. Continuing in this way for each successive period, the total number of permutations of the resulting set of 40 input prices amounts to 89^{10}. The number m, therefore, runs into trillions.[2]

6   Not much imagination is required to enable us to realize that we need not spend the best years of our lives in attempting to calculate the net benefit figures for each of these m permutations. A relatively small sample of two or three hundred of such permutations chosen at random should suffice for producing a normal distribution of net benefit figures that is not very different from the normal distribution of the m net benefit figures.

Such a sample, it should be evident, is generated as follows: one chooses at random – or set the computer to choose at random – only one of the three alternative future prices of input K_1 in the first period and only one of the three alternative future prices of each of the remaining three inputs, K_2, K_3, K_4, in that period. We continue doing the same for each of the nine remaining periods, so choosing at random a set of 40 different prices in all. From each of the set of 40 input prices, a particular net benefit figure is calculated.

When this operation is repeated two or three hundred times, the resulting two or three hundred calculated net benefit figures, when ranked according to magnitude, should reveal a normal distribution with many of the same characteristics as those in the distribution of the whole population of m net benefit figures. Should there be any doubt about this, one continues drawing random samples. If after, say, another hundred or so such samples are taken, no significant change in the distribution can be observed, we may conclude that the sample distribution is satisfactory.

7   It cannot be gainsaid that this ingenious stratagem for dealing with future uncertainty has an appeal to the theoretical mind. The problem, however, is that of

---

2 Even if there were only two input prices to consider in each period, and only two guesstimates for each input price, the total number of permutations of the resulting 20-price set would come to over one million.

securing plausible guesstimates of the price movement of the relevant materials over a longish time span. Quite apart from having to make allowance for inflation over future years, the prices of some materials that may be used as inputs for the project might well be quite volatile over time. Yet, even for the less volatile input prices, forecasts of their future movements are not likely to be held with any confidence beyond a decade or so.

It must be concluded that this stratagem for dealing with future uncertainty can be useful only under limited circumstances: where, for instance, the time span of the project is relatively short and where, in addition, it is reasonable to expect little variation in the relevant input and output prices over the allocated time span of the project. Moreover, even if the resultant range of cost–benefit figures is held with a fair degree of confidence, it would be acceptable, or more acceptable, only if the demand for each of the *goods* produced by the project was unlikely to deviate much from its anticipated growth path.

8   In Western economies with a large private investment sector and a well-organized capital market, the economist may plausibly adopt the return on private investment (stratagem iv) as the appropriate opportunity yield for the returns on investments in the public sector.

Assuming that the risk run by each type of private investment can be arranged as a probability distribution, some average of the range of expected or actuarial rates of return on private investments may be adopted as the opportunity yield in evaluating each of the anticipated annual returns of a public project at some common point of time, either present or future.

9   It has been argued, however, that, where the funds for investing in a public project are raised wholly from tax revenues, this yield in the private investment sector may be replaced as the appropriate opportunity yield for public investment purposes only if the (subjective) cost of risk-bearing is the same for the taxpayer as it is for the individual private investor. The argument[3] is that, if the benefits and costs are to be measured, as they should be in terms of compensation variations – willingness to pay a maximum sum for benefits received, willingness to accept a minimal sum for losses incurred – the (subjective) costs of risk-bearing must be subtracted from the net benefits of the investment project in order to obtain a correct measure of its value to the recipient. According to this analysis, where the number of taxpayers is large, the risk borne by each one in respect of any particular public investment project becomes negligible. In contrast, the risk-bearing costs of a similar project to a limited number of private investors can be appreciable. Hence, it is concluded, it is not so much the government's pooling of investment risks from its undertaking of a large-number of investment projects that justifies the ignoring of the risks – or not only such investment pooling – but rather the fact of spreading the risk of any single investment over a very large number of

3 By Arrow and Lind (1970).

taxpayers.[4] As a corollary, it follows that a public investment with an expected rate of return below that of a private investment may yet be economically superior, for what is relevant in the comparison is not the expected rates of return *per se* but the expected rates of return net of the (subjective) costs of risk-bearing.[5]

Assuming that increased investment in the public sector entails reduced expenditure in the private sector, the above argument is valid wherever funds are raised by tax revenues (not by selling government securities), and wherever the public agency is restricted in the use of its investable funds to specified projects.

10   Obviously the riskier the type of private investment, the higher the expected rate of return – a consequence both of risk-aversion and the tax disadvantages of investing in projects that yield highly variable returns.[6] But whatever the reasons for the higher gross rates of return expected on riskier private investments, the conclusion remains unaffected. If the placing of public funds in the riskier type of private investment can, in fact, realize higher gross returns over time, then – in the absence of the Arrow–Lind conditions – no public investment ought to be undertaken that is expected to yield gross returns that are any lower.

To illustrate, if the A-type of private investment has an expected yield of 10 per cent before tax and the B-type of investment, which is riskier, has an expected yield of 14 per cent before tax, then, for society as a whole, continued investment only in the A-type investment produces a return of 10 per cent, whereas continued investment only in the B-type investment produces a return of 14 per cent.[7] If a succession of specific public projects is expected to yield, say, 12 per cent, then, in undertaking them, the agency is indeed forgoing the opportunity of earning an additional 2 per cent by investing instead in the B-type investment

Of course, one might do better yet if more information could be secured at low cost. If it were possible to know in advance the actual return to be realized on each particular B-type investment that the government could undertake as an alternative to a given public project, then such actual private yields – which would vary over time from one B-type of investment to another – could properly be used as the appropriate opportunity yield rather than the overall actuarial rate of return on all risky B-type investments. Such information, alas, is just not available at low cost: if it were, there would be no problem of uncertainty. The information we can

4 If the assumptions of rationality and full information are relaxed, we can justify neglecting the risk-costs of public investment in so far as the taxpayer experiences no anxiety about possible losses simply because he overlooks any connection between a loss incurred by a public investment and a possible increase in his tax payments.

5 A amendment to the Arrow–Lind thesis was made by Fisher (1973). He points out that, in so far as the risks involved are external diseconomies, or 'public bads', the damage experienced by each person does not diminish with the increase in the number of people who, also, will be the beneficiaries of the public investment.

6 The individual investor in risky projects may, however, be able to overcome the tax disadvantages to some extent by spreading his investment over a number of such projects.

7 Ignoring the tendency for the return to decline as more B-type investment is undertaken.

more reasonably hope for is an average rate of return for the B-type investment when a fair number of such investments have been undertaken. And, under given conditions, we might reasonably anticipate that this average rate, say 14 per cent, will continue over the near future. Only if this 14 per cent can reasonably be expected to continue up to the terminal year of the public project in question, however, can it be regarded as the appropriate opportunity yield in any public investment criterion. If the return on this B-type investment is expected to rise or fall over that period, modifications have to be made accordingly.

11   Care must be taken in the use of this highest actuarial rate of return, say, ρ, that is to be adopted as the basis of the social opportunity yield in public investment criteria. Only where the political constraint is such that the public agency has the option of wholly reinvesting at ρ all the returns of any project, is ρ to be used as the appropriate reinvestment rate (in the absence of superior public reinvestment opportunities). The reader will recall from our treatment of investment criteria in Part V that, in some cases, the public agency is constrained to distribute the benefits in cash or kind direct to the public, i.e. it is not permitted wholly to reinvest these returns in the private investment sector. Since, in these other cases, the usual behaviour assumption that is adopted has it that the public saves only a fraction of the cash return paid out to the recipients, which fraction saved may be supposed to be added to investment in the private sector.

12   We must remind ourselves, however, that we have assumed that a Western country has a large private investment sector. The larger this sector, the more appropriate it is to use the highest actuarial rate of return that may confidently be expected from private investments as the opportunity yield for public investment projects, at least in the absence of political constraints bearing on the alternative uses of public funds.

In countries where the private investment sector is not large, the employment of some average of yields on private investments (as the opportunity yield for public investment projects) is not appropriate, and we must seek further information to enable us to make plausible assessments of expected rates of return on alternative uses of the funds available for public projects. If such an assessment is not possible, we may have to fall back on using the community's rate of time preference as the opportunity yield in evaluating public investments. But if we do take this step, we must concede that we have lost sight of the uncertainty problem.

13   Thus, although this last of the four stratagems – the employment of some average of the actuarial yields on private investment as the opportunity yield on public investments – is the simplest way of coping with future uncertainty, it can hardly be recommended as an effective stratagem.

An average of the actuarial rates of return on a chosen set of private investments may make allowance for the future variability of this chosen average *only* if the range of the future variability is not much different from the past. But, of course, there can be no presumption that this will tend to be the case. The private investor knows this or, if he does not, he ought to. And in tacitly accepting this unavoidable future uncertainty, he is, in effect, a gambler.

In contrast, the economist entrusted with advising the political decision makers by producing net-benefit estimates of particular public investments cannot be so cavalier in this respect. He is obliged to deal explicitly with the unavoidable uncertainty of the relevant variables over the future. He must select some stratagem that places limits on the possible movement of the range of annual net-benefit estimates over the future. And, wherever possible, he must also consider the costs of using any method that might possibly reduce the incidence of uncertainty over the future.

Part VIII

Further notes

44 A summing up

1 A characteristic of the modern age is the inordinate respect which the production of figures commands. Nothing impresses people more than quantification of some sort, be it surveys, statistics, merit rankings, indices of economic or social trends, or money measures of gains and losses.

It is not surprising, then, that there is seldom a debate today about the propriety of some economic measure without someone calling for a CBA. Apparently, among politicians and the public at large, the belief persists that economists are also practitioners of a sort of black art, which enables them not only to rank economic alternatives, but also to calculate the actual magnitude of gains or losses arising from any proposed economic change.

Although the practising economist is, of course, aware that the regard in which he is held by the innocent public would not stand up well to close scrutiny, he accepts it as incumbent upon him to put himself out to go to some lengths in the attempt to produce reasonably reliable estimates of gains and losses of introducing economic measures, plus some idea of the confidence that can be reposed in his findings.

Bearing in mind such good intentions, let us now sum up our views on the practice of CBA by addressing ourselves briefly to three main aspects: (i) the methods adopted in CBA for selecting and processing the relevant data, in particular the economic concepts and techniques to be used; (ii) the ways and means of gathering data, whether from econometric studies, surveys or questionnaires; and (iii) the proposals for coping with uncertainty over the future of the movements of the relevant variables.

2 With regard to the second aspect, the ways of gathering the required data, ample space is given to it in several popular textbooks on CBA, the proposals being illustrated by innumerable examples. Also provided there are series of exercises intended to sharpen the student's understanding of the matter treated in successive chapters. Containing, as they do, a plethora of examples, tables, graphs, etc., there is much to be said for the usefulness of these ambitious manuals.

Important as this second aspect is, we have nonetheless confined ourselves in this volume chiefly to the first and more controversial aspect – to both a detailed exposition and a critical assessment of the economic concepts and techniques that we have argued are proper to the practice of CBA. Our decision to concentrate on what may be called theoretical constructs may be justified in view of the fact that, in general, the existing treatment of this primary aspect is far from satisfactory and is, indeed, often misleading.[1]

3 Although the occasional textbook appears in which the authors vaunt their 'broad church' approach, we have no hesitation in rejecting as erroneous any manifestation of eclecticism in respect of techniques to be employed in CBA. No one doubts that a cavalier attitude in this respect makes it easier to come up with figures, indeed with sets of figures. But the question to be faced in such cases is that of the meaning to be attached to the figures.

As indicated earlier, our notion of the validity of the economic concepts and techniques that may be used in a CBA turns on its conformity with the maxims long accepted in mainstream economics, namely, (i) that the value the economist is to place on any good or bad affecting a person is no more or less than that which the person himself places on it, and (ii) that, within some defined community, the net social benefit of any economic change is equal to the algebraic sum of the individual valuations of all who, in one way or another, are affected by the change.

These maxims which go to form the only acceptable foundation on which CBAs can be raised also have the incidental but singular merit of making the findings of a cost–benefit calculation easily understood by the elected policy makers in the community. And this understanding must be augmented by making it clear that, although the calculation of a positive net social benefit may be *said* to meet a Pareto criterion, it is generally one that only realizes a *potential* potential Pareto improvement for the community.[2]

So informed, the community's decision makers are enabled to make, if not wise policy decisions, at least decisions that accord with their broad economic goals.

In this connection, moreover, we have sought to make it evident why, in any such calculation, the economist is to restrict himself to the economic data only. In

1 Among the more common errors still to be found in the many textbooks on the subject, we may mention: the alleged measure of 'excess loss' or 'deadweight loss' believed to be incurred when a project is to be financed by raising excise (or even income) taxes; the measurement of 'producers' surplus' regarded as a sort of rent to producers; occasional blurring of the difference between resource cost and opportunity cost; the employment of a statistical measure of the value of a life lost, or of a disease, disablement or other misfortune; the licentious adding or subtracting of consumer surpluses without attention to the pertinent *ceteris paribus* clauses; a failure to emphasize the difference between the CV^{12} and CV^{21} measure of a good and bad which can be crucial to the cost–benefit calculation, especially in projects affecting the environment; the arguments purporting to show that the DPV method is to be preferred above the IRR method and, more generally, a naïve treatment of the ways future net benefits are to be discounted.

2 A project that affects the welfare of only a small community for a short period (no longer than three or four years) may be able, however, to realize a potential Pareto improvement.

particular, he is to eschew recourse to any weighting of money values, whether distributional weights or socio-political weights. The economist should, of course, be ready to inform policy makers about the distributional *consequences* of introducing specified economic measures. But it is entirely up to the policy makers themselves whether an otherwise beneficial project or measure should be rejected in consideration of the regressive distributional effects of its implementation, or vice versa.[3]

4   A penultimate word about those expected external effects that we know about yet which currently elude reliable methods of measuring their dollar value. Granted that the economist cannot include them in his calculus, he can at least make clear the area of ignorance. Thus, after seeking to measure all that can be measured with honesty, he can, first, also provide a physical description of these unmeasurable spillovers, and some idea of their significance. Second, he may offer a guess, or a range of guesses, at the value of damage to be expected. He will certainly want to avoid spurious quantification – spurious because based on invalid concepts. Third, and as a development of the preceding suggestion, he can have recourse to what have been called elsewhere (Mishan, 1969a) 'contingency calculations', these being the estimates of a critical magnitude for these unmeasurable spillovers which will just offset the excess benefits of a project that is calculated in disregard of them.

To illustrate, if the cost–benefit calculation of a new airport produces an excess benefit over cost of some $10 million per annum for the next t years, but only by ignoring the aircraft noise it generates, the increased traffic congestion it causes and the increased loss of life that is expected to follow, the economist can impress the authorities and the public with the importance of these consequences by making hypothetical estimates of a critical *average* loss per person, or per family, based on rough calculations of the numbers of people likely to be affected. Thus, (a) if it were reckoned that about half a million additional families would suffer in varying degrees as a result of the newly located airport, an annual compensatory sum averaging as little as $20 per family would wholly offset the excess benefit. Again, (b) if the new airport becomes responsible for adding to the road congestion within the region of the airport, so as to cause an average delay of one hour a week to about one million motorists, this delay alone, if valued at 20 cents an hour, would wholly offset the $10 million of excess benefits of the project. Similarly for loss of life, and any other remaining side effects.

Even though the estimate of the number of people affected is speculative, provided it is not altogether implausible, the resulting contingency calculations may

---

3 It is perhaps unnecessary to remark that cost-effective analysis, which seeks to determine the lowest resource cost of meeting specified goals (or else the largest increase of some good, or largest reduction of some bad, for a given resource cost) has some affinity with the maxims of mainstream economics. Other than occasional recourse to a discounting or compounding procedure, cost-effectiveness is a less sophisticated discipline than CBA.

well cast doubt as to the economic feasibility of the scheme – enough doubt, at least, to delay a decision until estimates of these less tangible, but socially import-ant, features of the scheme can be made with greater assurance. However, there may be instances in which the per person, or per family, valuation of the spillover deriving from the contingency calculation will be so large as to place the economic infeasibility of the scheme beyond doubt.

5   Turning to the third aspect of CBA entails removing the provisional accep-tance of our estimates of annual net benefits over the future. Here we are bound to recognize the difficulties of coping with unavoidable uncertainties in the movements of the relevant prices and other variables in the years to come.

Clearly, one cannot expect the various proposals for coping with future uncer-tainty to be as satisfactory as those proposed for a valid framework of CBA. For one thing, of the variety of methods proposed for dealing with future consequence, none can be securely anchored in the individuals' own choices. In consequence, none can be vindicated by reference to the maxims of mainstream economics. However we may rank them, all methods proposed are, by necessity, arbitrary. The choice, in any given instance, of one technique rather than another for dealing with such uncertainty will therefore depend on the economist's own assessment of the project and the sorts of benefits and costs to be measured.

The fact that many public projects are directed to environmental improvements – to the reduction of pollution, of effluent, or to the creation of national parks, and the value of collective goods, which take the form of benefits in kind (much easier to calculate than the terminal value of annual cash payments) – the valuation of the former benefits over the future is less affected by the vicissitudes of the market or of economic events generally.[4]

4 There are also other projects that wholly or in part create collective goods, yet whose benefits are far more difficult to evaluate, because they are also sure to generate a variety of externalities over the future. Included among such projects are the creation of dams, irrigation systems, and canals.

Appendix 1
Brief historical background to CBA

CBA is currently an established technique that is widely used in both governments and international organizations. Although certain underlying concepts of the technique originated from Europe in the 1840s, the use of CBA in environmental economics is a relatively new occurrence, becoming established only after regulations were set by the US government which made the use of CBA mandatory in certain circumstances in the 1930s.

The two underlying concepts which originated from Europe are the concept of consumer surplus and the concept of externality. The concept of consumer surplus was argued by Jules Dupuit in 1844, when he pointed out that the users of roads and bridges in France enjoyed benefits in excess of the tolls they paid for the usage (Dupuit, 1844). In the 1920s, Pigou (1952: 183–92) effectively developed the concept of externality by arguing that there is a difference between private economic production and public economic product, citing child labour, maternity leave for working mothers, alcohol, war and factory pollution,

CBA in environmental applications took on a significant role with the enactment of the US Flood Control Act of 1936 which, among other things, stated that any flood control project should be deemed desirable if the benefits to whomsoever they may accrue are in excess of the estimated cost. Although no specific guidelines were given on the implementation of the standard, the Act effectively paved the way for the assessment of projects on the basis of calculating their net benefits and the entire social assessment of the net benefits instead of solely basing it on the financial appraisal, which looks at the interests of only the producers.

Owing to the lack of specific and concrete guidelines, inconsistent sets of standards and procedures were developed and implemented by the various agencies involved in the development of water resources. This gave the impression that each agency's main objective of the CBA was to justify the projects that each agency wanted to carry out instead of providing critical evaluations of the merits of the projects.

In order to ensure consistent and standardized practices and guidelines across different agencies, an inter-agency group was formed in 1946. Called the US Federal Inter-Agency River Basin Committee's Subcommittee on Benefits and Costs, it produced the *Proposed Practices for Economic Analysis of River Basin Projects* (1950; revised 1958) or more commonly known as the *Green Book*.

This publication together with the *Budget Circular A-47* by the Bureau of Budget in 1952, not only attempted to standardize practices among the agencies and bring them in line with economic theories, they also caught and encouraged academic interest.

A firm theoretical *framework* for CBA was finally established with works by three eminent economists (Eckstein, 1958; Krutilla and Eckstein, 1958; McKean, 1958) which methodically utilized neoclassical welfare economics in relation with CBA. The 1960s and 1970s saw the rapid development of CBA as numerous books and papers on the topic appeared, all trying to accomplish the deceptively simple objective of determining whether a proposed project's benefits exceeded costs and, if so, by how much.

Use of CBA became more institutionalized and widespread from 1960 onwards, as governments in the US, Canada and the UK required formal CBA before the commencement of certain policies and projects. In the US, President Lyndon Johnson implemented a planning-program-budget system (PPBS) throughout the federal government in 1965 which contributed to the widespread use of CBA. In Canada, Sewell *et al.*'s *Guide to Benefit–Cost Analysis* (1965) and the implementation of a PPBS system in 1967 led to popular use of CBA. In the UK, the institutionalization of CBA took place after the release of the 1967 *Government White Paper*, and CBA was used for the M1 motorway project, the 1970s Channel Tunnel Proposals and the Third London Airport, among many other projects. The academic contributions by Mishan (1971) on CBA and normative economics (1981) added significantly to the growing literature.

In addition to being adopted by governments, CBA was also formally adopted by several international organizations – the OECD in 1969, the UN in 1972 and the World Bank in 1975 (Squire and Van der Tak, 1975). At the Earth Summit in Rio de Janeiro in 1992, it was agreed that country application of financial support for public sector projects be subjected to passing the cost–benefit test as far as possible.

In 1980, US President Ronald Reagan signed Executive Order 12291, in which the efficiency criterion was explicitly required in the preparation of Regulatory Impact Analysis for regulations that are expected to have an annual effect of $100 million or more on the economy. This executive order was replaced by Executive Order 12866, signed by President Clinton in 1993. This new order is similar to the former, requiring that all the costs and benefits of available regulatory alternatives be considered in the process of deciding whether to proceed with certain regulations. This order has continued to remain relevant and in force.

Appendix 2
The normative interpretation of a CBA

There is a temptation for economists eager to advance the status of their discipline to argue that, irrespective of the results of distributional effects, a potential Pareto improvement may in fact lay claim to commanding a consensus within a Western society and, if so, to be a component of virtual constitution. If so regarded, a potential Pareto improvement would have no less a constitutional legitimacy as a political decision within a democratic society. The grounds for such a claim are as follows.

First, there exist within Western societies economic institutions – such as progressive taxation and the system of welfare assistance – that act over time to translate the potential economic improvement into an actual Pareto improvement. Although it would be unreasonable to suppose that literally everybody in the community would actually be made better off by a change that met the Pareto criterion, it is not unreasonable to suppose that the bulk of the population affected by the change would be better off and that not many would be worse off.

Second, even though it may be the case that, for each change sanctioned by the Pareto criterion, a number of people will be made worse off, a succession of such changes is not likely to inflict losses on the same group. Over time, therefore, there can be a presumption that everyone or nearly everyone will be made better off by consistent application of the Pareto criterion.

Third, where the Pareto criterion countenances a change in which a group of people among the lower income brackets suffer a loss, political decision makers can generally be counted upon either to reject the scheme or else to arrange adequate compensation for the losers.

Persuasive though these arguments are, they are not conclusive. For lack of a better one, a majority may be willing to abide by the Pareto criterion, but others will continue to have reservations. One particular reservation has, in fact, no direct affinity with the above considerations. It arises, instead, from a scepticism about the basic maxim which accepts as the ultimate data for the economist the subjective valuations of the individuals comprising the population in question.

Within a modern growth economy in which the so-called 'Joneses effect' is in evidence, in which personal attire is markedly exhibitionist, in which norms of taste are declining, and in which a growing proportion of its output is trivial if not regrettable, the valuations of individuals in forming a collective decision have less to recommend them. Certainly, there is greater reluctance today among segments of the public to accept the judgement of the market in the face of substantial expenditures on commercial advertising designed to influence the valuations placed on goods by individuals. One can bring to mind consumption activities that flourish in the atmosphere of the 'new permissiveness' that are held by a large proportion of the population to be degrading at the same time that they are believed by others to be innocuous or liberating.

In addition to such instances of an incipient fragmentation of a consensus about the propriety of consumer goods and activity, there is another reason for doubting the worth of individual valuations. The untoward consequences of consumer innovations – one thinks in this connection of food additives, chemical drugs and pesticides, synthetic materials and a variety of novel gadgets – tend to unfold slowly over time. Their valuation by the buying public at any point in time may therefore bear no relation to the welfare anticipated. Indeed, the very pace of change today – the rapidity with which new models appear year after year – makes it virtually impossible for the public to learn from its experience. In sum, society can have little confidence that the valuations people place on goods have a close correspondence to their subjective wants – at any rate, close enough to justify their use, on the standard argument, as indicators of claims on society's resources.

In these circumstances, a promotion of the claim that the Pareto criterion commands a consensus is unwarrantable. The welfare economist must settle for a criterion that – although quite meaningful and occasionally commendable – cannot be sure of advancing social welfare or of meeting a consensus. The Pareto criterion continues to serve, albeit in a more humble capacity. It is seen to require simply that the sum of the valuations be positive, a requirement which need have no normative connotations.

Thus, the figure which the cost–benefit economist offers to the decision makers is no more than a summation of all individual valuations of a particular project or change, calculated at a point in time. This time is usually the present time, to which the value of expected benefits over future periods is reduced by a discounting procedure. Simply by providing ΣV (where the Vs may be interpreted as compensating variations) for the specified projects and ranking them accordingly and as required by the decision makers, the economist may regard himself as quite neutral in any official debate on the respective merits of the projects. He has, that is, no warrant for asserting a *social* ranking or preference for any of the projects arising from his findings.

This is a modest but useful task. And, as we are learning, not an easy one to discharge conscientiously. The findings of a cost–benefit study are properly regarded as a contribution to the political decision-making process, a contribution, incidentally, that governments and their public continually demand and whose significance they perhaps tend to overrate.

Appendix 3

The alleged contradiction of the Kaldor–Hicks criterion

1   The once-famous critique of the Kaldor–Hicks criterion harks back to Scitovsky's demonstration in 1941 that the ranking from using the Kaldor–Hicks test could in fact be reversed: a movement from I to II, using the Kaldor–Hicks test would show position II to be economically superior; at the same time, having reached position II, a movement back to I would show the latter to be superior.[1]

Because this seeming paradox is familiar enough to the student of economics and in any case, it is pertinent only within a general equilibrium analysis – as distinct, that is, from a partial equilibrium context common to a cost analysis – we deal with it briefly.

What must be demonstrated here is how a movement from one collection of goods Q_1 to another collection Q_2, one that realizes a potential Pareto improvement, is compatible with the reverse movement, one from Q_2 to Q_1, which also realizes a potential Pareto improvement.

2   The Scitovsky 'paradox' is easiest to illustrate and resolve using the geometry of goods space, measuring the amount of good X on the horizontal axis and the amount of good Y on the vertical axis. Let I_1 in Figure A3.1 be the community indifference curve passing through the initial collection of goods Q_1 comprising Y_1 of good Y and X_1 of good X. This collection of goods can be thought of as being divided between two persons (or two groups of persons), A and B, in a manner indicated by point d_1 on the contract curve from O to Q_1 of the box diagram, $OY_1Q_1X_1$. The tangency of d_1 between A's indifference curve I_A and B's indifference curve I_B is, by construction, parallel to the tangency of the community curve I_1 at Q_1.[2] As the alternative collection Q_2 is above the I_1 community indifference curve, it is possible to improve the welfare of everyone by moving to

---

1 Although this seeming paradox was first demonstrated by Scitovsky using the standard two-person two-good box diagram, it was, in fact, mentioned earlier by Pigou in his *Economics of Welfare* (1952).

2 A simple geometric technique for the construction of community indifference curves (that meet the optimal exchange condition) has been explained in Mishan (1957).

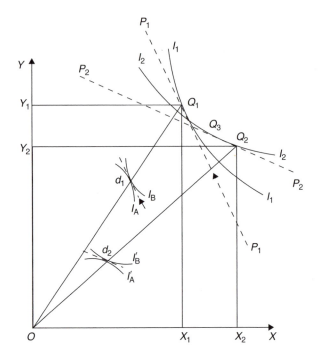

Figure A3.1

the Q_2 position (allowing always for sufficient divisibility). It is possible, that is, to make both A and B better off in Q_2 than in the Q_1 position.

However, *having moved* to Q_2 on this recommendation,[3] the resulting distribution of this Q_2 collection might be one such as is represented by point d_2 on the OQ_2 contract curve of the box diagram $OY_2Q_2X_2$, A's welfare (greater than it was in the Q_1 position) being represented by A's I'_A indifference curve, and B's welfare (less than it was in the Q_1 position) being represented by B's I'_B indifference curve. Again, the slope of the mutual tangency of I'_A and I'_B is, by construction, parallel with the tangent of the community indifference curve I_2 passing through Q_2. With this distribution resulting from the movement from Q_1 to Q_2, the slope at Q_2 is such that the I_2 curve passes below Q_1. And from this we infer that a movement from Q_2 to Q_1 realizes a potential Pareto improvement: beginning with the d_2 distribution of Q_2, that is, a movement to Q_1 can make both A and B better off.[4]

---

3 Though *without* intervening in the resulting distribution so as, by transfer payments, actually to make both A and B better off.

4 If, instead, we constructed Figure A3.1 so that I_1 passed *above* Q_2 and I_2 passed *above* Q_1, the reverse paradox is illustrated: that Q_2 is potentially Pareto inferior to Q_1, and also that Q_1 is potentially Pareto inferior to Q_2.

The same apparent paradox results if, instead of community indifference curves, we make use of the relative prices arising from the respective distributions of the two collections of goods. The relative prices for Q_1 is represented by the slope of the line P_1P_1 tangent to the I_1 curve at Q_1 and, at these relative prices, it is clear that Q_2, being to the right of this price line, is valued more highly than the Q_1 collection of goods. Once the community has moved to Q_2, however, the resulting relative prices are represented by the line P_2P_2 tangent to the I_2 curve at Q_2. At these relative prices, it is equally clear that Q_1, being above the P_2P_2 line passing through Q_2, is valued more highly than the Q_2 collection of goods.

3   Now the likelihood of such a reversal actually occurring in an economy producing a large number of goods and with a population of millions of people is far smaller than that conveyed by the impression of a two-good two-person diagram. Nonetheless, it remains a disconcerting possibility and one that has to be taken seriously in attempts to prove such general economic propositions as, for instance, that international trade is better for a country than autarchy or that an optimal position is better for the community than a non-optimal one.

The resolution of this 'paradox' in 1973 is of some interest in this connection and results in a caveat about proofs of general welfare propositions. For in all such reversal cases, as illustrated in Figure A3.1, there will be a unique hypothetical collection of goods Q_3 (being the point of intersection in the Figure of community indifference curves I_1I_1 and I_2I_2). And along the contract curve of this Q_3 collection, two distinct distributions will be found, one of them corresponding with the welfare combination associated with the equilibrium Q_1 collection, the other corresponding with the welfare combination associated with the equilibrium Q_2 collection. It follows that, what first appears as two 'contradictory' collections of goods, Q_1 and Q_2, may be reduced to two distinct distributions of a single (hypothetical) collection Q_3. The only valid ranking of Q_1 and Q_2, therefore, is a distributional ranking – if an acceptable distributional criterion can be found.[5]

4   This form of the 'paradox' has long been popular in the literature on welfare economics, where the search continues for propositions that will hold within a general equilibrium context. Such a 'paradox' and its resolution, however, apply only to allocative comparisons of different equilibrium collections of goods, as illustrated in Figure A3.1. Where, in contrast, we are restricted to an exchange economy, and the positions I and II to be compared are no more than different (efficient) distributions of a single collection of goods, it is simply *not* possible to demonstrate that the sum of compensating variations is positive in the movement from distribution I to distribution II, much less that it is also positive for the reverse movement from II to I and, therefore, constitutes a 'paradox'.

Attempts made to demonstrate this 'paradox' for alternative distributions of a *single* collection of two or more goods founder on a logical inconsistency: it

5 The complete exposition of this paradox resolution is found in Mishan (1973).

transpires that the exact compensating variations involved in the movement from distribution I to distribution II (or from II to I) entail amounts of the two or more goods for each person that, when added together, amount to a collection that is entirely different from the original collection. In sum, the alleged distributional comparison of a single collection is inadvertently transformed into a comparison of two collections of goods. And we already know that there is no difficulty in contriving a 'paradox' for two different collections of goods.[6]

---

6 A detailed demonstration of the invalidity of the existence of a distributional 'paradox' for a single collection of goods can be found in Mishan (1976b).

Appendix 4

The problem of second-best

1   It is a commonplace that, within a general equilibrium context, the necessary conditions that result from maximizing a social welfare function subject only to a production-boundary constraint may be interpreted as equal to the marginal-cost pricing rule for all goods.[1] The Second-Best Theorem, as formulated by Lipsey and Lancaster (1956), concludes that, if but one additional constraint is imposed on the welfare function (and in the real world there will be many), the necessary conditions that emerge from the maximizing procedure are different from those identified with the marginal-cost pricing rule and, in general, are surprisingly complex.

In the simple mathematical proof of the theorem, the authors first confirm that the necessary conditions that emerge from the maximizing of a welfare function subject only to a production boundary can be shown as equal to the condition that the ratio of any two prices be equal to the *ratio* of their corresponding marginal costs, a condition that, of course, is also met when the price of each good in the economy is equal to its marginal cost. Nonetheless, the ratio condition implies that, if there is a constraint additional to the production boundary, say the price of good x alone is set irremovably 20 per cent above its marginal cost, optimality will only be met if all other goods in the economy are produced to the point where their prices are also 20 per cent above their corresponding marginal costs.[2]

---

1   Other necessary conditions that are subsumed in an overall optimal position of the economy – the exchange optimum and the production optimum – are treated in detail in Mishan's 'A survey of welfare economics' (1960). See also his "Second thoughts on second best" (1962b).

2   Their general proof proceeds as follows: in order to maximize some function

$$F(x_1, x_2, \ldots, x_m)$$

subject to a single constraint

$$\phi(x_1, x_2, \ldots, x_m)$$

using the Langrangian method, maximize $W = F - \lambda\phi$. The necessary conditions will include $F_i = \lambda\phi_i$ or $F_i/F_j = \phi_i/\phi_j (i = 1, 2, \ldots, m)$. However, if now an additional constraint is introduced, say $F_1/F_m = k\phi_i/\phi_m$, where $k \neq 1$, the Langrange method requires that we maximize the function

$$W' = F - \lambda\phi - \mu(F_1/F_m - k\phi_1/\phi_m)$$

and the necessary conditions become much more complex (Lipsey and Lancaster, 1956). Also see Ng (2004: ch. 9, s. 9.1 and 9.2).

It may be expedient to elaborate on this last statement, as it is occasionally asserted that the stricter condition, that prices for all goods be set *equal* to their corresponding marginal costs, since for overall optimality it is necessary to ensure equality also between the marginal product of the factor and its marginal valuation to the factor owner, say, to the worker.

If, for example, the hourly wage of a specific type of labour is $10, whereas the value of its marginal product is $12, it may be argued that, by allowing the worker to increase the number of hours he works, a net social gain can be affected. The worker, for instance, may agree to work an hour longer for $10.50, another hour for $11 and so on, until the wage he receives for the nth hour is equal to the social value of his marginal product. Hence, by adding this condition, both the worker and the consumers are made better off.

This argument would be valid if, in perfect competition, each worker could indeed determine the number of hours he works in each activity by reference to the wage offered. But whether he is paid by the hour or by piece rates, the worker never does, in fact, determine the weekly hours he will work – even if overtime work is offered, the number of additional hours is circumscribed. In general, then, the worker has to accept as a condition of his employment the number of hours per day and the number of days per week that go with the job (along with specific overtime opportunities, if any). The choice of the number of hours per week, and their distribution over each day and week, are not extended to the worker in the operation of modern industry. He has to measure the weekly pay package, along with other conditions, in one activity with those offered by another or, in the last resort, with remaining unemployed. Thus, he compares the alternatives open to him on an all-or-nothing basis.

It follows that marginal adjustments of the amounts produced by various firms are not by the hour, or by the piece, of one or more workers. They are in fact made only by the entrance of additional workers or by their departure from the firm.

Given this situation, an optimal position is attained – one in which no further 're-shuffling' of factors can increase the aggregate value of the output produced – when all goods prices are proportional to their corresponding marginal costs.

2   The Second-Best Theorem incidentally disposes, if it were ever necessary, of the naïve proposition that an excise tax imposes a 'deadweight' or an 'excess' loss on the economy – inappropriately demonstrated in a partial equilibrium context using a simple demand and supply diagram. From such demonstrations, it is occasionally alleged that a CBA must take account of such an excess loss when it is, in part at least, financed by the levying of (additional) excise taxes.

For such a proposition to be valid, it is necessary that every good in the economy, save that (or those) being taxed, be priced at marginal cost – a most unlikely situation. What is more, if it so happened that all other goods were already priced at m per cent above their corresponding marginal costs, the levying of an excise tax of m per cent on the good or goods originally priced at marginal cost would bring the economy into an optimal position: far from being a burden, it would be a benefit. This would be so, in some degree at least, if a weighted average of the prices of all other goods was about *m* per cent. In the absence of any such situation, however, it cannot be known whether the excise taxes in question will be a loss or a benefit to society, much less its measure.

3   We may take it for granted that, in any modern economy, there will be a number of irremovable constraints – arising from excise taxes and subsidies, from strong monopolies and from industries that exploit 'cheap' labour – at least for some time. It follows from the Second-Best Theorem that there is no longer a simple rule that, if followed by the remaining goods in the economy, will ensure a second-best solution. Worse, owing to the complexity and extent of the data required to formulate the valid second-best rule, we can never even hope to discover it.

To make matters still worse, there appeared in the same year as the Second-Best Theorem an article (Mishan, 1957) highlighting the problem of the 'First-Best' solution. Lancaster and Lipsey, it will be recalled, developed their theorem by positing a unique welfare function. Where there is no more than a single boundary constraint, a unique optimal position will indeed emerge. Mishan's analysis, in contrast, showed the existence, in general, of a relationship between the distribution of welfare of any batch of goods and the relative prices resulting. In consequence, any point along some segment of the production boundary becomes a potential optimum for the economy, one that can be realized by a particular distribution of welfare among the members of the community. Indeed, it is this relationship between relative goods prices and distribution in each and every batch of goods within some segment of the production boundary that is responsible for what is known as the "Scitovsky paradox", discussed in Appendix 3.

In view of the undue influence exerted by the Second-Best Theorem on economists concerned primarily with the allocation of resources, it is as well to emphasize that in CBA – where, within a partial economic context, the question to be addressed boils down to the magnitude of the net benefit to society of introducing one or several goods into the economy – one is no longer seeking a price–marginal cost ratio to be applied to *all* remaining goods in the economy given, as irremediable, the ratios of the one or two deviant sectors that will bring the consequent sub-optimal economy as close as possible to the assumed unique optimal position. Rather the contrary, the economist must now accept *as a constraint* the range of different ratios that prevail in *all* the goods in the economy. He must then select the ratio for the one or several goods to be produced by the project that will bring the economy as close as possible to an optimal position, given the existing level of employment.

In other words, given the level of social welfare pertinent to the exising sub-optimal position of the economy, the cost–benefit analyst is to set the outputs of the project's several goods at marginal-cost ratios that will maximize the increase in social welfare. Contrary to what may be expected, the solution to the problem is quite simple.

This is easily understood by breaking the problem into two parts. First, we measure the tangible *ceteris paribus* gain of the introduction of the one or several goods by the project, generally in terms of the increase of their consumer surplus when their outputs are extended to the point at which their social prices are *equal* to their corresponding marginal opportunity costs. We then turn to the more elusive measure of the increase, if any, of that given tangible measure of gain, by some adjustment in these project outputs so that their social prices are somewhat above, or else below, their corresponding marginal opportunity costs.

By employing the same calculus used in establishing the Second-Best Theorem, it also emerges that there is no feasible method of discovering which way the adjustment should go, much less by exactly how much.

This negative result can be made yet more telling by two further reflections. Even if, following some divine revelation, this 'ideal' social price–marginal opportunity cost ratio were then applied by the economist to the outputs of the project, the movement from the initial outputs (at which social price is *equal* to its marginal opportunity cost) cannot be expected to be really worthwhile. In a modern economy in which scores of thousands of finished and intermediate goods are produced, each with its own price–marginal cost ratio (more accurately, its social price–marginal opportunity cost ratio), the divinely indicated adjustment would make so negligible a difference that it would be virtually imperceptible to the individuals comprising society.

Add to this (bearing in mind that, in fact, we will not be able to discover this 'ideal' ratio) that the assumption of a unique optimal position of the economy, as assumed in the Second-Best Theorem, is unwarranted. As shown by Mishan (1957), any number of points on the production boundary of the economy can become an optimal position by a particular redistribution of income that will also, in general, alter all relative prices. Thus, there is no avoiding the conclusion that no perceptible gain may be presumed from any divergence from the cost–benefit analyst's habitually setting outputs at social price equal to marginal opportunity cost when measuring, over time, the gains in consumer surplus from the goods introduced by the project.

Appendix 5

Origins of the Hicksian measures of consumer surplus

1   Marshall's (1924) definition of the individual's consumer surplus, the amount of money a person is willing to pay rather than go without the thing over that which he actually pays, though it has strong intuitive appeal, is not altogether satisfactory: for it implies a constraint on the quantity to be bought. The sum of money the consumer is willing to pay, say, for a licence to buy the good at some given price rather than go without it, depends on how much he is expected to buy. And if, as Marshall implicitly assumed, the amount of the good he is to buy – on paying for this licence – is the *same amount* as that which he buys at the price *in the absence* of any need for a licence, then he *will not*, generally, pay as much for the licence as he would if, instead, he were allowed to buy as much of the good as he wanted. His having to pay for a licence makes him worse off, and if his income effect were positive, he would then – at the same price – choose a smaller amount than if he could buy freely without a licence. Consequently, if he is constrained to buy the initial (larger) amount, he will pay less for the licence.[1]

2   Such considerations prompted Hicks's definition (1939) of a *compensating variation* measure of the consumer's surplus. For the privilege of being able to buy the good at the existing price, *in whatever amount he chooses*, the consumer is willing to pay some maximum sum – his compensating variation. In 1943, Henderson pointed out that the exact measure proposed by Hicks would differ

---

1 Marshall's dissatisfaction, and eventual disillusion, with the concept of consumer surplus, arose from his utility analysis. Aware that the fall in the price of a good which made the consumer better off had some effect on the amount he would buy, Marshall tried to circumvent the problem by holding the individual's marginal utility of income constant. But this was plausible only for minute changes in the individual's welfare. Moreover, in extending the concept to the market, Marshall's choice of working in terms of cardinal and interpersonal utility proved cumbersome and unconvincing.

Once Hicks introduced the more operational distinction between income and substitution effects. It became evident that it was real income, and not the marginal utility of money, that was to be held constant. And despite popular belief to the contrary, these are not alternative methods of expressing the same condition. A constant marginal utility of money does not imply constant real income, and vice versa.

according to whether the consumer had to pay for the opportunity of buying the good at the given price or whether, instead, he was to be paid for abandoning this opportunity. This distinction is illustrated by reference to the indifference curve for a single individual in Figure A5.1.

The good x is measured along the horizontal axis, to be introduced into the economy at a fixed price given by the budget line Y_0X_0. OY_0 measures money income over a period during which the prices of all goods other than x remain constant. Prior to the introduction of good x, the individual's money income Y_0 corresponds to a real income indicated by the indifference curve I_0. Once x is introduced at the price given by the budget line Y_0X_0, the individual chooses the point Q_1 on the higher indifference curve I_1, and therefore consumes OM_1 of x.

The difference made to the person's real income, $I_1 - I_0$, is unambiguous. Ambiguity arises simply because we are to measure the real gain in terms of money income, as defined, along the vertical axis. Hicks's compensating variation, CV, is equal to Y_0Y_1, for if the consumer is made to pay this sum in order to be permitted to buy x at the price (given by the slope of Y_0X_0), he could just reach Q_0 on his original indifference curve I_0. That is, if he is to be exactly as well off as he was originally before x was introduced, Y_0Y_1 is the maximum sum he can afford to pay for the privilege of buying x at the given price. And if called upon to pay this maximum, the amount of x that he would in fact buy is given here by OM_0.

Turning to Henderson's distinction, we now ask a different question: what is the minimum sum the consumer will accept to give up entirely the opportunity of buying the new good x at the market price, given by the slope of Y_0X_0? The

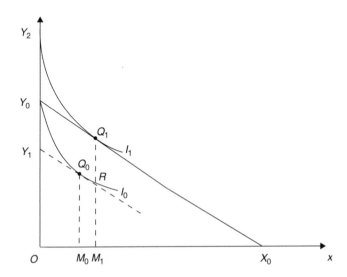

Figure A5.1

answer is a sum equal to Y_0Y_2. For adding this sum to his initial income OY_0, his total income becomes OY_2 and this income, without any x, is on his indifference curve I_1. He is then just as well off as he would have been if, at his original income OY_0, he was able to buy x at the given price. This measure of consumer's surplus was called by Hicks (1944) the equivalent variation, EV, inasmuch as, in the absence of x, such a sum provides the consumer with an equivalent improvement in his welfare.

Provided the income effect is positive ('normal'), Q_1 will be to the right of Q_0 on the parallel budget lines. OM_1 will therefore be larger than OM_0, and Y_0Y_2 will be larger than Y_0Y_1.[2]

3   More generally, the definition of CV is the sum of money to be paid by the consumer when the price falls; or to be received by him when the price rises – which, following a change in the price, leaves him at his initial level of welfare. The EV, conversely, is that sum of money to be received by the consumer when the price falls; or to be paid by him when it rises – which, if he were exempted from the change in price, would yet provide him with the same welfare change. These two measures have already been illustrated in Figure A5.1 for the special case of the introduction of a new good x at a given price, rather than for a change in the existing price of x. They are now illustrated in Figure A5.2 for the case of a fall in the existing price of x.

Initial money income is again represented by OY_0, initial real income being given by the indifference curve I_1 which is reached by the tangency of the price line p_1 at Q_1. If the price of x falls to p_2, the tangency of the p_2 price line at Q_2 raises the consumer's real income from I_1 to I_2. His CV is then equal to Y_0Y_1, this being the maximum sum he could afford to pay for the lower price p_2 without being any worse off. For if he pays this sum, so reducing his money income to OY_1, the now lower price p_2 enables him to reach B on his original I_1 curve. His EV, conversely, is equal to Y_0Y_2, this being the minimal sum he will accept to forgo the opportunity to buy what he wants at the lower price p_2, for with this sum, his total income would be equal to OY_2, and with this income and the old price p_1 he could just reach the higher indifference curve I_2 at C. This increase in his welfare is exactly equal to that which he could attain with this new price p_2 and with his original money income OY_0. Once more, Y_0Y_2 will exceed Y_0Y_1 for a 'normal' good x, as drawn, the reverse being true if x, instead, were an 'inferior' good.

We can now go through the same exercise for a rise in the price of x. With income OY_0, we begin with the consumer being faced with p_2 and, therefore, choosing point Q_2 on indifference curve I_2. A rise in the price of x to p_1 now induces his to take up the position Q_1 on the I_1 indifference curve. Our definitions would therefore measure the CV of such a price rise by Y_2Y_0, this being the minimum

---

2 The reader will note that these relationships hold irrespective of whether marginal utility of real income is diminishing, constant, or increasing, these three possibilities being consistent with any given indifference map of the individual.

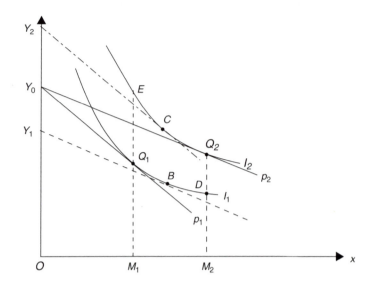

Figure A5.2

sum that would restore the individual's welfare to its original level I_2 when the price rises to p_1. The EV is now to be measured as equal to Y_0Y_1, this being the maximum sum the consumer is prepared to give up if he is exempted from the higher price p_1. For giving up this sum and retaining the old price p_2 would enable him to reach I_t (at B), which is the level of welfare he reaches if he is not exempted from the rise in price to p_1.

4 These two measures, the CV and the EV, are all that are needed in ordinary circumstances. Solely as a matter of curiosity, however, we might wish to go back to Figure A5.1 for a precise measure of the definition put forward by Marshall. This turns out to be a sum equal to the vertical distance Q_1R, this being the maximum sum the consumer will pay for the privilege of being able to buy x at the given price *provided* he is constrained to buy OM_1 of x – this amounts of x being that which the consumer actually buys when he is permitted (without having to pay anything for the privilege) to buy freely at the given price. For if he moves along the price line from Y_0 to Q_1 and is then obliged to stay with the quantity OM_1 of x, he must give up Q_1R in order to be at R on his original indifference curve I_0. This measure Q_1R is smaller than Y_0Y_1, as indeed it should be, since the consumer would pay less for the privilege of being able to buy x if he were compelled to buy a particular amount of it (here OM_1) than if, instead, he could choose whatever amount of x he wished.[3]

---

3 This is true (that is the Marshallian measure is smaller than the CV) irrespective of whether x is a 'normal' or an 'inferior' good.

Thus, the Marshallian measure differs from the CV measure only in its having a quantity constraint attached to it. Extending the Marshallian-type measure to a change in the price, we return to Figure A5.2. For a fall in price from p_1 to p_2, the relevant quantity constraint is OM_2, and the quantity-constrained CV is therefore measured as Q_2D. A quantity-constrained EV, requiring the consumer to purchase only OM_1 of X – this being the amount he buys at the original price p_1 without receiving any compensation – is measured as Q_1E.[4]

Again, for a rise in price from p_2 to p_1 these measures are reversed. Q_1E becomes the quantity-constrained CV, and Q_2D becomes the quantity-constrained EV. Q_2D is smaller than Y_0Y_1, and Q_1E is larger than Y_0Y_2.

In this short account of the origins and development of Hicks's measures of consumer surplus, the reader will notice that we follow the contemporary literature in adopting the term proposed by Hicks, the equivalent variation, in this and the following three Appendices, whereas in the text we refer to it as the CV[21] – the compensating variation for the movement back from state 2 to state 1 is necessary to maintain the state 2 welfare.

---

4 It is clear from Figure A5.2 that the quantity-constrained CV measure Q_2D is smaller than the unconstrained CV measure Y_0Y_1, which is as it should be, because he would always pay less for a constrained privilege than for an unconstrained one. For the analogous reason that he would want to receive a larger compensation if he were to be constrained with respect to quantity than if he were not to be so constrained, the quantity-constrained EV measure EQ_1 is larger than the ordinary EV measure Y_0Y_2.

Appendix 6

Marginal curve measures of consumer surplus

1 The two more popular measures of consumer's surplus, CV and EV, can be represented on the marginal diagram, Figure A6.1. I_0' is the marginal indifference curve corresponding to indifference curve I_0 in Figure A5.1 in Appendix 5. In fact, I_0' is the curve of the first derivative of I_0 with respect to x. Similarly, the marginal indifference curve I_0' is the first derivative of the I_1 curve of Figure A5.1. For convenience, both marginal indifference curves are represented as straight lines in Figure A6.1. And, since in Figure A5.1 I_1 is indicative of a higher level of welfare than I_0, the assumption of a 'normal' good x requires that marginal indifference curve I_1' be drawn above (or to the right of) I_0'.[1]

If we regard individual welfare as continuously variable, the indifference curves are infinitely dense and so also, therefore, are the marginal indifference curves. For illustrative purposes, however, we could select an arbitrary number of marginal indifference curves, I_{01}', I_{02}', and so on, as indicated by the broken lines in Figure A6.1.

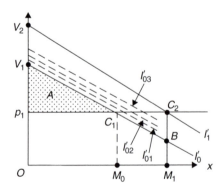

Figure A6.1

---

1 If, instead, the income effect on x were negative, the reverse would be true; the I_1' marginal indifference curve would be below the I_0' marginal indifference curve.

We shall return to this diagram presently, after taking a closer view of the origin and of the point M_1 by means of an incremental diagram, Figure A6.2. The story opens with no x being available and our consumer having I_0 welfare. The maximum sum he will pay for a single unit of x is shown as the first unit column, with height v_1. Let us suppose that he pays this maximum sum, in which case his welfare remains unchanged at level I_0. He is then offered a second unit of x. The maximum he can now afford to pay for this second unit is given by the height of the second column, v_2. Again, we suppose that he is required to pay this maximum, so retaining his original welfare at I_0, and a third unit of x is offered to him, for which he can pay as much as v_3, the height of the third column. If we continue in this way, he will eventually, after purchasing M_0 units of x, have offered as much as v_{m0} for the M_0th unit of x.

If he buys M_0 units of x on these terms, he will be no better off after buying them than he was before he bought any x. His level of welfare, that is, remains at I_0. Now, let the price p_1 be set at height v_{m0}. The sum of the portions of the solid columns that stick up above the price line (their dotted segments) must now be interpreted. Since his payment of this sum, in addition to price p_1 per unit for OM_0 units of x, is such that he is no better off than he was originally without x, this sum is to be regarded as the CV for introducing x at a price p_1. It is the maximum sum he will be able to pay for the privilege of buying x at p_1 without his being any worse off than he was originally. In Figure A6.1, with continuous curves, this CV is represented as the area of the shaded triangle A.

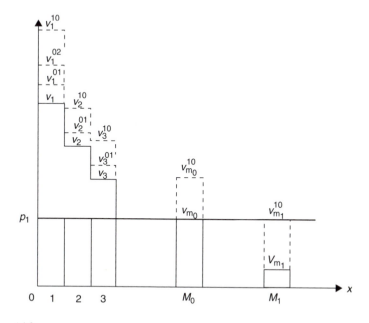

Figure A6.2

2   Let us now return to our consumer in a more charitable humour and allow him to buy all the x he wants at the introductory price p_1. His welfare, or real income, increases from I_0 to I_1, and – because his real income effect is assumed positive – he buys more of x: in fact OM_1 of x in Figure A6.1.

Looking at things in the light of the incremental diagram Figure A6.2, we notice that, because of this increase in real income, the value of the final M_1th unit is now valued at v_{m1}^{10}, equal to price p_1, and not at the smaller value v_{m1} – the maximum he would have paid for the M_1th unit on the first procedure, which retained his welfare at the level I_0. Indeed, because of the increase in the level of his welfare from I_0 to I_1 when he is allowed to buy x freely at p_1 (and ends up buying OM_1 units), the valuation of all preceding units of x is raised; the M_0th unit being valued at v_{m0}^{10}, the third unit being valued at v_3^{10}, and the first unit being valued at v_1^{10}, and so on. The stepped line joining the top of these revised columns in Figure A6.2, from the first to the M_1th unit, can be represented, however, by the segment V_2C_2 of the continuous marginal indifference curve I_1' in Figure A6.1. Once the consumer has been allowed to buy all he wants of x at price p_1, and his welfare rises from I_0 to I_1, the area $OV_2C_2M_1$ is the exact measure of what the OM_1 units of x are worth to him.

If the privilege of buying x at p_1 were now withdrawn, he would have to be returned his expenditure on OM_1 units of x, or $Op_1C_2M_1$. But unless he were also paid a sum equal to the area of the triangle $p_1V_2C_2$, he would be worse off than he was with the privilege of buying all he wanted at price p_1; his welfare, that is, would be below I_1. The triangle $p_1V_2C_2$ is, then, the measure of his EV. It is the minimum sum that is needed to make him as well off when the privilege of buying x at p_1 is withdrawn as he was when he enjoyed that privilege.[2]

3   We now return, once more, to Figure A6.2 in order to throw more light on two issues that are somewhat obscure. As mentioned, beginning with welfare at level I_0, the maximum the consumer will pay for the first unit of x is given by the height v_1 of the first solid column. But if, instead of paying this maximal sum, he pays no more than the price p_1, he makes a surplus on this first unit equal to the column segment p_1v_1. As a result, his welfare rises, say, to I_{01} (greater than I_0), and the maximum he is now prepared to pay for the second, third and subsequent units of x is – on the assumption of a positive income effect – raised somewhat to

---

2 The reader might care to note that the quantity-constrained CV – corresponding to the Marshallian definition of consumer's surplus – is smaller than the Hicksian CV. In Figure A6.1, it can be represented as the shaded triangle A *less* the triangle C_1C_2B, because the quantity constraint requires of the consumer that, in paying a maximum for the privilege of buying x at p_1, he continue to buy OM_1 units (and not the OM_0 units he would have chosen to buy). Since the marginal indifference curve I_0' shows the maximum he is prepared to pay for these additional M_0M_1 units of x, and shows that this maximum for each such unit is below the price p_1, his welfare can be maintained – after paying a sum equal to the triangle A – only by refunding him the losses he must sustain on the additional M_0M_1 units, a total loss given by the triangle C_1C_2B.

v_2^{01} for the second unit, to v_3^{01} for the third unit of x and so on. Let him now be offered a second unit of x at the same price p_1, and he makes as a surplus on this second unit an amount equal to $p_1 v_2^{01}$. His welfare has risen by another increment to, say, I_{02}, and the maximum sum he will pay for successive units also rises. For the third unit, he will now pay as much as v_3^{02} (above v_3^{01}, but not shown in the figure) and so on. Proceeding in this way, determining the resulting maximum sum the consumer will pay for each successive unit prior to allowing him to buy it at price p_1, we can trace a locus that has been called (Hicks, 1944), the 'marginal valuation', MV, curve. Its relation to the marginal indifference curves of Figure A6.1 could be shown here but, in order not to clutter up the picture, we have reproduced the main features of Figure A6.1 in Figure A6.3, and shown this MV curve as the line joining V_2 to C_2.

This MV curve is not, however, to be identified with the demand curve, for in order to generate a demand curve for x, we trace the path of consumer purchases by gradually *lowering the price* from V_1 to p_1. Although both the MV and the demand curves pass through C_2 when the price is p_1, for all previous quantities of x the MV curve (for a 'normal' good) is above the demand curve, shown as the *dotted* curve joining V_1 to C_2. The reason is simply that, in tracing the locus of the MV curve, the consumer is deemed to buy each successive unit of x, from the first onward, at the actual price p_1. In contrast, the demand curve is generated by having the consumer pay a price that is first equal to OV_1 and, though gradually lowered, remains above p_1 until the final M_1th unit is bought. As a result, the surplus of welfare gained in the purchase of the first, second, third and subsequent units of x (save for the final M_1th unit) is greater for the MV curve procedure than for the demand curve procedure. At each unit of x, save the final M_1th unit, the consumer's valuation is, therefore, higher for the *MV* curve than for the demand curve.

4   In order to broach the second issue, we return to Figure A6.2, and recall that the maximum sum the consumer will pay for the first unit is given by the height v_1 of the first column. If he is permitted to buy this one unit at p_1, his CV for that

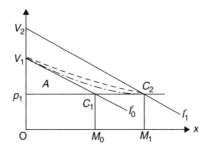

Figure A6.3

one unit is equal, as indicated, to the dotted segment of the column above the p_1 line. Suppose we now ask the question: what is the minimum sum he will accept in order to give up the privilege of buying this one unit of x at p_1? Now if this question is asked prior to his having bought any unit of x at a price (such as p_1) below his maximum valuation of a first unit, his welfare will still be at the I_0 level. The minimum sum he would accept to forgo having the one unit of x might then be thought equal to the maximum sum he would pay for it. But whether in fact he has bought this x unit at p_1, and his welfare has risen to the level I_{01} (greater than initial level I_0), or whether he has *not* yet bought this unit of x, and his existing welfare is still at I_0, makes no difference. The minimum sum he will require to forgo the unit he bought at p_1, or the opportunity to buy it at p_1, is in either case the same, and larger than the maximum sum he would pay to be able to buy a unit of x at p_1. For assuming that he has not yet bought any x at p_1, and his welfare is still therefore at I_0, the individual must ask himself the question: what is the level of welfare I *could* reach if I were permitted to avail myself of the opportunity of buying this unit of x at p_1? And the answer, as indicated above, is the level I_{01}, greater than I_0. The sum of money which, therefore, exactly compensates him for *not* being able to attain this I_{01} level of welfare (through the purchase of a unit of x at p_1) is equal to the column segment $p_1 v_1^{01}$.

This description of the sum of money, however, corresponds exactly to the definition of the EV – the sum which, if he is exempted from the economic change in question, provides him with the equivalent change in his welfare.[3] More generally, if no constraint is placed on the amount of x the consumer would wish to buy, the EV necessary to induce him to forgo the opportunity of buying x at p_1 is equal to the area of triangle $p_1 V_2 C_2$ in Figure A6.3.

5   Let us summarize these interpretations. The CV for introducing x at price p_1 is given by the shaded triangle A in Figure A6.1. Once x is introduced at that price, the consumer, in the absence of constraint, will buy OM_1 units and achieve a welfare level corresponding to indifference curve I_1. In order to persuade him to forgo this opportunity to buy x at p_1, which takes him to I_1 welfare, he must receive a minimum sum equal to the area of the large triangle, $p_1 V_2 C_2$. By definition, this is his EV.

If, however, he has already been given the price p_1, and the economic change consists of withdrawing it entirely, this same minimum sum, equal to triangle $p_1 C_2 V_2$, now represents the consumer's CV, being the sum that must be paid him in order to maintain his existing welfare at I_1. His EV in this circumstance is the smaller triangle A, this being the maximum sum he would pay to be exempt from

---

3 If, however, the economic change being contemplated is the exact opposite of this, i.e. the *withdrawal* of the opportunity of buying a unit of x at p_1 and, as a result, a reduction of the consumer's welfare level from I_{01}, the payment of this sum is the appropriate CV for such an economic change, for it is the sum the consumer must receive in order to maintain his existing level of welfare, I_{01}, following such a change.

losing the opportunity to buy at p_1, which payment would in fact reduce his level of welfare to I_0,[4] the level prior to the introduction of good x.

Confining ourselves to the CV and EV of introducing a normal good x at price p_1, it is clear that the area between the price and VE, the individual's demand curve is greater than the CV area and less than the EV area, i.e. for 'normal' goods, $CV < D < EV$. It is obvious that the smaller is the income effect, the smaller will be the difference between these areas regarded as measures of consumer's surplus. In the limiting case of zero effect, the three areas coincide.[5]

6   Finally, we can translate the CV and EV measures of Figure A5.2, featuring a fall in the price from p_1 to p_2 onto the marginal diagram of Figure A6.4. At p_1 the consumer is buying OM_1 units. At p_2 he is buying OM_2 units. The marginal indifference curves I_0', I_1' and I_2', are indicated as solid lines, and the demand curve passing through VDH as the dotted line.

The CV of the fall in the price from p_1 to p_2 is equal to the cost difference for OM_1 units of x, or rectangle p_1p_2FD, *plus* the triangle DFG. The EV for that fall in price is equal to the cost-difference for OM_2 units, or rectangle p_1p_2HJ *less* the triangle HJK. These measures of CV and EV are, of course, reversed for a price rise from p_1 to p_2.

The horizontal slice of consumer's surplus under the demand curve, the area p_1p_2HE is an approximation to either of the exact measures, being clearly greater

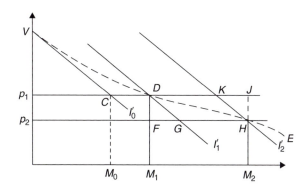

Figure A6.4

4 It should be self-evident that the maximum sum a consumer will pay to acquire a benefit (his CV) is the same maximum sum he will pay to hold on to it (his EV), i.e. to be exempt from its removal once he already has it.
5 If x had a negative income effect we should have $EV < D < CV$. Figure A6.3 would have to be revised by exchanging points M_0 and M_1, C_1 and C_2, V_1 and V_2. The demand curve joining the new V_1 to the new C_2 would then be steeper than either of the two marginal indifference curves. In the extreme case, the demand curve over a range slopes upwards from left to right.

than the CV measure, and smaller than the EV measure, for a price fall. Again, the smaller the income effect, the closer is the coincidence of the three measures. For a zero income effect, the measures coincide. Goods with zero income effect are hard to come by, but for a great many purposes the income effect involved is small enough for economists to make use of the area under the demand curve as a close approximation of the relevant benefit or loss.

Appendix 7

The concept and measure of rent

1 Although the concept of rent, in the specific sense of a surplus to factor-owners, is not so popular in CBAs as the concept of consumers' surplus, it is possible that, with growing awareness of allocation theory and growing refinements in techniques of measurement, it will become increasingly employed. The concept deserves more detailed treatment for another reason: the use of the area above the supply price of a factor is a less reliable proxy for the measurement of rent than is the area below the consumer's demand curve a proxy for his surplus. The reader will appreciate this remark more readily after the concept of rent has been defined.

Textbook definitions that are still in current use can be divided into two types. One conceives of rent as a payment in excess of that necessary to maintain a factor in its current occupation. The other would describe it as the difference between the factor's current earnings and its 'transfer earnings'—the latter term denoting its earnings in the next most highly paid use. As we shall see, the first type of definition is ambiguous because of the quantity constraint. The second type of definition is even more restricted, however, as its validity would require that, in the choice of occupation, men are motivated solely by pecuniary considerations. Indeed, it will transpire that, like consumer surplus, rent is a measure of change in a person's welfare and, again like consumer surplus, can have both a CV and an EV measure.[1]

2 As with the treatment of consumer surplus, our first recourse will be to the indifference map. Figure A7.1 indicates four quadrants of a diagram in which money income Y is again measured vertically, and the good L (which can be thought of as labour services) is measured horizontally. Any horizontal distance to the right of the origin O would measure the amount of L acquired by the individual; any horizontal distance to the left of the origin, the amount of L given up. Similarly, any distance above the origin measures the amount of income acquired, and any distance below it the amount of income given up. As distinct from the consumer

---

1 This account follows the treatment of rent proposed by Mishan (1958).

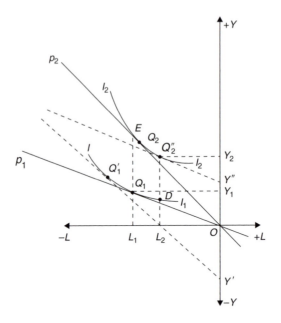

Figure A7.1

goods' situation which is depicted in the north-east quadrant, the factor supplies' situation is here depicted in the north-west quadrant.[2]

If we construct a price-line p_1 passing through the origin and tangent at Q_1 to the indifference curve I_1, the individual is represented as in his chosen equilibrium position, giving up OL_1 of this particular sort of labour and, in exchange, acquiring

2 This construction has three advantages over the more common leisure–income diagram which is placed in the usual north-east quadrant.

(i) The choice among available combinations of two goods, leisure (regarded as a homogeneous good) and money, fails to convey the more general notion of the individual as a demander and a *supplier* of any number of goods and factors, electing to provide a particular combination of them according to market prices. In general, each of the variety of factors the individual can offer requires a different skill and entails a different degree of hardship.

(ii) One avoids the artifice of a limit to the amount of the 'good' leisure, say 24 hours of the day, which artifice has the awkward result that an improvement in welfare is represented along one axis as equivalent to more than 24 hours of leisure a day. In the construction of Figure A7.1, the limit to the supply of any factor is governed directly by the shape of the person's indifference curves, and the measure of any welfare change is in terms of the one good, money income.

(iii) The indifference map of Figure A7.1, whose curves can be extended to cross the vertical axis, is the correct prior construction to that useful textbook diagram in which a downward-sloping curve from left to right crosses a price axis, to the right of which the line is interpreted as a demand curve for the good, and to the left of which the line is interpreted as a supply curve of it.

OY_1 units of money income. Let the market supply price for this sort of labour rise from p_1 to p_2, and the individual's new equilibrium is given by the combination Q_2 on the I_2 indifference curve. The resulting change from Q_1 to Q_2 may be divided, in the usual Hicksian way, into a pure substitution effect – a movement from Q_1 to Q_1' – and a pure welfare effect – a movement from Q_1' to Q_2. Although the welfare effect can, of course, go either way, it should be noticed that a positive welfare effect – implying a welfare-induced increase in the *demand* for a good or factor – constitutes a reduction in the *supply* of a good or factor. Thus, a positive, or 'normal' welfare effect, following a rise in the price of a factor, acts to reduce the amount put on the market. As we shall see, the 'backward-bending' supply curve of the factor owner is the outcome of a strong positive welfare effect overcoming the unambiguous substitution effect.

The increase in the individual's welfare that follows the rise in the price of his labour from p_1 to p_2 can be measured, first as a CV—here, the exact amount of money that has to be taken from him to restore his welfare to its original I_1 level. The measurement of the CV on the vertical axis is, therefore, OY'. It is the maximum sum of money he could give up for the opportunity of selling his labour at the higher price p_2. If he gives up this sum OY', he will have the negative income indicated by Y' and, with price p_2, he can just reach I_1 at Q_1'.

This increase in his welfare can also be measured as an EV – here, the exact amount of money which has to be given to him to ensure that, if the opportunity to sell his labour at p_2 is not extended to him he is still able to reach the new welfare level as indicated by indifference curve I_2. The EV is, therefore, measured as OY'' along the vertical axis. If he is paid this sum, he will be able to reach I_2 at Q_2'' with the original price p_1. It will be observed that, in the 'normal' case (positive welfare effect), the CV measure of an increase in welfare that follows a rise in the supply price exceeds the EV measure.

Since rent is frequently regarded as a surplus which may be partly or wholly appropriated without having any effect on the supply of factors, it is important to notice that – provided the welfare effects are not zero – wherever the individual has to pay an amount less than, or equal to, his rent (as measured, say, by his CV), the amount of factors he will offer will differ from the original amount. To illustrate, if, after the price has risen to p_2 and he supplies L_2 of the factor, the CV measure of his rent is equal to OY', as stated. Let him be taxed the full amount of this rent and, with the new price p_2, he will reach Q_1', and supply a larger amount of factors than before.

3 As with consumer's surplus, we could also trace out a quantity-constrained CV and EV. This constrained CV, sometimes associated with the Marshallian concept of rent, would be the sum of money the individual would surrender in order to retain p_2 when, at the same time, he was restrained from providing no more than OL_2 of the factor (this being the amount he chose to supply at p_2). This restriction on him choice of quantity, not surprisingly, reduces the sums he is willing to pay for the opportunity of having the higher price p_2 from OY' to Q_2D. Similarly, the constrained EV, the minimum sum he will accept to forgo p_2 when he is compelled to supply the original amount OL_1, is EQ_1, which is larger than the unconstrained EV of OY'. There is obviously nothing 'wrong' in using the quantity-constrained CV and EV. But on grounds of plausibility and convenience, they are to be rejected in favour of the CV and EV proper.

4   It is instructive to turn briefly to the case of the supply of a factor in two alternative occupations A and B. Although the individual might choose to work part time in each occupation, this is not always feasible owing to institutional arrangements. We shall therefore confine the analysis to the case of placing his factor L entirely in occupation A or entirely in B.

   Figure A7.2 represents a section of a three-dimensional indifference map, with the same vertical axis Y and two horizontal axes, L_a and L_b, crossing at right angles. If we imagine our three-dimensional figure were cut vertically into four equal parts, the figure is the space left after the removal of the vertical quarter in which L_a and L_b are both negative. Our attention is largely restricted to the upper, the positive, part of the diagram.

   The rate of pay in A is given by p_a, which is higher than p_b. If he chose to work in A at p_a, his earnings OY_a would be higher than his earnings OY_b, in B. Nevertheless, the individual chooses to place his factors entirely in occupation B, his equilibrium being Q_b on the indifference surface I_2 which is above the indifference surface I_1 on which is found his alternative choice, Q_a. Compared with the equilibrium he

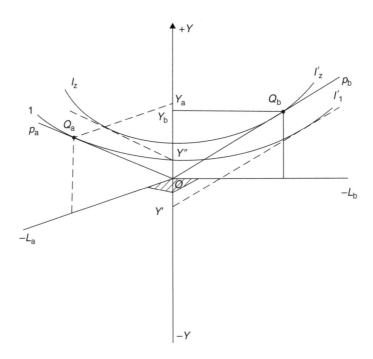

Figure A7.2

could reach in the *A* occupation, the individual enjoys a positive economic rent which, as an *EV*, can be measured as OY' – this being the maximum sum he is prepared to pay to remain in *B*, for, after paying as much as OY', he can just reach the I_1 indifference surface – the new, lower, level of welfare which he would reach if he had to move into the *A* occupation. Conceived as a CV, the rent is measured as a sum equal to OY'', this being the minimum sum the individual must be paid in order to induce him to transfer to occupation *A*, for, after receiving the sum OY'', he will be able, moving along p_a to reach the I_2 indifference surface – representing his original level of welfare.

It should be manifest that, because of his occupational preference for *B*, the positive rent from working in *B* rather than *A* is accompanied by a smaller money return. Indeed, the textbook definition of rent, turning on the difference between the factors' current earnings and their transfer earnings, would, in this instance, be negative for the worker who chooses the *B* occupation, whereas it is clearly a positive rent on the CV or EV definition.[3]

---

3 By a *positive* rent in this connection we mean an *increment* in his welfare from being in *B* rather than in *A*; an increment of welfare that can be measured either as the EV or as the CV of the move from *A* to *B*.

Appendix 8

Marginal curve measures of rent

1 The marginal curves I_1' and I_2' in Figure A8.1 correspond to I_1 and I_2 in Figure A7.1, except that, for conventional reasons, they are drawn from left to right. The I_0' marginal indifference curve in the figure corresponds to some original I_0 curve (not depicted in Figure A7.1) before any price was offered for the factor L. It is convenient, again, to draw these three curves as straight lines.

To fix our ideas, we shall suppose L to be labour of a given skill, measured along the horizontal axis in hours per week in a specific industry A, the prices of all other factors and goods being taken as constant.[1]

When the individual first contemplates employment in A, the I_0' curve is the locus of minimal payments required to induce him to offer there his successive

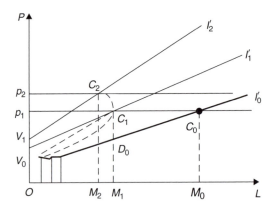

Figure A8.1

---

1 We could have used a larger diagram to disclose the nature of the marginal indifference curve I_0' by taking hourly increments of this labour and – parallel with our treatment of consumer's surplus – constructing successive columns, the heights of which would indicate the individual's valuation of each successive hour offered. Having gone through this process in connection with consumer's surplus in some detail already, we shall not repeat it – though we have drawn in the first three columns under the I_0' to remind us of the process.

increments of labour. If he receives these minimal payments, and no more, as he moves from left to right along the I_0', he is no better off at any point along it than he is at the beginning, prior to his employment there. The introduction now of an hourly wage p_1 enables us to represent triangular areas corresponding to his CV and EV.

2 The individual's CV is a sum of money equal to the area of the larger triangle $V_0C_0p_1$, determined as follows. The area beneath the I_0' curve up to the M_0th unit, equal to $OV_0C_0M_0$, is the minimum sum of money needed to induce him to work the OM_0 hours, whereas the rectangular area, $Op_1C_0M_0$, is what he would be paid for working the OM_0 hours. The *excess* of this rectangular area over that minimum sum, equal to the triangle $V_0C_0p_1$, is therefore the maximum sum he can afford to pay for having the opportunity to sell his labour in A at p_1. For if he pays this maximum sum in exchange for this opportunity of selling his labour at p_1, he is just able – by choosing to work OM_0 hours – to maintain his welfare at the original I_0 level, being then no better off than he was before the p_1 opportunity was presented to him.

His EV, in contrast, is a sum that is equal to the area of the smaller triangle $V_1p_1C_1$, explained as follows. We put the question: having availed himself of the p_1 price to offer OM_1 units of labour and reached the I_1 level of welfare, what is the maximum sum he is willing to pay in order not to have to do any work in A?[2] This is equal to the area $OV_1C_1M_1$ under the I_1' curve. However, if he gives up the opportunity to sell his labour at p_1, the total income he forgoes is equal to the rectangular area $Op_1C_1M_1$. And this loss of income exceeds the most that he is willing to pay by the area of the triangle $V_1p_1C_1$. In order, then, to retain this I_1 level of welfare (which he was able to reach with p_1) when p_1 is no longer available to him, he must receive a sum equal to the area of this triangle.[3]

By starting with a supply price equal to V_0 in Figure A8.1, a price at which the individual supplies nothing, and gradually raising the price to p_1, at which he supplies OM_1 units, we generate the dotted-line supply curve of labour joining V_0 to C_1. For a 'normal' good or factor being offered (one for which *less* is offered as welfare increases), the supply curve will be steeper than the relevant marginal indifference curves. For an 'inferior' good or factor, in contrast, the supply curve

---

2 Along any marginal indifference curve, a movement *rising upward* (to the right, as drawn in the figure) implies a *giving up* of units, the vertical height therefore measures the *minimum* sums required for successive units offered. A movement *sloping downward* (to the left, as drawn in the figure) implies the *acquiring* of additional units – or the withdrawal of units once supplied. The vertical height therefore measures the *maximum* sums he will pay for additional units.

The same interpretation holds for the consumer's marginal indifference curves, although downward-sloping is, in contradistinction to Figure A8.1, to the right, and upward-sloping is to the left.

3 The quantity-constrained CV, associated with the Marshallian measure, can also be represented in Figure A8.1. Once price p_1 is introduced, the amount the individual chooses to supply is OM_1. The most he is willing to pay to obtain this price p_1, while at the same time being constrained to purchase OM_1 units, is a sum equal to the area $V_0D_0C_1p_1$, which is clearly smaller than the unconstrained CV, $V_0C_0p_1$, as indeed it has to be.

will be flatter than the marginal indifference curves. In the 'normal' case, Hicks's marginal valuation curve (MV) will also be steeper than the marginal indifference curves. And since, for each successive unit offered, the welfare effect (until the M_1th unit is reached) is greater than that produced in generating the supply curve, the MV curve, indicated by the broken-line curve V_0C_1, will be above the supply curve.

3   We must now face the critical question: how well does the area between the price and the individual's supply price approximate the CV and EV measures of rent? Although the construction of diagrams of this sort can be somewhat arbitrary, it is well known that the supply curve can be much steeper than the marginal indifference curves and, indeed, can be backward bending – implying a welfare effect that is positive and large relative to the substitution effect. What makes the welfare effect so important in the factor market are the existing economic institutions under which people tend to place all their labour in single occupations. The welfare of each worker, therefore, depends exclusively, or largely, on the level of a single factor price. It is quite possible, in fact as well as in theory, that a further rise in price from p_1 to p_2 would (if he were allowed to choose) result in the worker's choosing to supply OM_2 units, a smaller amount of labour than the OM_1 units he supplies at p_1. The resulting supply curve, passing through $V_0C_1C_2$, though it lies between the CV and EV measures of rent, could be very different from either. This would be bad enough if either measure were acceptable as satisfactory for the purpose in hand. But in a CBA, guided by the criterion of a potential Pareto improvement, it is the CV measure that is usually employed.

Granted 'normal' welfare effects, a project that *raises* the supply price of the factor, on the one hand, produces a CV measure of rent that could be significantly *larger* than the area above the supply price. The consequent underestimation of the rent accruing to the factor-owner might, erroneously, preclude an economically feasible project. On the other hand, for a project that *lowers* the supply price of a factor, the area defined by the CV could be significantly *smaller* than the area above the supply curve. The consequent overestimation of the loss of rent resulting from using the area above the supply price as a proxy for the CV measure might then, again erroneously, preclude projects that are economically feasible.[4] How important is this consideration likely to be?

---

4 Under the same conditions, the conclusion for changes in the demand price is the opposite of that for the supply price. On the one hand, a project that *raises* the demand price of a good will, in the 'normal' case, have a CV (the minimum sum the consumer will accept as compensation) that is *larger* than the area under the demand curve. If the welfare involved is substantial, the consequent underestimation of the loss could result in a CBA admitting projects that do not meet the criterion.

One the other hand, for a project that results in a *reduction* of the price of a good to the consumer, the CV is smaller than the area under the demand curve. The consequent overestimate of the gain from using the area under the demand curve as a proxy for the CV might again admit projects that are not economically feasible.

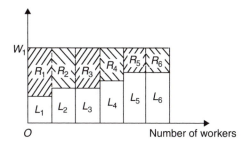

Figure A8.2

4   As indicated earlier, in modern industry it is the general practice to offer workers a 'package deal'; in its simplest form, a wage rate plus a constraint on the number of hours per day, and also on the number of days per week. Such constraints vary from industry to industry and in occupations within the industry, but this fact makes no difference to the analysis of rent in such circumstances.

Suppose the hours per week in the A industry are set at 40, except in the particular case in which the worker, when offered p_1 per hour, would have in any case chosen to work 40 hours, the constraint will be operative. If so, his CV under the 40-hour constraint will be smaller than it would be without it. Provided it is positive, however, he will accept the all-or-nothing offer and make some rent from it. The worker's CV under this constraint – the maximum sum he will pay in order to have the opportunity to work the 40-hour week in A at p_1 – is the excess of the weekly wage over the minimum payment he will require. And this minimum weekly payment he would accept is represented in Figure A8.2, as the area of a unit L column with height equal to such minimum sum. Since the figure ranks the columns in ascending order of height, column L_1 corresponds to the minimal sum of the first worker; he would accept a sum lower than all the others and, in consequence, makes the largest (constrained) CV rent. Letting the total pay for the 40-hour week be measured as OW_1 on the vertical axis, the CV measure of rent for the first worker is represented by R_1; the shaded extension of column L_1 to height W_1. Similarly, the areas of $R_2, R_3, R_4, \ldots$ indicate the rents of workers 2, 3, 4 and so on.

Clearly, the stepped line obtained by tracing the tops of the L columns indicates the beginning of the supply curve of labour for that industry. If we continued adding workers in ascending order of height, we should eventually engage a worker, say the nth worker, whose L column was just below, or equal to, the height of the W_1 line. All workers in the industry, save possibly the nth, will be making a rent.

Where large numbers of workers are involved, we may draw a continuous supply curve to the point of intersection with the weekly wage line, the total rent to the workers in this industry being the area enclosed between the wage line and the supply curve. A lengthening of the working week, or any other restriction, would be represented as an upward shifting of this supply curve. The equilibrium number of workers would fall, and the rents of each of the remaining number would be reduced.

We may conclude, tentatively, that, notwithstanding the difficulties discussed in connection with the *individual* supply curve, the constraints imposed by industry are such that the area above the supply curve of a particular type of labour to an industry offers a good measure of the rent enjoyed by the number employed. The gain or loss of rent resulting from a rise or fall in the weekly wage can now also be measured in the conventional way.

Appendix 9

The limited applicability of property rights

1 Unfortunately the real world is less accommodating than free-enterprise economists wish. Extending property rights to arable or pasture lands, to mineral and marsh lands, possibly also to some lakes and to stretches of a river, may work well to some extent. But in some cases it does not work well enough to prevent environmental damage occurring on a significant scale, and in others it is quite impracticable.

Property rights in forest lands, for example, do not work well – not unless trees are fast-growing and timber companies are restricted to areas so limited that, over the long term, profits depend upon continual re-afforestation.

Unfortunately, nearly all tropical rain forests, although officially under state control, tend to be treated as a commons. They continue to be destroyed rapidly both by large tractor-using companies in search of quick profits from the exports of hardwood to industrial countries, and also by migrant peasants who use 'slash and burn' methods in levelling thousands of acres of tall-tree forests in order to clear a space for farming. No account, in these activities, is taken of the loss to be borne by present and future generations, not only the irreplaceable loss of fauna and flora[1] but also the cumulative effect such destruction has on the Earth's atmosphere and climate upon which our survival depends.

Deep-sea fishing is another instance where, although property rights are conceivable, they would be far too costly to enforce. Systems of rationing the fish catch with the aim of conserving the fish population may seem more practical, but they are wasteful, unpopular with fishermen and difficult to monitor.

2 In other cases, the idea of allocating property rights is a non-starter. There is no way in which the atmosphere over any area of the Earth's surface can be parcelled out to companies or people so as to make them responsible for its maintenance. And as it is impossible to confer distinct portions of air space on individuals or corporations, the atmosphere above the Earth will be used – as it always has been in the absence of prohibitions or regulations of emissions – as a common sewer.

---

1 Loss of potential medical benefits from undiscovered use of plants.

Nor is anti-pollution legislation that effective. The required installation, say, of tall smoke stacks can reduce the amount of smoke and noxious particles suffered by the local population. But, as we now know, the wind-borne gases produced by burning fossil fuels move across national boundaries and settle in other countries in the form of acid depositions, so damaging their soil, forest lands and lakes.

Not only does our planet's atmosphere continue, in the main, to be used as a common sewer for a variety of man-produced gases, our oceans have also long been used for dumping waste and, in the past few decades, for extremely poisonous chemical and radioactive wastes.

Apart then from a few familiar instances – such as the cultivation of crops or of cattle and other animals – property rights have limited applicability, and none whatever to the more serious environmental problems.

Appendix 10
The rate of time preference

1 It is commonly alleged that the individual's rate of time preference, when positive – a preference for $100, say, this year rather than $100 next year – arises from impatience or myopia, allowing that he expects to be alive and well over the near future.

It is correct to state that, if a person is indifferent between receiving an additional 100 this year and an additional 105 next year and an additional $105(1.05)^2$ the year after, his rate of time preference is 5 per cent. If such individual were to receive 100 each year until some terminal year T, the value of this stream of benefits would be equal to $100(1.05)^T + 100(1.05)^{T-1} + \ldots + 100$, or $\sum_1^T 100(1.05)^t$ in the Tth year. Yet, from such statements, we are not able to infer whether, with respect to income or consumption over time, a person is impatient, prudent, or overcautious.

Ignoring the problem of uncertainty, let us consider the distribution of income over a number of years of a person A in an economy where there is no market for loans of any sort. We simplify further by representing person A's indifference curves as between only two years, y_1 measured along the horizontal axis of Figure A10.1, and y_2 measured along the vertical axis. (A third year y_3 is suggested by an arrowhead marked y_3, emerging from the origin, allowing the imaginative student to conceive of three-dimensional indifference surfaces covering a three-year time span which can, mathematically, be extended to any n years.)

Allowing the sum of, say, $40,000 to be distributed between years 1 and 2, all the possible divisions are indicated by all possible points along the 45 degree line D. Person A can choose to take all the available $40,000 in year 1, all of it in year 2 or, more likely, some of the $40,000 in year 1, and the remainder in year 2. If person A is a prudent person, he will choose to distribute the available income so as to receive $20,000 in each of two years, a division indicated by point Q_3, at which his highest indifference curve I_3 is tangent to the distribution line D. For at any other point along line D, he will be on a lower indifference curve.

Thus, at Q_3 on his I_3 indifference curve, person A is indifferent to receiving a given increment of income, say $100, in year 1 or receiving the same $100 increment of income in year 2. In so far as person A remains equally prudent – irrespective of the total available income dividing it equally between the two years – all points of tangency between his indifference curves and the relevant D lines will lie along a 45 degree ray, OR, passing through the origin. This OR ray,

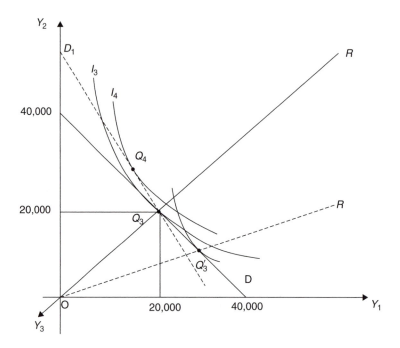

Figure A10.1

being equidistant at any point from each of the axes, is what identifies person A as being prudent – as valuing an additional dollar in year 1 as being exactly in value to him as an additional dollar in year 2.

Were person A an impatient person, he would instead have chosen a point Q_3' along the D line, a point below Q_3, so as to have more income available in year 1 than in year 2. Him being an impatient person would be represented by a ray OR' (the broken line in the figure) that is below the ray OR.[1]

2   Returning now to our prudent person A who chooses Q_3 division of his income between this year and the next, we suppose a loans market springs up, one that offers $105 next year for every $100 received this year – a return of 5 per cent per annum. Our prudent person A is now faced with a new opportunity to improve his welfare: in the absence of this new opportunity, he would be just as well off if, for parting with $100 of this year's income, he were to receive an additional $100

---

1 If the impatient person found himself initially at point Q_3, he would be worse off than if he were at Q_3'. Moreover, the slope of his indifference curve passing through point Q_3 along the D line would be steeper than 45 degrees, indicating that if he has to give up, say, $100 this year he will require more than $100 next year if his welfare is to be maintained.

next year. If, instead, he were to receive an additional $105, he would certainly be better off.

In Figure A10.1, the new opportunity line facing person A at Q_3 once the loans market is introduced is shown by the broken line D_1 through Q_3, which is steeper than the original line D. In consequence, person A moves to Q_4 on line D_1, this being on a higher indifference curve I_4. Once at Q_4 on his I_4 indifference curve, his rate of substitution will be 105 next year for 100 this year – his rate of time preference, that is, becomes 5 per cent per annum, equal then to the rate offered by the market.

Clearly, our prudent person A has not changed his character: he has only changed his behaviour in response to the new opportunity presented to him. Because at Q_4 he now has less income available this year, his indifference curve I_4 at that point will reveal that he will sacrifice, say, an additional $100 of this year's income only if he will receive at least an additional $105 next year.

What is more, if the truly impatient person, associated with the ray OR', chooses point Q_3' along line D in the absence of a loans market, the introduction of such a market, one offering a return of 5 per cent per annum, would be shown by a line steeper than line D – in fact parallel to line D_1 – passing through point Q_3'. At some point of the upper portion of this steeper line, the chosen point is on a higher indifference curve tangent to that line. This impatient person, in adjustment his income over time to the market for loans, also ends up with a rate of time preference equal to market rate.

We may conclude that the existence in the economy of a market offering a positive rate of return on savings can arise independently of the character of the savers, whether they be, all or some, impatient, prudent, or overprudent. Such a market can come into existence if there are people or businesses that want to borrow only for investment purposes.

Appendix 11

Selecting a set of investment projects for given political objectives

1 In selecting from a number of technically feasible investment projects that set which maximizes the excess terminal benefit, $TV(B) - TV(K)$, subject to a budget constraint, the method proposed here assumes normalization of the alternative investment options unless otherwise stated.

The features of the selection problem are, first, that there are several objectives to be achieved, single or complex, and second, that each of these objectives can be achieved by several alternative investment projects. For example, one of the objectives could be that of pest control over a certain area. Another could be that of flood control plus electricity generation.

Assuming the existence of a competitive economy with a high level of employment, with a ρ greater than r, the problem becomes that of choosing from the array of all the technically feasible investment projects available – a number of alternative projects (not necessarily the same number) for each of the political objectives – those that together produce the largest excess terminal benefit subject to the budget constraint. We must bear in mind, however, that, although we are to ensure that all the investment projects to be compared have the same time span, as indicated in the preceding chapter, they will not necessarily have the same initial outlay.

2 In setting up the problem, some general guidelines should be followed:

(i) The same objective to be realized in more than one area is to count as a different objective.

(ii) If, within a single area, two or more objectives are achieved by only one of the investment options, these two or more objectives are to be treated as a single objective.

(iii) If, for any objective that provides two or more services, there are m alternative investment options providing these services but in different proportions, they are to count as m alternative investment options.

If, for example, it is possible that, within the same area, one investment project provides flood control alone, another provides both flood control and electricity, and a third provides flood control and electricity also, but in different proportions, there are three investment options to be counted.

Turning to the question of finance, the more general approach is that the finance to be made available for the investment projects selected, no greater than the politically determined budget constraint, may be raised by taxation or borrowing or both. But, beyond the budget, some additional finance may be provided by not renewing some of the already existing public enterprises (their amortization funds then becoming available to contribute to the outlay of one or more of the investment options).

3 Restricting ourselves first to a budget that is raised only by taxation and/or borrowing, we proceed by dividing the *excess* terminal benefits ETB of each investment option by the terminal value of its outlay, which gives us the per dollar ETB for each investment option, its DETB.

We now place in a single row all the DETBs of those investment options that are able to provide one particular objective, there being as many rows as there are objectives. The array of the resulting DETBs forms the data that we have to work with.

We can illustrate the selection process under the simple assumption that there are but three political objectives to be attempted: (A) a passenger and traffic bridge across the river Flo in a particular locality for which there are three alternative investment options, as shown in Table A11.1; (B) a dam across the river Flo that will generate electricity for a nearby urban area, for which there are five investment options, as shown in Table A11.1; (C) a dam further down the river Flo that provides both flood control and electricity to another urban area, for which there are four alternative investment options.

To the right of the array of DETB figures in Table A11.1 are bracketed figures giving the terminal value, in $ million, that is required for that particular investment option – 12 in all in Table A11.1. The DETB figures themselves are all positive as, indeed, they have to be if the investment option is Pareto efficient, i.e. each of the investment options included in the table produces a greater terminal value than that of its terminal opportunity cost.

Suppose the budget available is $5 million, inasmuch as the figures in the brackets are the terminal values of the outlays, this initial budget of $5 million must be compounded forward to the common terminal year T at P to become, say, $7 million. Thus, the problem reduces to that of choosing no more than one of the alternative options in each row of the table so as to produce the highest aggregate terminal value of outlays that does not exceed $7 million.

Table A11.1 Investment options

A	0.05(4.8)	0.20(1.5)	0.30(2.0)		
B	0.10(4.5)	0.20(4.0)	0.40(4.0)	0.45(3.0)	0.50(3.5)
C	0.22(5.0)	0.25(4.0)	0.30(2.5)	0.35(3.0)	

If, for instance, we pick the DETB of 0.22 in row C and that of 0.30 in row A, the two options together require a terminal outlay equal to $5 million plus $2 million, altogether $7 million, which exhausts the terminal value of the budget. The excess terminal benefit of using these two investment options come to (0.22 × $5 million) plus (0.30 × $2 million), a total excess terminal value of $1.7 million. We could, instead, pick the DETB of 0.5 in row B and the DETB of 0.35 in row C which together produce a larger excess terminal benefit of $2.8 million while using up terminal outlays equal to $6.5 million.

And so we could continue picking other sets of one, two or three investment options, but no more than one from each row, to obtain the highest excess terminal benefit subject to the terminal budget constraint of $7 million. It would be quicker, however, to devise a computer programme wherever there were a large number of objectives and many alternative investment options for each objective. [1]

4   We now turn to the case in which the budget, $7 million in the above example, may be supplemented by the funds made available by a discontinuing of a number of existing public projects that could otherwise be renewed. To simplify, we shall continue to suppose the existence of the data in Table A11.1 but, in addition, we suppose that there are three existing public projects: X_1, X_2 and X_3, that have now reached their terminal year and which therefore can either be renewed or else their recouped outlays be used instead to finance one or more additional investment options. If, at most, all three of these existing public projects were discontinued, the terminal value of their outlays would, let us say, add $3 million to the $7 million budget.

Clearly, it would be economically inefficient to discontinue X_1, X_2 or X_3 (so as to make additional funds available for achieving the objectives) if its DETB, which has to be forgone, exceeds that of the one or more investment options it supplants. To illustrate, if the X_1 renewable public project is the only one with a lower DETB than any of the 12 investment options being considered for the three objectives A, B and C, it would certainly be economic to discontinue it first and to use the amortized funds, amounting to its initial outlay, to finance one or more of the investment options. Should it so happen that the terminal value of X_1's outlay were equal to $4 million, this much of the available budget would be enough to finance one or more of the investment options, or possibly less than enough.

---

1   The problem can be formalized, bearing in mind that for each of the Q_i objectives ($i = 1, 2, \ldots, n$) there can be many I_j alternative investment options ($j = 1, 2, \ldots, m$), where m is the largest number of alternative investment options for any one or more objectives); also that we can admit *no more than one* of the alternative investment options for any one objective.

If T_{ij} denotes the DETB of the jth investment option that can achieve the ith objective, K_{ij} the terminal value of its outlay, and K the terminal value of the budget that is available (equal to $7 million in the above example), then we are to maximize

$$\sum_{i=1}^{n}\sum_{j=1}^{m} T_{ij}K_{ij} \leq K. \tag{A11.1}$$

Consequently, some juggling about to alight upon the best mix of investment options that does not exceed a maximum terminal value of $10 million must be anticipated.

Once there were a large number of objectives to meet, each attainable by quite a few alternative investment options, it would be advisable to design a computer programme.[2]

2 The problem can again be formalized (using the notation and caveats in footnote 1) as follows:

$$\text{maximize} \sum_{i=1}^{n} \sum_{j=1}^{m} T_{ij} K_{ij} \le K + M \tag{A11.1}$$

and *also*

$$\text{maximize} \sum_{q=1}^{g} T_q M_q \le M \tag{A11.2}$$

(g being equal to 1 *or* 2 *or*, ..., or g, as required by the problem.)

Where $M_1, M_2, \ldots, M_g$ are the respective terminal values of the outlays of public projects $X_1, X_2, \ldots, X_g$ that may be renewed *or discontinued*, their corresponding DETB being $T_1, T_2, \ldots, T_g$. The maximum allowable for the terminal values of those public projects that are discontinued is (politically) fixed at M. Moreover, economic efficiency requires that each of the T_q chosen in (A11.2) not be greater than any of the T_{ij} selected in (A11.1).

Appendix 12
The value of human life

1 As Sir Thomas Browne solemnly observed in his *Religio Medici*, 'Heresies perish not with their authors but, like the river Arethusa, though they have lost their currents in one place, they rise up in another'. So also with the economist's valuation of life, the heresy being regression to the belief that the economic value of a human life is somehow to be related if not to the utility of his expected earnings, capital or consumption, then to some contrived economic index. Such recipes for cooking up an economic value of human life may bear comparison with the calculation of the value of a two-week honeymoon for a loving couple by reference to their anticipated outlays over the period (including forgone earnings) plus, perhaps, some allowance being made for the frigidity of one or other of the spouses. For the figure arrived at on this assumption of the relevant data bears no logical relation to the value that might be placed on the anticipated honeymoon experience by either of the enamoured couple.

When it comes to valuing human life by reference to the effects of the expected economic activity of the individual, three nominal models are of interest in order of technical sophistication: those of Usher (1985), Conley (1976) and Arthur (1981). It would be tedious to attempt a summary description of the construction of these models which, however, may be worth ploughing through for the intellectual diversion – testimony to an increasing tendency among academic disciplines of too much technique chasing too few ideas.

We may also mention in passing a number of other ambitious models such as those of Cook and Graham (1977), Jones-Lee (1980) and Keeney (1980) that involve neither expected earnings, etc., nor yet direct willingness to pay, yet contrive to produce an economic value for a person's life.

Most of these models contain a crucial magnitude, call it Q, which is incorporated into a mathematical expression from which the value of a person's life is to be calculated – or, at least, set within bounds.[1] But the usefulness of the

---

1 Thus Q would be H^T in Conley's paper, WE in Arthur's paper and RL in Jones-Lee's paper. To be sure, the paper by Jones-Lee also introduces the concept of maximum acceptable risk, but he cannot obtain it from his RL figure. He must discover it from direct estimates or guess at it or else accept it as a residual from a direct estimate of his $\Delta v / \Delta p$, always assuming he can also place a reliable figure on his RL.

magnitude Q cannot be independently determined without recourse to empirical data.

Certainly, no method has been devised by which such models can be tested.[2] Nor is the purpose of such models evident. Operationalizing them is very difficult and, however plausible their assumptions or their actual estimates of the economic value of human life, they can hardly be said, or expected, to influence economic policy.[3]

2 The value of a life calculated from such a model may, of course, be 'tested' by reference to a CV[12] for a given change in risk (as indicated, and criticized in Chapter 36), but in that case, the model is superfluous.

3 Guided by such models – or else by (unwarranted) inferences from some average compensation required for accepting a given (additional) risk of death or injury in a particular activity – calculations have indeed been made for the value of a human life and, also, for the value of a range of injuries sustained by a person.

For instance, the value, or 'shadow price', of a human life has been calculated as equal to about $4 million, that of a brain injury equal to $119,000, that of a drowning or near-drowning $100,600, and so on for a range of injuries.

Accepting the mainstream economic principle that the value of an item (good or bad) to a person is that which he himself places on it, in order for such calculations to be valid, we should have to discover, say, that in 1989 a person would have been indifferent as between remaining alive and the receipt of about $4 million (which presumably he would donate to family and friends or charities). If he received $5 million in exchange for his life, his welfare would therefore have been increased. Similar remarks, of course, apply to all such calculations.

Needless to remark, no interviews have been reported that confirm the validity of such calculations. (See also Chapter 36, Section 5.)

Appendix 13

Deadweight loss or love's labour lost

1   When public investment is to be financed not by borrowing, but by taxation, wholly or partly – whether by excise taxes, income taxes or property taxes – an alleged consequence is the generation of a marginal Pareto loss, one that is referred to as a 'marginal excess tax burden' or 'deadweight loss'.

This alleged burden does not address itself to the amounts transferred by the taxes – the gain in spending power of the government being exactly equal (if we ignore collecting costs) to the loss of spending power of the taxpayers, but to what is sometimes called the 'distorting' effects of taxes, tariffs, subsidies, etc. As this term 'distorting' effects is used somewhat licentiously, it makes for clearer thinking to focus directly on the relevant issue: will the taxation in question move the economy as a whole closer to, or further from, an overall optimal position? And if we can determine which way, can we also measure the change in total welfare? It should be obvious that answers to these questions are related to the analysis used in establishing the Second-Best Theorem, as discussed in Appendix 4.

2   Prior to the 1950s, economic textbooks occasionally illustrated the marginal excess tax burden of an excise tax t by a wedge, equal to height t, placed between the demand and supply curve of Figure A13.1. Originally, the equilibrium price was p_1 and the equilibrium quantity x_1. Following an excise tax equal to t, the equilibrium price rises to p_2, and the equilibrium quantity falls to x_2.

The amount transferred from consumers and producers together is then equal to $t \times Ox_2$ – with producers paying the amount equal to $(Ox_2 \times p_1 p_0)$ and consumers paying the amount $(Ox_2 \times p_1 p_2)$. But the loss to both producers and consumers together exceeds the sum transferred to the government by the amount measured by the shaded triangles, the upper shaded triangle being a loss of consumer surplus, and the lower shaded triangle being a loss of producer surplus. Hence, the excise tax t entails an excess marginal burden as measured by the shaded triangles.

All very neat, and all very misleading. Quite apart from the unwarrantable concept of producer surplus, as discussed in Part II, such a partical-equilibrium conclusion cannot be extended to a general-equilibrium conclusion. A validation of the apparent marginal loss of consumer surplus from imposing an excise tax would require that all the remaining goods in the economy continue to be priced as equal to their corresponding marginal cost, and also that there be no income

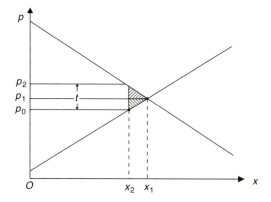

Figure A13.1

taxes. If it happens that, in the absence of income taxes, the prices of all remaining goods were above their marginal costs by the same proportion, $\frac{p_1 p_2}{O p_1}$, then a tax of $p_1 p_2$ on good x would restore the economy to a full optimal position (given fixed factors) as compared with the original sub-optimal position before good x was taxed. In that case, the excise tax on good x would be an excess marginal gain rather than an excess marginal loss.

Inasmuch as it is virtually certain that, in a modern economy producing many thousands of items, at any moment in time their prices will be above or below their corresponding marginal costs in varying degrees, there can be no assurance whether an excise tax on good x or on several other goods also will move the economy as a whole closer to or further from an optimal position, much less that the gain or less can be measured. This conclusion is reinforced when one bears in mind that in CBA it is not the ratio of market prices to their marginal costs that is relevant but (correcting for externalities) the ratio of the social valuation per unit (or 'social price') to the corresponding marginal opportunity cost.

It will be convenient in the remainder of this Appendix to refer to the former ratio as the market ratio and the latter as the social ratio.

3   An income tax, or rather an increase in income tax, is perhaps less elusive, if only an x per cent increase in a person's income tax is equivalent to a uniform tax on all goods (save leisure) of a bit more than x per cent.[1]

---

1 A tax of 1 per cent on a person's income is equivalent to him of $100x/100 - x$ per cent of all goods save leisure. Thus, an income tax of 1 per cent is exactly equal to a uniform tax on all goods (save leisure) of 1.02 per cent, an income tax of 5 per cent to a uniform excise tax of 5.26 per cent, and so on.

   If there is already a sizeable income tax but no excise taxes (or no comparable ones), an x per cent income tax is equivalent to a uniform excise tax of something more than 1.02 per cent.

Now, we already know that a deviation of the social price of a good from its marginal opportunity cost does not, of itself, tell us anything. In connection with optimal positions for the economy as a whole, what matters is the difference of this ratio from one good to another. If the ratios are the same for all goods, an overall optimal position (for fixed factor quantities) is reached, whether all social prices are equal to corresponding marginal opportunity costs, whether they are all 5 per cent, 100 per cent or, in general, x per cent above or below corresponding marginal costs.

The same logic applies to any other ratio pattern – other, that is, than a uniform ratio – and, therefore, to its corresponding sub-optimal position. Thus an increase in income tax of, say 10 per cent, is equivalent to a person of a uniform increase (of something more than 10 per cent) on the prices of all goods (save leisure). By simply hiking up all prices by the same percentage for all persons the original sub-optimal position remains unchanged.[2]

4   The only warrantable conclusions that we can draw from the above considerations are as follows:

(i)   In general, and bearing in mind that only the pattern of social ratios is relevant, it is uncertain whether the chosen range of excise taxes imposed to raise funds for the project will result, on balance, in a marginal excess burden or marginal excess gain for the community.

(ii)   Even where there may reasonably be a presumption of marginal excess burden or marginal excess gain, it is unlikely to be significant. For instance, in the absence of a national emergency, an average increase in income tax exceeding 5 per cent would be unusual in any modern democracy. Yet, for most democracies, the resulting increase in revenue would be more than enough to finance one or two large public projects.

(iii)   Whether the additional taxes raised to finance the public project(s) in question may be presumed, on balance, to issue in some deadweight loss or some 'deadweight gain', its *actual* figure will almost certainly elude measurement.

5   As a postscript, it may be added that, even if the economist were vouchsafed, by some divine power, the exact figure for the 'deadweight loss' or 'deadweight

---

2 It may, of course, be argued that the optimality condition which requires the value of a person's leisure to be equal to the social value of his marginal product is infringed by an income tax. We know, however, that perfect competition is not only possible with fixed factor quantities but also that in the modern economy fixed factors are generally the rule, not the exception. It follows that this labour–leisure condition is generally infringed, regardless of taxes: few workers can be offered the opportunity of choosing, each day, just how long they wish to work in a variety of differnt occupations.

Hence, the introduction (or increase) of an income tax cannot be held to infringe a condition that is, in any case, already infringed in its absence.

gain' from the raising of taxes specifically to fund the public projects in question, it is *most unlikely* – in view of the fact that the economist's measures of social gains and of opportunity costs are unavoidably only approximate, to say nothing of the allowances to be made for future uncertainties – that its inclusion in the cost–benefit calculation would materially affect the acceptability or otherwise of the public projects or of their ranking.

Appendix 14

CBA and the problem of locating environmentally noxious facilities – an informal discussion

1 A major concern of CBA is in the identification, quantification and valuation of environmental damage associated with proposed projects. Predominant among these environmental external effects are air pollution, water pollution and noise pollution causing hazards to human health and deterioration in environmental quality. These degradations in environmental quality are mainly the result of a lack of ownership rights such that there are no market transactions, and hence no market prices, to indicate values. People who have to put up with these noxious effects that are mainly the incidental by-products of a project go uncompensated. Therefore, it is the task of a CBA economist to measure these environmental disamenities as part of the social costs of a project.

The siting of locally noxious facilities such as sewage treatment works, city airports, electric power plants and incinerators is another important area where a CBA study would be helpful for decision makers. These are facilities that offer useful services to the general public and are often considered 'necessary' by society, but almost everyone agrees that they should be located at places outside their neighbourhoods: the so-called 'NMBY (not in my backyard) syndrome' (Popper, 1983).

A CBA study of an environmentally noxious facility based on a national accounting stance rather than a local or regional one would, invariably in most cases, lead to acceptance of the facility, bowing to the demands of a greater general public. People who live in the neighbourhood and are the direct recipients of the negative externality often go uncompensated under a Kaldor–Hicks efficiency criterion and, consequently, too many of these projects may be proposed.

2 What do garbage dumps, airports, sanitary landfill, sewage treatment plants, strip mines and nuclear power facilities all have in common? For one thing, these are facilities which, to a large extent, involve the public sector in full or partial ownership or have substantial government operating subsidies. Further, where the physical facility requires a fairly large tract of land, this would usually be acquired under the laws of compulsory acquisition. In the construction of hydro-electric power plants or any nuclear facility, a public utility regulatory agency is also typically involved. Thus, the public sector, whether acting as owner, financial

supporter or regulator, must decide, first, on the merits of having the facility and, second, after having decided for the facility, where it should be located.

The second characteristic of these environmentally noxious facilities is that they generally impose non-exclusive negative externalities in the immediate neighbourhood. Examples of such disamenities are pollution, displeasing aesthetics and even potentially life-threatening hazards, as in chemical plants, nuclear facilities and electrical transmission stations. While the greater public (at regional or national levels) enjoys the goods and services newly created, or outputs, at reduced monetary costs, it is the local residents who must put up with such non-exclusive disamenities.

As these environmentally noxious facilities are becoming larger in size and operation, they are more likely to be sited in remote areas or areas with a rural background. It is also in these areas that the potential for environmental and ecological conflict of a much larger scale becomes likely.

Concern over social, economic, and negative environmental impacts, from mega-projects has led to the increasing adoption of more open processes for discussions on project evaluation. These processes normally involve public participation and open forums to ensure that all parties can express their concerns. In some cases, strong local opposition may even succeed in having a proposed facility relocated elsewhere or redesigned for mitigation of its more negative impacts. While these cases are rare, it is without doubt that the decision process can be time-consuming and, in most cases, a costly exercise. In cases where, on the one hand, the local residents are opposed to the siting of the facility, the larger public, on the other hand, demands a faster response in meeting its needs. The characteristics of these environmentally noxious facilities are such that the problem of location involves more than the usual standard cost–benefit calculations, and may require a time-consuming process searching for a conflict-resolution instrument acceptable to all.

3   There are six commonly suggested conflict-resolution instruments for the siting and local acceptance of an environmentally noxious facility in a particular neighbourhood. These are: local regulations such as zoning; public hearing and environment impact assessments; licences and permits; compulsory acquisition of land with market compensation; mitigation policies; and general compensation.

4   Local governments or municipalities in most countries have the authority to impose certain bylaws and regulations pertaining to environment and land use. Zoning, for example, involves the division of land into districts that have different regulations. These regulations are in the form of legal constraints under which land use, rights and entitlements are defined and can be exchanged. These regulations are usually formulated and based on a master or comprehensive plan designed to protect and promote the health, safety and welfare of the local population.

Public-sector economists tend to favour zoning as an effective regulatory measure for promoting efficient resource allocation in areas of incompatible land use, especially where public–private interests conflict. Zoning is supposed to correct market imperfection in the presence of negative externalities so that it results in prices of land that equal the true marginal product without causing the prices of similar land to differ. Two types of zoning exist: separation-of-land use zoning divides an area into zones and permits only certain land uses in each zone, for example separate zones for residential, commercial and industrial use; exclusionary zoning restricts certain land uses altogether. For example, it may regulate the planting of trees and shrubs, billboards, colours, heights of buildings and other aesthetic considerations.

While zoning regulations do lessen conflicts in incompatible land uses, they do not by themselves extinguish any negative externalities emanating from an environmentally noxious facility imposed on the surrounding neighbourhood. To the extent that less favoured areas or municipalities are used for siting environmentally noxious facilities, the question is whether property owners in such areas should be compensated for bearing the negative externality. Zoning can also be too complex and costly a measure to result in optimal land uses because of lengthy and elaborate zoning processes.

Thus, zoning regulations neither protect nor compensate residents of less favourably zoned areas. Also, where mega-projects involving state or federal authorities are concerned, local governmental regulations become relatively ineffective: land can be re-zoned, special permits can be granted, the law can be invoked and political pressures can be applied.

5   International lending agencies (for example, the World Bank) increasingly require that explicit attention be given to the environmental impact of proposed projects and that this be included in any loan applications (Earth Summit, 1992). Environment impact assessments are a means to avoid post-facility consequences which have been unanticipated or underestimated (Fischer and Davis, 1973; Schofield, 1987). In the process of accounting, measuring and valuing environmental impacts of projects, opportunities are provided for informal public hearings, review and comments from professionals, and meetings with various interest groups. Although less than perfect solutions, environment impact statements are meant to identify negative environment changes early, so that mitigation, modification of the scale of the project, relocation of the facility or even dropping the proposed project entirely can be undertaken (Ortolano, 1997; Lee and Kirkpatrick, 2000).

To the extent that environment-impact assessments are public information, environmental litigation by strong local opposition may not be uncommon. The cost of such actions (temporary injunctions) is the delay in initiating projects and, along with it, the project benefits. Often, a ready presumption is that citizen participation and judgement lack scientific rigour in estimating environmental impacts, but it must also be recognized that the values of planners or evaluators need not coincide with the values held by the people. The evaluations should reflect the values of all the people potentially affected by a proposed project or facility and not just some of the people, in this case, the planners and the outside residents.

While evaluation methods such as checklists, matrices, networks, map overlays and computer simulation provide very useful aids to decision making, assessment can be improved further by infusing them with information on public attitudes, and especially those of the local residents of a neighbourhood facility, *early* in the design and planning stages. Most environment-impact assessments tend to overlook this useful view. Better and more informed decision making requires both quantitative and qualitative assessments (for example, more local public opinion surveys and forums). To the extent that forums are incorporated into an environment-impact assessment, these are very useful conflict-resolution instruments. For large-scale projects involving government funding, environment-impact assessments are now required in Indonesia and Malaysia.

6   As with all large-scale installations, environmentally noxious facilities normally require some form of building and operational licence or permit. This is another conflict resolution instrument which carries with it opportunities for public hearing and involvement. Depending on the strength of the arguments and evidence provided by project opponents, the proposed facility may be reduced in scale, relocated or even abandoned.

Licensing and obtaining permits, however, requires considerable documentation and, at times, comprehensive surveys, such that delays in project benefits and outputs are inevitable. In the United States, for example, a study has shown that, in the extreme case of a proposed siting of a nuclear power facility, the construction-permit review or resolution stage may take up to eight years to be completed (Randall, 1987). While extreme care and effort must be taken in deciding on the location of nuclear facilities, in other less life-threatening situations the important question must be whether the demands of the larger society can afford the delays brought about by such procedures.

7   Compulsory acquisition of land where private owners are compensated with market values for their land is another widely used conflict-resolution instrument, which may, however, result in losses of welfare to private landowners. Compulsory acquisition recognizes the need for the legal–state machinery to compel reluctant landowners to dispose of their land for a public purpose. It is also used to prevent unjust enrichment on the part of private landowners who are only prepared to give up their land for a price several times higher than the market price of the land. Without such a legal power, a private landowner would be 'in a position to hold the (proposed) scheme and name his price' (*Fraser v. R.* [1963] SCR 455).

In most instances, compulsory acquisition recognizes the comparative method of valuing property. This involves a comparison of data collected from various sales of similar properties in the same or similar localities.

It must be emphasized, however, that compulsory land acquisition can only be justified if the public benefits outweigh the private costs inclusive of the losses

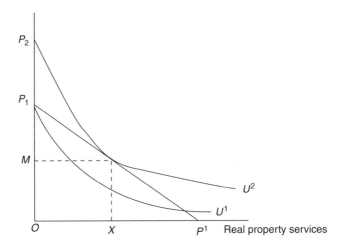

Figure A14.1

to dispossessed landowners. The rationale of paying market compensation is that the money sum awarded to the expropriated landowners would enable them to purchase a similar property and, consequently, be made no worse off. Society can then make use of the land resource for whatever public purpose it has in mind that would confer a positive net benefit, thereby increasing social welfare.

However, it is well known that land, unlike most goods and services traded in the market, is not identical, and hence the implicit assumption behind market compensation, namely availability of near or perfect substitutes, is clearly unrealistic. Land is unique. Apart from physical differences, neighbourhood qualities and length of occupancy, there would still be the psychological cost of relocation to a different community, for which disturbance damage awards do not presently allow.

Insufficient compensation payments would also mean too many public projects may be implemented. That market compensation for compulsorily acquired land may result in undervaluation is illustrated in Figure A14.1.

The vertical axis describes the varying levels of money income, while the horizontal axis shows the varying levels of real property services accruing to the landowner. Before the land was compulsorily acquired, the landowner enjoyed U^2 level of welfare with OX property services and OM level of money income or wealth. The property owned by the landowner has a market price given by the slope of the line P_1P^1. The landowner can sell the land OX at this price but has chosen not to do so, because he would be worse off. If he sold the land, he would end up enjoying a lower welfare U^1, with zero property services and OP_1 level of money income. Thus, if the basis for compensation for compulsory acquisition of land is that of market value, the loss in welfare ($U^2 - U^1$) may occur. Adequate compensation in OX land is, in fact, equal to OP_2.

This conflict-resolution mechanism can be highly efficient if a method can be devised to compensate dispossessed landowners for their actual loss incurred. Negative externalities imposed by an environmentally noxious facility can be internalized by also compulsorily purchasing adjacent land from their property owners and paying actual loss compensation. A buffer zone would then be created. More conscious efforts should be made to obtain property with compensation payments made agreeable to both sides: bid pricing from alternative locations may be made known to landowners so that unreasonableness and unwarranted enrichment can be minimized. A value-to-owner compensation standard may be applied (Knetsch and Borcherding, 1979). This conflict-resolution instrument has much potential and deserves more research by way of implementation acceptable to all affected parties

8 Measures to mitigate environmental degradation and negative externalities are commonly relied upon as a useful conflict-resolution instrument in facility siting. These mitigation measures usually involve some redesigning of the facility or improved monitoring and decision procedures to reduce actual or perceived risks arising from the facility. Such measures may include the provision of a sealed covering for a sewage treatment facility (to reduce unpleasant odours and air pollution), the placing of reinforced materials around chemical storage tanks (to reduce chances of a leakage) or the installation of continuous monitoring devices within and around the facility.

Apart from those mitigation measures, which usually involve some kind of engineering or technological options, there are also mitigation measures which aim to regulate the operation of the facility through local residents' participation by way of their representation on the facility's governing board. This type of institutional mitigation measure is useful if the facility is primarily of the hazardous kind, as in the case of nuclear power stations and toxic chemical plants, for they represent efforts to reduce the level of mistrust between the facility operator and the host community. These measures also aim to raise the level of comprehension among local residents as to the actual statistical risks of accidents, and the measures that are being taken to prevent them (Gregory and Kunreuther, 1990).

Institutional mitigation measures seem to be consistent with what has been called 'procedural rationality', which refers to the processes upon which a decision outcome is determined. If the process upon which a decision is based is perceived to be flawed or biased, agreement on facility siting between the local residents and its owner or operator becomes almost impossible. Together with compensation schemes, mitigation policies would seem to play an important complementary role in promoting the local residents' likelihood of accepting a proposed noxious facility (Quah and Tan, 2002).

9 Concern over the negative external impacts arising from the siting of an environmentally noxious facility has led to the adoption of more open processes for project evaluation and, in some jurisdictions. For example, in British Columbia, Canada, and in Massachusetts, United States, compensation schemes or mitigation actions are now required as part of local development. Existing compensation plans require public participation in the form of public hearings and submissions so as to identify, measure and internalize major worries and concerns held by local residents.

One simple compensation scheme proposal (scheme I) calls for local governments to submit sealed bids indicating the minimum compensation sum that they would be willing to accept from a higher-level government or quasi-government body to locate an environmentally noxious facility within their vicinity. The bids are then compared and the facility will be built in that jurisdiction which has submitted the lowest bid. If all the bids are perceived to be too high, plans for the facility will be shelved, reduced in scale and a rebid conducted or new sites proposed (O'Hare et al., 1983; Randall, 1987).

Along similar lines, another compensation scheme (scheme II) might call for *all* municipalities to submit sealed bids, again indicating the minimum compensation sum that they would require for hosting the facility *but* compensation to be received would come from *all* the remaining non-host communities (Quah and Tan, 2002).

Thus, whether a particular community is geologically or physically suitable to host a noxious facility is immaterial or irrelevant to scheme II, as what is being recognized here is that the negative externalities imposed on the host community should be borne by *all* communities, because the output of the noxious facility is enjoyed by all. Just as in the case of a public good, where provision is normally made by government and paid for by general taxes, the same treatment applies here, where each municipality can be regarded as an 'individual entity' consuming the public good. As in scheme I, the eventual host community would be the one that offers to accept the facility at the *least* compensation sum.

Such a 'compensation auction' method would provide some means of assessing the actual and perceived external diseconomy brought about by the siting of the facility on the local residents and ensure that the optimal location was selected in terms of minimizing social cost. If the compensation auction method were to be conducted systematically, transaction costs in the form of delays and local opposition to the facility would be greatly minimized.

A major assumption of both compensation auction methods, however, is that local governments must have some idea how to estimate the actual and the perceived welfare loss on the part of their residents and their own municipalities. Such assessments can be difficult, and some losses are not readily identifiable. Aspects such as aesthetic nuisance and social pollution are intangible social costs. However, other items, such as the costs of treating pollution, expenditure on the required expanded infrastructure (roads, additional lighting, etc.) and compensation for land acquisition, are more easily measured and submitted for compensation. This, in turn, necessitates an agreed-upon structure and methodology for environment-impact assessments and CBA between local governments and the federal or state government. Where disputes occur, an arbitration compensation board may be set up, whose decisions may be final.

However, both compensation auction schemes I and II may induce strategic bidding on the part of municipalities. In order to avoid hosting the proposed noxious facility, they may bid high. Concomitantly, there may also be municipalities bidding more than their true social costs, hoping to gain from compensation in the event that they are selected as the host community. However, at least in scheme II, there is an element of restraint in that, if a municipality strategically bids high, either to gain more than the social costs imposed or to avoid hosting the facility, the municipality may not be selected if there is at least a bid lower made by other municipalities and, worse still, the municipality concerned would have to pay for the social costs (on an equal basis with other municipalities) to the municipality that was selected under scheme II. For more work on compensation auctions, see Quah and Tan (1999).

10 Assuming that social costs to the local residents can be measured, there is also the question of whether the compensation received by the local government is equitably distributed to its residents in proportion to the harm suffered. Upon receiving the compensation, the local government may choose instead to reduce property taxes or provide increased services for its residents. Again, just as in the provision of some public goods, for which every individual pays through taxes, through the acceptance of a public bad, in this case a local bad, every individual receives a reduction in municipal taxes or property taxes or both. It might be argued, however, that those residents who are directly affected by the negative externality as measured by their residential or business proximity to the facility, and those residents who lose their land through compulsory acquisition, should receive more compensation commensurate with their larger loss. And, while there are, admittedly, difficulties whenever actual compensation payments have to be made, say, to more than a few hundred families disturbed by aircraft noise, their dwellings being near an airport, one could think of compensation as being a function of decibel rating or distance to the airport.

Valuing intangibles such as peace and quiet, unpolluted air and water, aesthetic beauty and visibility is not an easy task. But to ignore such valuations or to ascribe descriptive features of them in some CBAs and environment-impact analyses is to reduce them to a value of zero. The result is that people tend to take these intangibles for granted. There are quite a number of methods that have been devised by economists to measure and value such intangibles. Methods such as contingent valuation, hedonic pricing, travel cost and revealed preference have been used extensively and are continually being refined.

11 There is a crucial need to establish clear guidelines and criteria for compensation if claims are allowed. This is to minimize delays in the construction of the proposed facility by avoiding the probability or likelihood of entertaining a floodgate of claims or even litigation. Making the criteria known would also aid opponents of an environmentally noxious facility in understanding the basis upon which to make claims. A well-defined set of criteria will also avoid political controversies and rent-seeking behaviour of some parties, including municipalities.

Another advantage in establishing clear compensation criteria over negotiated claims with each party was suggested by Skaburskis (1988) in that, if the developer is a public utility, the executives, being less answerable to the market, would quite naturally be inclined towards overcompensation in order to maintain a more 'peaceful' environment and to speed up the construction of the facility. To make up for this, higher rates for the output produced would be charged to the utility's customers.

No compensation claim should be allowed for the fact that employees (consisting of outside residents) of the facility will be using existing public goods and services provided by the local government if congestion has not yet set in. Further, the savings made by the project developer because of proximity and accessibility to the local neighbourhood services should not be a factor in settling compensation claims. Using uncongested public goods and services does not create costs. Compensation should be paid only where impacts create real costs and not in cases where they involve a transfer of income or wealth. Changing the quality of the local environment and hence the reduction in values to local residents should be compensatable. Pecuniary externalities should not be compensated. The compensation scheme should require the project developer to pay for harmful effects arising from the facility, but it should also allow the owner of the facility to receive payment for beneficial impacts. Thus, only the net costs of the project should be included in the compensation package. Compensation claims should be based on significant external impacts. Those impacts that are small or remote relative to the required costs of assessing their magnitude should be excluded. Just as in standard CBA, double counting of project impacts should be avoided. For example, the owner of the facility should pay the damage done to local roads less the amount paid indirectly through the local tolls or taxes on its trucking or transport services. For more information on sets of efficiency criteria, see Skaburskis (1988) and Quah and Tan (2002).

12   Policy makers will, however, also be concerned with equity. If redistribution of income and wealth is an important goal of the federal or state government, the compensation sum received by the local government should be distributed and used more in favour of the welfare of the lower income groups, the elderly and the disabled in the local community. Ideally, people adversely affected by the negative environmental impacts should be compensated directly if they can be identified and the extent of their sufferings measured easily. Equity grounds alone would dictate that compensation claims by landowners adjacent to the facility should receive priority considerations.

Mishan (1977b: 250) has argued that the lower income groups are especially disadvantaged when it comes to spillover effects. This is because

> The rich have legal protection of their property and have less need of protection from the disamenity by others. The richer a man is the wider is his choice of neighbourhood . . . In contrast, the poorer a family, the less opportunity it has for moving from its present locality. To all intents, it is stuck in the area and must put up with whatever disamenity is inflicted upon it.

One might argue, therefore, that it is the economically disadvantaged jurisdiction that would more often be the selected site for locating an environmentally noxious facility. The local residents would, in most likelihood, be unable to mount and sustain an effective opposition. This factor, together with the prospects of increased employment and money income, would almost certainly sway the arguments in favour of the location of the facility.

Bibliography and further reading

Abelson, P. (2003) 'The Value of Life and Health for Public Policy', *Economic Record*, 79: 2–13.

Adler, M. and Posner, E. (eds) (2000) *Cost–Benefit Analysis: Legal, Economic, and Philosophical Perspectives*, Chicago, IL and London: University of Chicago Press.

Anderson, R.J. and Crocker, T.D. (1971) 'Air Pollution and Residential Property Values', *Urban Studies*, 8: 40–8.

Arrow, K.J. (1966) 'Discounting and Public Investment Criteria', in Kneese, A.V. and Smith, S.C. (eds) *Water Research*, Baltimore, MD: Johns Hopkins University Press.

Arrow, K.J. and Lind, R.C. (1970) 'Uncertainty and the Evaluation of Public Investment Decisions', *American Economic Review*, 60(3): 364–78.

—— (1972) 'Uncertainty and the Evaluation of Public Investment Decisions: Reply', *American Economic Review*, 62(1): 171–2.

Arthur, W.B. (1981) 'The Economics of Risks to Life', *American Economic Review*, 71(1): 54–64.

Balassa, B. (1974) 'Estimating the Shadow Price of Foreign Exchange in Project Evaluation', *Oxford Economic Papers*, 26: 147–68.

Baumol, W. (1968) 'On the Social Rate of Discount', *American Economic Review*, 58: 788–802.

—— (1972) 'On Taxation and the Control of Externalities', *American Economic Review*, 62: 307–22.

Becker, G. (1965) 'A Theory of the Allocation of Time', *Economic Journal*, 75: 493–517.

Beesley, M. (1965) 'The Value of Time Spent Travelling: Some New Evidence', *Economica*, 32: 174–85.

Bierman, H. and Smidt, S. (1988) *The Capital Budgeting Decision: Economic Analysis of Investment Projects* (7th edn), New York: Macmillan.

Blaug, M. (1985) *Economic Theory in Retrospect* (4th edn), Cambridge: Cambridge University Press.

Boardman, A., Greenberg, D., Vining, A. and Weimer, D. (2001) *Cost–Benefit Analysis: Concepts and Practice* (2nd edn), Upper Saddle River, NJ: Prentice-Hall.

—— (2006) *Cost–Benefit Analysis: Concepts and Practice* (3rd edn), Harlow: Pearson.

Bradford, D. (1975) 'Constraints on Government Investment Opportunities and the Choice of Discount Rate', *American Economic Review*, 65: 887–99.

Brent, R. (1990) *Project Appraisal for Developing Countries*, Hemel Hempstead: Harvester Wheatsheaf.

—— (1996) *Applied Cost–Benefit Analysis*, Cheltenham: Edward Elgar.

Broome, J. (1978) 'Trying to Value a Life', *Journal of Political Economy*, 9: 91–100.

Buchanan, J. (1965) 'An Economic Theory of Clubs', *Economica*, 32: 1–14.

Buchanan, J. and Stubblebine, W. (1962) 'Externality', *Economica*, 29: 371–84.

Burrows, P. (1979) *The Economic Theory of Pollution Control*, Oxford: Martin Robertson.

Campbell, H. and Brown, R. (2003) *Benefit-Cost Analysis: Financial and Economic Appraisal Using Spreadsheets*, Cambridge: Cambridge University Press.

Campen, J. (1986) *Benefit, Cost, and Beyond: The Political Economy of Benefit–Cost Analysis*, Cambridge, MA: Ballinger.

Carson, R., Meade, N.F. and Smith, V.K. (1993) 'Contingent Valuation and Passive Use Values: Introducing the Issues', *Choices*, 8(2): 5–8.

Clawson, M. (1959) 'Method of Measuring the Demand for and Value of Outdoor Recreation', *Resources for the Future*, Washington, DC: Brookings Institution.

Clawson, M. and Knetsch, J. (1966) *The Economics of Outdoor Recreation*, Baltimore, MD: Johns Hopkins University Press.

Coase, R. (1960) 'The Problems of Social Cost', *Journal of Law and Economics*, 3(1): 1–44.

Coleman, J. (1984) 'The Possibility of a Social Welfare Function', *American Economic Review*, 56: 1105–22.

Conley, B.C. (1976) 'The Value of Human Life in the Demand for Safety', *American Economic Review*, 66(1): 45–55.

Cook, P.J. and Graham, D.A. (1977) 'The Demand for Insurance and Protection: The Case of Irreplaceable Commodities', *Quarterly Journal of Economics*, 91: 143–56.

Cropper, M. and Oates, W. (1992) 'Environmental Economics: A Survey', *Journal of Economic Literature*, 30: 675–740.

Currie, J., Murphy, J. and Schmitz, A. (1971) 'The Concept of Economic Surplus and Its Use in Economic Analysis', *Economic Journal*, 81: 741–99.

Dardis, R. (1980) 'The Value of a Life; New Evidence from the Marketplace', *American Economic Review*, 1970: 1077–82.

Dasgupta, P. and Heal, M. (1979) *Economic Theory and Exhaustible Resources*, Cambridge: Cambridge University Press.

Dasgupta, P., Marglin, S. and Sen, A. (1972) *Guidelines for Project Evaluation*, New York: United Nations.

Davis, O. and Whinston, A. (1965) 'Welfare Economics and the Theory of Second Best', *Review of Economic Studies*, 32: 1–14.

Dinwiddy, C. and Teal, F. (1996) *Principles of Cost–Benefit Analysis for Developing Countries*, Cambridge: Cambridge University Press.

Dorfman, R. (1962) 'Basic Economic and Technological Concepts', in Maass, A., Hufschmidt, M.M., Dorfman, R., Thoms, H.A., Marglin, S.A. and Fair, G.M., *Design of Water Resources Systems*, London: Macmillan.

Dorfman, R., Samuelson, P.A. and Solow, R.M. (1958) *Linear Programming and Economic Analysis*, New York: McGraw-Hill.

Dreze, J.H. (1974) 'Discount Rates and Public Investment: A Postscriptum', *Economica*, 41: 52–61.

Duesenberry, J. (1949) *Income, Saving and the Theory of Consumer Behaviour*, Cambridge, MA: Harvard University Press.

Dupuit, J. (1944) 'De la mesure de l'utilite des travaus publics', *Annales des Points et Chaussées*, translated by R. Barback (1952) in *International Economic Papers*, 2: 83–110.

Eckstein, O. (1958) *Water Resources Development*, Cambridge, MA: Harvard University Press.

Eisner, R. and Strotz, R. (1961) 'Flight Insurance and the Theory of Choice', *Journal of Political Economy*, 69: 355–68.

Ellis, H. and Fellner, W. (1943) 'External Economies and Diseconomies', *American Economic Review*, 33: 493–511.

English, M. (1984) *Project Evaluation: A Unified Approach for the Analysis of Capital Investments*, New York: Macmillan.

Farrell, M. (1958) 'In Defence of Public Utility Price Theory', *Oxford Economic Papers*, 10: 109–23.

Feldstein, M. (1964a) 'Net Social Benefit Calculation and the Public Investment Decision', *Oxford Economic Papers*, 16: 114–31.

—— (1964b) 'The Social Time Preference Discount Rate in Cost-Benefit Analysis', *Economic Journal*, 74: 360–79.

—— (1972) 'The Inadequacy of Weighted Discount Rates', in Layard, R. (ed.), *Cost–Benefit Analysis: Selected Readings*, Harmondsworth: Penguin.

Fischer, D. and Davis, G. (1973) 'An Approach to Assessing Environmental Impacts', *Journal of Environmental Management*, 1: 207–27.

Fisher, A. (1973) 'Environmental Externalities and the Arrow–Lind Public Investment Theorem', *American Economic Review*, 63(4): 722–5.

Flowerdew, A. (1971) 'The Cost of Airport Noise', *The Statistician*, 13: 23–35.

Foster, C. and Neuburger, H. (1974) 'The Ambiguity of the Consumer's Surplus Measure of Welfare Change', *Oxford Economic Papers*, 26: 66–77.

Freeman, A. (1971) 'Air Pollution and Property Values: A Comment', *Review of Economics and Statistics*, 53, 415–16.

—— (1977) 'A Short Argument in Favour of Discounting Intergenerational Effects', *Futures*, 4: 7–9.

Friedman, M. and Savage, L.J. (1948) 'Utility Analysis of Choices Involving Risks', *Journal of Political Economy*, 56: 279–304.

George, I. (1978) *Modern Cost–Benefit Methods*, Basingstoke: Macmillan.

Glaister, S. (1974) 'Generalised Consumer Surplus and Public Transport Pricing', *Economic Journal*, 84: 849–67.

Gramlich, E. (1990) *A Guide to Benefit–Cost Analysis* (2nd edn), Upper Saddle River, NJ: Prentice-Hall.

Green, H.A.J. (1961) 'The Social Optimum in the Presence of Monopoly and Taxation', *Review of Economic Studies*, 29: 66–77.

Gregory, R. and Kunreuther, H. (1990) 'Successful Siting Incentives', *Journal of Civil Engineering*, 60: 73–5.

Hanemann, W. (1991) 'Willingness to Pay and Willingness to Accept: How Much Can They Differ?', *American Economic Review*, 81: 635–47.

Hanley, N. and Spash, C. (1993) *Cost–Benefit Analysis and the Environment*, Cheltenham: Edward Elgar.

Harberger, A.C. (1968) 'On the Opportunity Cost of Public Borrowing', *Economic Analysis of Public Investment Decisions: Interest Rate Policy and Discounting Analysis*, Hearings before the Joint Economic Committee, 90th Congress, 2nd Session, USGOP, Washington, DC.

—— (1971a) 'On Measuring the Social Opportunity Cost of Labour', *International Economic Review*, 89: 23–33.

—— (1971b) 'The Three Basic Postulates for Applied Welfare Economics: An Interpretive Essay', *Journal of Economic Literature*, 9: 785–97.

Hause, J.C. (1975) 'The Theory of Welfare Cost Measurement', *Journal of Political Economy*, 83: 1145–82.

Haveman, R.H. and Krutilla, J.V. (1968) *Unemployment, Idle Capacity and the Evaluation of Public Expenditure*, Washington, DC: Resources for the Future.

Henderson, A. (1943) 'Consumers Surplus and Compensating Variation', *Review of Economic Studies*, 8: 117–21.

Hicks, J.R. (1939) *Value and Capital* (2nd edn, 1944), Oxford: Clarendon Press.

—— (1944) 'The Four Consumers' Surplus', *Review of Economic Studies*, 11: 31–41.

—— (1956) *A Revision of Demand Theory*, Oxford: Clarendon Press.

Johansson, P.-O. (1993) *Cost–Benefit Analysis of Environmental Change*, Cambridge: Cambridge University Press.

Jones-Lee, M. (1980a) 'Maximum Acceptable Physical Risk and a New Measure of Financial Risk Aversion', *Economic Journal*, 90: 49–72.

Jones-Lee, M. (1980b) 'Maximum Acceptable Physical Risk and a New Measure of Financial Risk Aversion', *Economic Journal*, 90: 550–68.

Kahneman, D. and Tversky, A. (1979) 'Prospect Theory: An Analysis of Decisions under Risk', *Econometrica*, 47: 263–91.

Kaldor, N. (1939) 'Welfare Propositions of Economics', *Economic Journal*, 49: 549–52.

Keeney, R. (1980), 'Equity and Public Risk', *Operations Research*, 9: 45–56.

Knetsch, J. (1989) 'The Endowment Effect and Evidence of Nonreversible Indifference Curves', *American Economic Review*, 79: 1277–84.

—— (1995) 'Asymmetric Valuation of Gains and Losses and Preference Order Assumptions', *Economic Inquiry*, 33: 134–41.

—— (2003) 'Environmental, Ecological, and Behavioural Economics', in Dovers, S., Stern, D.I. and Young, M. (eds), *New Dimensions in Ecological Economics: Integrative Approaches to People and Nature*, Cheltenham: Edward Elgar.

Knetsch, J. and Borcherding, T. (1979) 'Expropriation of Private Property and the Basis for Compensation', *University of Toronto Law Journal*, 29: 237–40.

Knetsch, J. and Sinden, J. (1984) 'Willingness to Pay and Compensation Demanded: Experimental Evidence of an Unexpected Disparity in Measures of Values', *Quarterly Journal of Economics*, 99: 507–21.

Krutilla, J. (1967) 'Conservation Reconsidered', *American Economic Review*, 54: 777–86.

Krutilla, J. and Eckstein, O. (1958) *Multiple Purpose River Development, Studies in Applied Economic Analysis*, Baltimore, MD: Johns Hopkins Press.

Layard, R. and Glaister, S. (eds) (1994) *Cost–Benefit Analysis* (2nd edn), Cambridge: Cambridge University Press.

Lee, N. and Kirkpatrick, C. (2000) *Sustainable Development and Integrated Appraisal in a Developing World*, Cheltenham: Edward Elgar.

Leibenstein, H. (1966) 'Allocative Efficiency vs X-Efficiency', *American Economic Review*, 56: 392–415.

Linnerooth, J. (1979) 'The Value of Human Life: A Review of the Models', *Economic Enquiry*, 17: 52–74.

Lipsey, R. and Lancaster, K. (1957) 'The General Theory of Second Best', *Review of Economic Studies*, 24: 11–32.

Little, I.M.D. (1957) *A Critique of Welfare Economics* (2nd edn), Oxford: Oxford University Press.

Little, I.M.D. and Mirrlees, J. (1968) *Manual of Industrial Project Analysis in Developing Countries*, vol. 2, OECD.

Loomis, J. and Walsh, R. (1997) *Recreation Economic Decisions: Comparing Benefits and Costs* (2nd edn), State College, PA: Venture Publishing.

Marglin, S. (1963a) 'The Opportunity Costs of Public Investment', *Quarterly Journal of Economics*, 77: 274–89.

—— (1963b) 'The Social Rate of Discount and the Optimal Rate of Investment', *Quarterly Journal of Economics*, 77: 95–111.

Marglin, S.A. (1976) *Value and Price in Labour Surplus Economies*, New York: Oxford University Press.

Marshall, A. (1924) *Principles of Economics* (8th edn), London: Macmillan.

Margolis, J. and Guitton, H. (eds) (1969) *Public Economics*, London: Macmillan.

McKean, R. (1958) *Efficiency in Government through Systems Analysis, with Emphasis on Water Resource Development*, New York: John Wiley.

Meade, J. (1962) 'External Economies and Diseconomies in a Competitive Situation', *Economic Journal*, 64: 54–67.

Mishan, E. (1952) 'The Principle of Compensation Reconsidered', *Journal of Political Economy*, 60: 312–22.

—— (1957) 'A Reappraisal of the Principles of Resource Allocation', *Economica*, 24: 324–42.

—— (1958) 'Rent as a Measure of Welfare Change', *American Economic Review*, 49: 386–94.

—— (1960) 'A Survey of Welfare Economics 1939–1959', *Economic Journal*, 70: 197–265.

—— (1962a) 'Welfare Criteria: An Exchange of Notes', *Economic Journal*, 72: 234–44.

—— (1962b) 'Second Thoughts on Second Best', *Oxford Economic Papers*, 14: 205–17.

—— (1963) 'Welfare Criteria: Are Compensation Tests Necessary?', *Economic Journal*, 73: 342–50.

—— (1965a) 'Reflections on Recent Developments in the Concept of External Effects', *Canadian Journal of Economics and Political Science*, 31: 3–34.

—— (1965b) 'The Recent Debate on Welfare Criteria', *Oxford Economic Papers*, 17: 219–36.

—— (1967a) 'Interpretation of the Benefits of Private Transport', *Journal of Transport Economics and Policy*, 1(2): 184–9.

—— (1967b) 'Pareto Optimality and the Law', *Oxford Economic Papers*, 19: 255–87.

—— (1967c) 'A Normalisation Procedure for Public Investment Criteria', 77: 777–96.

—— (1969a) *Welfare Economics: An Assessment*, Amsterdam: North-Holland.

—— (1969b) 'The Relationship between Joint Products, Collective Goods, and External Effects', *Journal of Political Economy*, 77: 329–48.

—— (1969c) *Welfare Economics: Ten Introductory Essays*, New York: Random House.

—— (1970) 'What is Wrong with Roskill?', *Journal of Transport Economics and Policy*, 4: 221–34.

—— (1971a) 'Pangloss on Pollution', *Swedish Journal of Economics*, 73: 1–27.

—— (1971b) 'The Postwar Literature on Externalities: An Interpretative Essay', *Journal of Economic Literature*, 9(1): 1–28.

—— (1973) 'Welfare Criteria: Resolution of a Paradox', *Economic Journal*, 83: 747–67.

—— (1974) 'Flexibility and Consistency in Project Evaluation', *Economica*, 41: 81–96.

—— (1976a) 'Choices Involving Risk: Simple Steps Toward an Ordinalist Analysis', *Economic Journal*, 86: 759–77.

—— (1976b) 'The New Welfare Criteria and the Social Welfare Function', *Economisch en Sociaal Tijdschrift*, 30(5): 775–83.

—— (1977a) 'The Plain Truth about Consumer Surplus', *Zeitschrift für Nationalökonomie*, 37(1): 1–24.

—— (1977b) 'Property Rights and Amenity Rights', in Dorfman, R. and Dorfman, N.S. (eds), *Economics of the Environment: Selected Readings*, New York: W.W. Norton.

—— (1977c) 'Economic Criteria for Intergenerational Comparisons', *Futures*, 9(5): 383–404.

—— (1977d) *The Economic Growth Debate: An Assessment*, London: Allen & Unwin.

—— (1980a) *Introduction to Normative Economics*, New York: Oxford University Press.

—— (1980b) 'The New Welfare Economics: An Alternative View', *International Economic Review*, 21: 691–705.

—— (1981) 'The Value of Trying to Value a Life', *Journal of Public Economics*, 15: 133–7.

—— (1982) 'The New Controversy about the Rationale of Economic Evaluation', *Journal of Economic Issues*, 16: 29–47.

—— (1985) 'Consistency in the Valuation of Life: A Wild Goose Chase?', *Social Philosophy and Policy*, 2: 133–37.

—— (1988) *Cost–Benefit Analysis: An Informal Introduction* (4th edn), London: Unwin Hyman.

—— (1993) *The Costs of Economic Growth* (2nd edn), London: Weidenfeld & Nicolson.

Montgomery, M. and Needleman, M. (1997) 'The Welfare Effects of Toxic Contamination in Freshwater Fish', *Land Economics*, 73(2): 211–23.

Moore, P.G. (1968) *Basic Operation Research*, London: Pitman.

Mulligan, P. (1977) 'Willingness to Pay for Decreased Risk from Nuclear Plant Accidents', Working Paper No. 3, Energy Extension Program, Penn State University.

Mumy, M. and Hanke, E. (1975) 'Public Investment Criteria for Underpriced Products', *American Economic Review*, 66: 289–300.

Musgrave, R.A. (1963) *Foundations of Economic Analysis* (2nd edn), Cambridge, MA: Harvard University Press.

—— (1969) 'Cost–Benefit Analysis and the Theory of Public Investment', *Journal of Economic Literature*, 7(3): 797–806.

Nash, J. (1950) 'The Bargaining Problem', *Econometrica*, 18: 155–62.

Needleman, L. (1976) 'Valuing Other People's Lives', *Manchester School*, 44: 309–42.

Ng, Y.K. (2004) *Welfare Economics: Towards a More Complete Analysis*, Basingstoke: Palgrave.

Nichols, A. (1969) 'On the Social Rate of Discount: Comment', *American Economic Review*, *American Economic Association*, 59(5): 909–11, December.

Nichols, D.A. (1970) 'Land and Economic Growth', *American Economic Review*, *American Economic Association*, 60(3): 332–40, June.

Nwaneri, V.C. (1970) 'Equity in Cost–Benefit Analysis', *Journal of Transport Economics and Policy*, 4: 238–56.

O'Hare, M., Bacow, L. and Sanderson, D. (1983) *Facility Siting and Public Opposition*, New York: Von Nostrand Reinhold.

Ortolano, L. (1997) *Environmental Regulation and Impact Assessment*, Chichester: John Wiley.

Page, T. (1977) *Conservation and Economic Efficiency*, Baltimore: John Hopkins University Press.

Paul, M. (1971) 'Can Airport Noise be Measured in Money', *Oxford Economic Papers*, 23: 297–327.

Pauwels, W. (1977) 'The Possible Perverse Behaviour of the Compensating Variation as a Welfare Ranking', *Zeitschrift fur Nationalokonomie*, 38: 369–78.

Pearce, D. and Nash, C. (1983) *The Social Appraisal of Projects*, Basingstoke: ELBS and Macmillan.

Pigou, A.C. (1952) *Economics of Welfare* (5th edn), London: Macmillan.

Popper, F. (1983) 'The Political Uses of Risk Analysis in Land Use Planning', *Risk Analysis*, 3: 255–63.

Portney, P. and Weyant, J. (eds) (1999) *Discounting and Intergenerational Equity*, Washington: RFF Press.

Prest, A.R. and Turvey, R. (1965) 'Cost–Benefit Analysis: A Survey', *The Economic Journal*, 75: 683–735.

Puttaswamaiah, K. (ed.) (2000) *Cost–Benefit Analysis: Environmental and Ecological Perspectives*, Piscataway, NJ: Transaction.

Quah, E. and Tan, K. (1999) 'Economics of NIMBY Syndrome: Siting Decisions', Environment and Planning C, *Government and Policy*, 16: 255–64.

—— (2002) *Siting Environmentally Unwanted Facilities: Risks, Trade-Offs and Choices*, Cheltenham: Edward Elgar.

Ramsey, D.D. (1969) 'On the Social Rate of Discount: Comment', *American Economic Review*, 59: 919–24.

Randall, A. (1987) *An Economic Approach to Natural Resource and Environmental Policy* (2nd edn), New York: John Wiley.

Samuelson, P.A. (1954) 'The Pure Theory of Public Expenditure', *Review of Economics and Statistics*, 36: 387–9.

—— (1963) *Foundations of Economic Analysis* (2nd edn), Cambridge, MA: Harvard University Press.

Sandmo, A. and Dreze, J.H. (1971) 'Discount Rates for Public Investment in Closed and Open Economies', *Economica*, 38: 395–412.

Schofield, J. (1987) *Cost–Benefit Analysis in Urban and Regional Planning*, London: Allen & Unwin.

Scitovsky, T. (1941) 'A Note on Welfare Propositions in Economics', *Review of Economic Studies*, 9: 77–88.

Scott, M.F.G. (1974) 'How to Use and Estimate Shadow Exchange Rates', *Oxford Economic Papers*, 26: 169–89.

Sewell, W.R.D., Davis, J., Scott, A.D. and Ross, D.W. (1965) *Guide to Benefit–Cost Analysis*, Ottawa: Queen's Printer.

Sinden, J.A. (1967) 'The Evaluation of Extra Market Benefits: A Review', *World Agricultural Economics and Rural Sociology Conference*, Abstracts, 9: 1–16.

Skaburskis, A. (1988) 'Criteria for Compensation for the Imports of Large Projects', *Journal of Policy Analysis and Management*, 7: 668–86.

Small, K., Winston, C. and Yan, J. (2003) 'Preferences for Travel Time and Reliability', Working Paper, University of California (Irvin).

Solow, R.H. (1974) 'The Economics of Resources or the Resources of Economics', *American Economic Review*, 64: 1–14.

Squire, L. and van der Tak, H. (1975) *Economic Analysis of Projects*, Baltimore, MD: Johns Hopkins Press.

Sugden, R. and Williams, A. (1978) *The Principles of Practical Cost–Benefit Analysis*, Oxford: Oxford University Press.

Sydsaeter, K. and Hammond, P. (2005) *Further Mathematics for Economic Analysis* (2nd edn), Harlow: Pearson Education.

Takayama, A. (1994) *Analytical Methods in Economics*, Hemel Hempstead: Harvester Wheatsheaf.

Tang, S. (1991) *Economic Feasibility of Projects: Managerial and Engineering Practice*, New York: McGraw-Hill.

Throsby, D. (1970) *An Introduction to Mathematical Programming*, New York: Random House.

Tipping, D.G. (1968) 'Time Savings in Transport Studies', *Economic Journal*, 78: 843–54.

Usher, D. (1985) 'The Value of Life for Decision Making in the Public Sector', *Social Philosophy and Policy*.

Viscusi, W. and Aldy, J. (2003) 'The Value of Statistical Life: A Critical Review of Market Estimates Throughout the World', *Journal of Risk and Uncertainty*, 27: 5–76.

Walsh, R. (1986) *Recreation Economic Decisions: Comparing Benefits and Costs*, State College, PA: Venture Publishing.

Walshe, G. and Daffern, P. (1990) *Managing Cost–Benefit Analysis*, Basingstoke: Macmillan.

Weisbrod, B.A. (1968) 'Income Redistribution Effects & Benefit–Cost Analysis', in Chase, S.B. Jr (ed.), *Problems in Public Expenditure Analysis*, Washington, DC: Brookings Institution.

Wilkinson, R.G. (1973*) Poverty and Progress: An Ecological Model of Economic Development*, London: Methuen.

Zeckhauser, R. (1975) 'Procedures for Valuing Lives', *Public Policy*, 23: 419–64.

Index